The English

General Editors
James Campbell and Barry Cunliffe

This series is about the European tribes and peoples from their origins in prehistory to the present day. Drawing upon a wide range of archaeological and historical evidence, each volume presents a fresh and absorbing account of a group's culture, society and usually history.

Already published

The Etruscans
Greame Barker and Thomas Rasmussen

The Lombards
Neil Christie

The Basques
Roger Collins

The English
Geoffrey Elton

The Gypsies
Angus Fraser

The Bretons
Patrick Galliou and Michael Jones

The Goths
Peter Heather

The Franks
Edward James

The Russians
Robin Milner-Gulland

The Mongols
David Morgan

The Armenians
A.E. Redgate

The Huns
E.A. Thompson

The Early Germans
Malcolm Todd

The Illyrians
John Wilkes

In Preparation

The Sicilians
David Abulafia

The Irish
Francis John Byrne and Michael Herity

The Byzantines
Averil Cameron

The First English
Sonia Chadwick Hawkes

The Normans
Marjorie Chibnall

The Serbs
Sima Cirkovic

The Spanish
Roger Collins

The Romans
Timothy Cornell

The Celts
David Dumville

The Scots
Colin Kidd

The Ancient Greeks
Brian Sparkes

The Picts
Charles Thomas

The English

Geoffrey Elton

BLACKWELL
Oxford UK & Cambridge USA

First published 1992
Reprinted 1993
First published in paperback 1994
Reprinted 1995, 1999

Blackwell Publishers Ltd
108 Cowley Road
Oxford OX4 1JF, UK

Blackwell Publishers Inc
350 Main Street
Malden, Massachusetts 02148, USA

British Library Cataloguing in Publication Data
A CIP catalogue record for this book is available from the British Library

Library of Congress Cataloging in Publication Data
Elton, G. R. (Geoffrey Rudolph)
The English / Geoffrey Elton
p. cm. — (The Peoples of Europe)
Includes bibliographical references (p.   ) and index.
ISBN 0–631–17681–0 (HB: acid-free paper)
ISBN 0–631–19606–4 (PB: acid-free paper)
1. National characteristics, English. 2. England—Civilization.
I. Title. II. Series
DA118.E48   1993
942—dc20   92–19106

Typeset in 11 on 12.5pt Sabon
by Hope Services (Abingdon) Ltd
Printed and bound in Great Britain
by T J International Ltd, Padstow, Cornwall

This book is printed on acid-free paper

Contents

List of Plates

List of Figures

Preface

When the editors and publisher invited me to contribute a volume on the English as one of the peoples of Europe, to stand beside books on Franks and Basques and so forth, I explained that I could not produce a book in the style of the series. I am neither an archaeologist nor an early-medievalist, and unhappily not even a social historian. I can only hope that the editors will not come to regret their generous acceptance of my reservations and conditions. For what in the end has emerged is a survey skipping over the centuries – an essay and definitely not a treatise. I have attempted to discover the characteristics that manifested themselves over that long history as the identifying marks of that collection of mortals who in the fifth century of our era settled in what became known as England, and who underwent a string of experiences that even as they changed still emphasized the outward cohesion of a people. Inevitably, given my formation and preferences, I was bound to concentrate on political and ideological events. I do not apologize for going counter to a good many current convictions concerning the things that matter about social groupings. Family relationships or habits of procreation seem to me historically less than fascinating; they tell us about this or that human being but not about a given collection of them, and they do not really change through time. After all, so many attempts to define the commonplaces of human behaviour in historical categories have proved mistaken.

At any rate, that is what I am here presenting: the English through a millennium of their public lives and outward experience. That story really ends in the early nineteenth century when long-established characteristics underwent astonishing transformations. A changed people emerged into modern times. The last chapter makes an effort to indicate those changes without attempting a proper study of the last two centuries; even more than the first five chapters, it is forced to skim the surface. I have throughout been aware of the risks I was running, but I thought and still think the effort worth trying. Against one likely charge, however, I should like to enter my defence. If it is thought that I have painted an unduly favourable picture of the English, this is not the consequence of an unthinking and somewhat old-fashioned patriotism. It is because they so appeared to one who came upon them from the outside. I was well over seventeen years old when I landed in England on St Valentine's Day in 1939, and I knew virtually nothing of that country, not even its language. Within a few months it dawned upon me that I had arrived in the country in which I ought to have been born, a conviction surprisingly reinforced by two and a half years spent in the ranks of His Majesty's Army. In a way, this book tries to pay a debt of gratitude, but it does so after careful reflection and after personal experience of other peoples.

For the five substantive chapters I have tried to acquaint myself with the present state of knowledge (which, I am well aware, is constantly moving onwards); to have done so for the sixth would have meant adding years and volumes to the enterprise as well as fudging the significant terminal date of the English as they had been. I have thought it desirable to accept full responsibility for what is here said, and I have therefore not troubled my many friends among the experts. But I am deeply grateful for the assistance they gave me in print, an assistance which the footnotes inadequately recognize.

Geoffrey Elton
Cambridge, December 1991

Postscript What happened after I handed in the typescript calls for specific acknowledgement. I owe a burden of gratitude to Miss Ginny Stroud-Lewis for collecting and laying out the illustrative material. I also received most valuable queries and corrections from Mr James Campbell (editor of this series) for the medieval section, and from Dr John Stevenson for the modern. I apologize to both for not accepting all their suggestions. In particular I must exonerate Mr Campbell from all responsibility if any errors persist in the first chapter. On some disputable points I adhered to the views I had formulated, and it is possible that I was wrong in places. Mr Campbell did his best, and I apologize.

Abbreviations

BIHR   Bulletin of the Institute of Historical Research
EHR   English Historical Review
HJ   Historical Journal
JBS   Journal of British Studies
JEH   Journal of Ecclesiastical History
PP   Past and Present
SCH   Studies in Church History
TRHS   Transactions of the Royal Historical Society

1

The Emergence of England

'The effective creation of the Kingdom of England may be dated from A.D. 927', the year in which Athelstan, king of Wessex and Mercia, took over the Danish and English parts of Northumbria and thereby in effect also accepted the existence of a separate kingdom of Scotland.[1] This settlement of the island resulted from half a millennium of conflict, growth, advance, setback and so forth: a most confused and confusing story. In that time, the marauding bands of barbarians from the regions around Friesland and the mouth of the Elbe had settled into peasant communities, had formed political structures in which leaders of war-bands became kings who issued codes of law in between proving their continued taste for fighting, and had been captured by the Christian God sent out by the papacy at Rome. Above all, the mixed collections of Germanic raiders had become acceptably subsumed under the name of the English – not indeed a nation nor a truly coherent people but a gathering of various tribes and non-tribal bodies willing to be so described. The name was in a manner an accident. Among those German invaders the real description of origin spoke of both Angles and Saxons (the Jutes of Kent, popular in the older accounts, are today reckoned disputable), and of the two Saxon was the better and more apposite patronymic. The decisive maker of the English people was the Venerable Bede who belonged to the Angles of Northumbria, and Pope Gregory's pun about Angles and angels also contributed to the triumph of

[1] *Handbook of British Chronology* (Royal Historical Society, 1986), 25.

the English name. Confused by all this, the nineteenth century
dithered between Anglo-Saxon and Old English. Here we shall
speak of the Anglo-Saxons who by stages turned into the
English, the subject of this essay.[2]

From the first those future English were thus far from racially
pure or simple, a fact also manifest among the other, fundamentally Germanic, people who from the early fifth century
onwards overran the Roman empire. And the emergence of an
English collectivity took a long time. Even Alfred, who reigned
from 871 to 899, was by no means yet safely a single king of
such a body, though a 'paradox' has been identified: 'there *is* a
remarkably precocious sense of common "Englishness", and
not just in politically interested circles.' Bede's application of
the name marched in step with the usage employed by such
other churchmen as Eddius, biographer of St Wilfrid, or
Boniface, the apostle of the Germans: by the later seventh
century, the idea of a single name had spread widely among the
clergy, the bearers of literacy.[3] It is therefore necessary to keep
in mind the absence of any practical reality behind the idea that
prevailed until the early tenth century, when indeed all the
strands finally coalesced into the emergence of an English
nation – then but not before. In the end, England and the
English were put together by agencies from above: by a central
political authority (kingship) and a unifying ideological structure (the Christian Church).[4]

The Anglo-Saxon conquest of a large part of the British Isles
was, of course, a part of that westward flood of the Germanic
peoples – sometimes tribes or *naciones* in the early-medieval
sense, sometimes almost accidental collections of uprooted
inhabitants from various regions – which in the fourth, fifth and
sixth centuries destroyed the Roman empire and produced a
series of often temporary political structures emerging from
permanent settlement. The Anglo-Saxon share in this upheaval

[2] Cf. Michael Richter, 'Bede's Angli – Angles or English?' *Peritia* 3 (1984), 99–114;
Patrick Wormald, 'Bede, the *Bredwaldas* and the origin of the *Gens Anglorum*', in
Ideals and Reality in Frankish and Anglo-Saxon Society, ed. P. Wormald et al. (1983),
99–129.

[3] Wormald, 'Bede', 120, 122, 126.

[4] H. R. Loyn, *The Governance of Anglo-Saxon England* (1984), p. xiv. I find recent
arguments saddling the Anglo-Saxons with Celtic wives and inherited institutions less
persuasive than the views here summarized, but I know I may be wrong.

was on the whole characterized by coming somewhat later than most of the rest, in the main a consequence of the fact that they decided to colonize an island which had to be invaded by sea. True, Saxon raiders had been active as early as the 360s, descending upon the shores of Britain in accidental collaboration with Irish raiders in the west, while the Romans' failure to subdue the whole island produced increasing inroads by Picts and Scots across the northern walls. But proper immigration and settlement came only after the Romans had altogether withdrawn from Britain early in the fifth century, and therefore involved struggles with native – Celtic – principalities rather than the overthrow or absorption of imperial remnants. Unlike the Goths, Lombards, Franks and Burgundians, the Anglo-Saxons thus did not take over Roman regions and did not encounter the traditions of the late empire. This had particular consequences in three ways: the Anglo-Saxons did not inter-marry with the indigenous population; they inherited no institutions of government and public order; and they took much longer to abandon their heathen gods and adopt Christianity.

The Making of the English

Despite some opinion to the contrary, it seems pretty certain that the Germanic invaders did not mix significantly with the Celts (Britons), whom in two generations of conflict they pushed back into the western and northern uplands. Personal names and the names of settlements would seem to bear this out, and the fact that the names of such major natural features as rivers at times preserve Celtic origins does not affect the issue. Above all, the Anglo-Saxon language, in its various manifestations, preserved extraordinarily few words borrowed from the Celtic.[5] At the same time, the invaders did not meet the sort of demotic Latin that dominated the intercourse of all peoples in Italy, Spain or Gaul; in English circles, Latin was

[5] The Anglo-Saxons have been described as poor linguists, forcing the native Britons to become bilingual (H. Mayr-Harting, *The Coming of Christianity to Anglo-Saxon England* [1972], 31). A pretty conceit, perhaps, rather than a serious judgement, though some will argue that the problem kept re-emerging in English history.

from the first a strictly learned language, acquired from writings rather than speech, and more commonly also used to write rather than speak. From this odd fact sprang the early and impressive growth of Anglo-Saxon itself, a vernacular employable in areas that elsewhere tended to be dominated by Latin. Many native cultures wrote poetry in their vernaculars, but the Anglo-Saxon language could not only produce *Beowulf* but also cope with the technicalities of the law and government, as well as with the demands of Bible learning and historiography.

Thus the emerging English could from the first lay claim to a high degree of native self-sufficiency, a condition which readily breeds arrogant self-satisfaction. It must therefore be stressed that their condition did not constitute racial purity or anything even remotely resembling a united national character, those things that nineteenth-century fantasies so readily ascribed to them.[6] In particular, they were not a single breed but a collection of diverse tribesmen roving in mixed bands that ultimately settled separately in convenient farming regions. As I have already said, until Bede presented them as one people living under a number of regional princes they looked much more like regionally diverse groups speaking forms of a language which, though manifestly related, differed sufficiently from one another to put communication in question. Before the Norman Conquest those various though related languages had turned into dialects of one Anglo-Saxon, or Old English, language which itself was the product of a written civilization. The consolidation that lay behind this development also enabled the Anglo-Saxon occupants of Britain first to survive and then to incorporate the next wave of assaults from overseas – the Viking raids which began in the eighth century and culminated in the brief establishment of a Danish dynasty on the originally Anglo-Saxon English throne in the eleventh. Although the inhabitants of the eastern and north-eastern sectors – the so-called Danelaw – remained distinguishably Danish for quite a while and left permanent linguistic traces in landscape and governmental terminology, this did not prevent the full flowering of an English kingdom indifferent to the king's origins: Danish Cnut was as fully king of England as was

[6] Cf. Hugh A. MacDougall, *Racial Myths in English History: Trojans, Teutons and Anglo-Saxons* (1982).

English Athelstan. One English characteristic which reappeared not infrequently in later history thus made itself felt quite early on. Though living on an island created a sense of separateness from other nations, in actual fact the nation of England was from the start of mixed origin and thereafter readily absorbed and assimilated further additions to the mixture. The only exception to this adaptability lay to the west and north-west: from the first, the lines were clearly drawn between Celts and Germans. The other failure to take over the whole island resulted from an accident: of the various lesser kingdoms that the Wessex kings knit together into the kingdom of England only the parts to the north of Northumbria remained independent, and they in due course coalesced into the kingdom of Scotland.

The Early Kings

The reduction of tribal or accidental groups into one nation was, however, above all the work of a succession of ambitious rulers – of kings. The whole history of the Anglo-Saxon settlements has from the first – from the days of Celtic observers like Gildas and Nennius, and from their own chronicle tradition – been written as the history of these so-called kings. Their constant appearance and reappearance, their rivalries and disputes, easily create the impression that these units of the so-called heptarchy (the seven supposedly tribal kingdoms) constituted the reality. And among them ascendancy might seem to move from the king of this part to the king of that, with eras of dominance ascribed to Kent, Northumbria, Mercia, ultimately Wessex. Though much of this enduring picture was created by the chroniclers and historians of the day, most of it, it seems to me, comes from the fact that those princelings are called kings; kingship has a powerful aura in English history, and its later reality has been too readily cast back upon those Anglo-Saxon quasi-rulers.

Of course, ultimately a real kingship did emerge from the miasma of the Dark Ages, but the process took time. The invaders were not organized in proper tribes, and unquestionably included entrepreneurs who stemmed from neither the

Angles nor the Saxons of the Continent, though those two linguistic units predominated: they were simply people driven forth to find new regions to colonize, and such organization as they commanded consisted of families or kin-groups that moved as bodies. As they settled they needed leadership in a situation of danger and confusion, and the chieftains who made it were those who proved most successful at the kind of warfare involved. What shaped the units that emerged was geography, not history or anthropology, and the emergence took some three to four generations to manifest itself. But by the end of the sixth century the so-called kingdoms existed, their boundaries still fluid and their relations governed by rivalry for farmland and by the ambitions of those commanders of war-bands. As now this, now that region gained a measure of superiority, later observers draped an elegant mantle of hegemony over the shoulders of this ruler or that: hence the notion of the *Bretwalda*, overlord of the southern half of the island, recently identified as 'less an objectively realized office than a subjectively perceived status'.[7] But kings like the murderous Penda of Mercia (633–56), or his supposedly saintly killer Oswy of Northumbria (642–70), let alone the briefly effective Æthelbert of Kent (*c.*550–616), did not lord it over a temporarily unified Anglo-Saxon realm; they merely impressed the chroniclers (and sometimes Bede) by their special achievements – the acceptance of the Christian mission in the case of Kent, successful marauding and killing in the case of the rest. A hundred years after Penda's death the ruler of Mercia was another kind of man – Offa (758–96) whose rule resembled real kingship a good deal more, to the point where he attracted respect from the Carolingian rulers of the Franks. But even then unification was a long way off, and temporary ascendancy is all one can find.

There was one element embedded in these kingships that gave them the roots of the real thing: the rulership which sprang from successful leadership in the early conquests and settlements immediately descended through families, and kings came to hold their position by inheritance rather than by personal quality and distinction. This is remarkable enough, though to some degree the same phenomenon seems traceable also in

---

[7] Wormald in 'Bede' 118. That essay clears up a lot of mist.

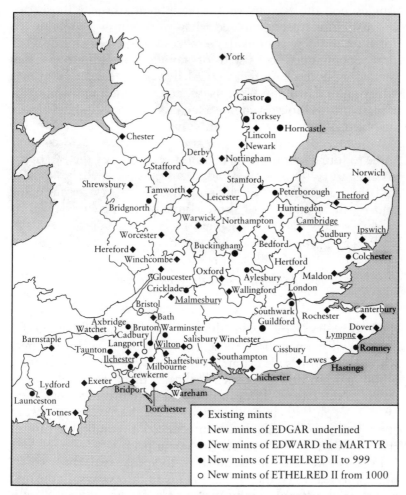

York

Caistor

Torksey

Horncastle

Chester

Lincoln

Newark

Derby

Nottingham

Stafford

Norwich

Shrewsbury

Tamworth

Stamford

Leicester

Peterborough

Thetford

Bridgnorth

Huntingdon

Warwick

Northampton

Cambridge

Ipswich

Worcester

Buckingham

Bedford

Sudbury

Hereford

Winchcombe

Hertford

Colchester

Gloucester

Oxford

Aylesbury

Maldon

Cricklade

Wallingford

London

Bristol

Malmesbury

Bath

Southwark

Rochester

Canterbury

Axbridge

Bruton

Warminster

Guildford

Dover

Watchet

Cadbury

Lympne

Barnstaple

Langport

Wilton

Salisbury

Winchester

Romney

Taunton

Cissbury

Ilchester

Shaftesbury

Southampton

Lewes

Milbourne

Hastings

Lydford

Crewkerne

Chichester

Exeter

Bridport

Launceston

Wareham

Totnes

Dorchester

♦ Existing mints

New mints of EDGAR underlined

● New mints of EDWARD the MARTYR

● New mints of ETHELRED II to 999

○ New mints of ETHELRED II from 1000

Figure 1 Mints, 957–1016 (from David Hill, An Atlas of Anglo-Saxon England, *Oxford, Blackwell, 1981. Reprinted by permission of Basil Blackwell).*

some others of the Germanic kingdoms that carved up the Roman empire, but I have seen no explanation for the early appearance of the one principle that links Anglo-Saxon kingship with the established monarchies of the High Middle Ages.[8]

[8] The highly interesting discussion by J. M. Wallace-Hadrill, *Early German Kingship in England and on the Continent* (1971), seems to take the practice of descent by family inheritance for granted.

Plate 1 Coinage from the reign of Æthelred.

(Did it perhaps owe something to the manifestly powerful position of women in all those kinship groups; was it mothers who planned the succession?) It is, in any event, this descent by blood and kin that gives such reality as there was to the kings down to the later eighth century, and in return the kings were able to exploit their accession by such descent to impose a species of genuine rule which introduced a remarkable case of state-building in the later Anglo-Saxon period.

Even before kingship became, so to speak, real, those chiefs of regions exercised their office mainly in three ways. In the first place, they offered a physical centre for the regional self-consciousness which in due course would produce a sense of local nationhood. That is to say, they gathered around themselves and their families a primitive court of men and women committed to their service and drawing benefits therefrom. From these usually wandering courts there radiated elements of administration: kings and their courts had to be fed, peace had to be kept, armies had sometimes to be raised and organized. All this naturally varied in degree and effectiveness, but within it lay the germs of a full-scale government superimposed on the traditional local organizations of kinship and

Plate 2 King Athelstan presenting a copy of Bede's works to St Cuthbert, the seventh-century English saint, Winchester, c.930. Corpus Christi College, Cambridge, MS. 183, fol.1v. (Reproduced by kind permission of The Bodleian Library, Oxford.)

village. The king's thegns found him his warriors; the king's reeves – a pretty ill-defined and flexible set of men committed to carrying out the royal orders – formed the breeding ground of a genuinely nation-wide system of government by and under the king.

Secondly, these kings were as a rule leaders in war, obviously a function only notional if the office was for a time in the hands of a woman or a child, but always built into the essential concept of the whole notion. Kings had to be warriors because for some 300 years after the first settlement the chief thing remembered about them and their people was the constant warfare. What between the contests for ascendancy, the conflicts of personality, and the piecemeal extension of English rule at the expense of the Celtic borderlands, warfare was near enough continuous, and the number of kings who died in their beds barely outnumbered those who were killed in battle or murdered without the cover of a battle. It was a far from civilized society, and that despite the elements of culture that grew quite strikingly at the same time. Freemen were buried with their weapons, the one thing that truly identified their individuality, and even if this custom did not celebrate genuine military achievements it enshrined a dominant warlike tradition.[9] And all free men owed military service when called upon to gather for war by those overlords who called themselves kings. The surprising number of royal saints (many of them women) were less genuine martyrs for their religion than the casualties of wars whom interested parties within the struggling Christian clergy (more about them later on) could claim as champions after their violent deaths.

Of course, this state of endemic battling did not arise solely from the competition of all those chieftains. The island remained exposed to attacks from outside, especially from Ireland and from the region that later came to be known as Wales. And just as it seemed, in the days of Offa whose dyke from the Dee to the Severn identified a permanent frontier in the west, as though something like order might be imposed by the ascendancy of Mercia, a new wave of attacks began with the raids of Norsemen or Vikings – Danes in the east and Norwegians in the north-west. Peace does seem to have been rare and never secure, so that the military role of kings had a lot going for it. In passing one may note that these conditions helped to promote an essentially monastic structure for Christianity when it arrived: monasteries were havens of approximate peace, protected by religious awe quite as much as by walls. To some extent this apparent prevalence of war may be a

---

[9] It has been shown that weapon burials testify to superior standing in society, rather than point to military ranks spending their lives fighting (H. Hänke, ' "Warrior Graves": The Background of the Anglo-Saxon Weapon Burial Rite', *PP* 126 [1990], 22–43).

consequence of the records: what was best remembered and most commonly written down was the marauding and the fighting. But there was certainly enough of it in a society still distinctly rude and barbaric for that selection in the memory to represent a truth.

That it was not, however, the whole truth appears strikingly in the third major function of kingship. Anglo-Saxon kings, or at least quite a number of them, acted also as givers of law, or perhaps rather as collectors and definers of the legal customs of their communities. Legal codes were one of the specialities of those kings. Such ordering and setting down of dooms can occasionally be matched in other Germanic settlements, but the Anglo-Saxons stand out in the regular and repeated production of what look like legislative summaries, starting (so far as survival runs) with the laws of Æthelbert of Kent towards the end of the sixth century. The most important case was that of Wessex, where King Ine formulated a very detailed code about a century later; in both Kent and Wessex subsequent lawgivers adopted and adapted the early efforts. Absence of peace did not equal anarchy; those legal codes constituted perhaps the most positive and most lasting activity of royal rulers.

Naturally, the laws, being written down and preserved, provide splendid information on the kind of society with which we are dealing.[10] The first remarkable thing about them is the language in which they were originally composed. Those kings and their advisers used the vernacular; unlike all the rest of western Europe they escaped the bureaucratic imposition of Latin. The relatively late date of the conquest and distance from Rome played their part in this, but what matters is the effect: a society which managed to organize itself from within its own conventions and resources. So far so impressive: but a closer look at the laws so defined tends to remind one once again of what a mixture of the primitive and the sophisticated this society contained. The laws, so called, are predominantly concerned to define penalties for various crimes

[10] For a shrewd set of comments on the laws cf. H. G. Richardson and G. O. Sayles, *Law and Legislation from Æthelbert to Magna Carta* (1966), ch. 1. The book certainly contains some extravagances in detail and in general interpretation (cf. J. C. Holt's review in *History* 55 [1970] 232–3), but its critical attitude to the Anglo-Saxon codes is refreshing.

Plate 3 *Unarmoured mounted spearmen in an early eleventh-century psalter: a close copy of early ninth-century illustration. (The British Library, London.)*

and transgressions, more especially theft, though physical injuries and even killing are given some houseroom. Take the laws of Ine, set down around 690, which were to form the basis for the settling of the realm by Alfred and his successors. Since Ine began by announcing that he had taken the advice mainly of members of his clergy, it comes as no surprise to find the details concerning Christian observance heading the list and extreme in their savagery. Working on a Sunday will get a slave flogged and a free man enslaved. But after that we hear virtually only of money fines, varied with the standing of the offender and the offended, as well as with the nature of the offence. This leads to some odd juxtapositions. Killing a man (or a woman) is redeemed by the payment of *wergild* to his or her kin, but a *ceorl*, previously accused in vain and at last caught in the act of stealing, will lose a hand or a foot. The earliest laws make it plain that folk custom is being organized with the benefits coming to the victim and his kin, but by stages the king inserts himself both as a deviser of laws (legislation is still too grand a term) and as beneficiary who takes his share of the fine. Like other aspects of government, the laws and their enforcement depend on the action of kings, even though genuinely royal courts do not make their appearance until the ninth century. Most cases are heard and settled in folk-moots of one kind or another – usually the court of the hundred – by the community; there are no lawyers, and a man's equals or superiors judge him unprofessionally. This, of course, is why kings found it necessary to offer the guidance provided in their so-called laws.[11]

In their essence, these Anglo-Saxon law codes resembled the tribal and regional systems found among all the Germanic peoples and their settlements, and the reliance on communal courts also does not differ much from the *Schöppengerichte* which were still active in sixteenth-century Germany when they battled against princely courts trying to impose the civil law derived from Rome. (By that time, as we shall see, the king's jurisdiction had long taken virtually exclusive charge in

---

[11] The laws of Æthelred of *c*.1000 (*English Historical Documents 500–1042*, ed. Dorothy Whitelocke [1955], 403ff.) demonstrate the attainment of a well-organized trial procedure: item 3.1 in effect testifies to the institution of a jury of presentment, while the roots of a trial jury are indicated in item 13.2.

England.) But two things about the laws of the Anglo-Saxons deserve special notice. In the first place, to say it again, they were written in the vernacular; despite the part played by the Church in securing the elementary form of codification, Latin did not enter into the game. The laws of the Franks survive from the mid-sixth century, but only in Latin.[12] Despite the notable regional differences, a reasonably coherent form of the English language therefore existed at the time, available for the relatively sophisticated needs of government; it also came to suffice for the impressive production of formal charters, issued by kings and sometimes lesser landowners and mostly extant because they created endowments for monasteries which kept a record of their title-deeds. And secondly, we should surely be a little more surprised than historians of Anglo-Saxon England commonly are to think about these quite primitive communities dealing almost exclusively in money fines, some of them very large. From the late sixth century, at any rate, Kent possessed sufficient circulating coins to make such rules sound sensible, and this phenomenon continued impressively through the rest of the Anglo-Saxon era. The Anglo-Saxon communities relied almost exclusively on coins minted in the realm, and quite a few have also been found in hoards on the Continent. Coining became one of the prerogatives of kingship; from the tenth century, kings called in all money every few years for recoining, combining profit with rectitude. But this surprisingly sophisticated practice derived from several centuries of a developed money economy, practised in what were almost exclusively agrarian settlements with trade – internal or external – taking very much a back seat. The emergence of princely ascendancy both assisted and benefited from this native production of generally accepted coins.

The Role of the Church

Kings constituted one agency engaged in turning the settled bands of peasant warriors into a people; the other, as powerful, was the Church, emerging as both the product and the

---

[12] Edward James, *The Franks* (1988), 12.

promoter of long labours devoted to turning those heathens into Christians.[13] In actual fact, the island which the Germanic invaders began to settle from the middle of the fourth century onwards was nominally Christian, the whole Roman empire having formally embraced that faith some 120 years earlier. Nor was that adherence purely nominal: the Celtic inhabitants practised and preserved a species of that religion. Indeed, the Anglo-Saxon arrival coincided with the final success of the Christianizing missions carried out in Ireland by St Patrick, a Celt from northern Britain, and while the Anglo-Saxons remained pagan the new Christians of Ireland (not for the last time) tried to return the compliment by sending out their missionaries across the sea. The task proved to be more difficult than one might have supposed, in great part because the old and the new inhabitants so resolutely refused to mix. Theodoric the Ostrogoth (474–526) arrived in Italy as a Christian, and Clovis the Frank (c,464–511) turned Christian the moment he had established his rule over Gaul, but the invaders of what was to become England abandoned their old religion only slowly and by stages. In 563, the Irishman Columba founded a missionary monastery on Iona, off the west coast of Scotland, and in 597 St Augustine's mission, organized from Rome by Pope Gregory the Great, arrived in Kent. However, it took the better part of a century to convert even the ruling sort, and the real Christianizing of these slow and stubborn people took close on 200 years of spasmodic advance and retreat. However, there were advantages in this lack of urgency. The Goths lost their chance of a lasting hold on Italy because in their early eagerness they had picked on the doomed form of the Christian religion known as Arianism: this produced the alliance of the Roman pope with the Roman emperor at Constantinople which destroyed Theodoric's successors. Clovis, a crafty politician very suitably elected patron saint of all French politicians, in effect submerged the possible innovation of a Frankish realm in a re-creation of Roman Gaul in new hands and thereby fixed the lines of French development for centuries in ways adverse to peace and freedom. The Anglo-Saxons waited, courted by Irish monks from the west and north, and by Roman emissaries from

---

[13] See esp. Mayr-Harting, *The Coming of Christianity.*

the south. Northumbria – Bede's Northumbria – in effect became the first truly Christian kingdom in the island, and in the time of that assertive and self-important saint, Bishop Wilfrid, looked likely to impose a Christianity derived from the Celtic monastery. Rome thought otherwise, and the Synod of Whitby (664) terminated the Irish and Celtic pressure, leaving the Anglo-Saxon Church to look to Rome and to be organized quite efficiently by Archbishop Theodore who, arriving at Canterbury in 669 at the age of sixty-seven, contrary to all the probabilities still had twenty-one years to set his stamp on the Church in England. The work was done thoroughly and well, so much so that by the 720s it was possible for an Anglo-Saxon missionary, St Boniface, to undertake the conversion of Saxony and parts of Germany east of the Rhine in the service of both Rome and the Carolingian Franks. After Whitby, and thanks to Theodore, the English Church and clergy remained in close contact with the centres of western Christianity, while the Celtic fringe and Ireland retreated into a form of stagnant isolation. Some of those close contacts quite regularly involved journeys by both churchmen and noblemen to Rome, but more arose from the dispatch of presents and books to the distant brethren – the sort of thoughtfulness that helped to provide Bede with his excellent library at the monastery of Jarrow.[14] Some lesser Anglo-Saxon kings took to abandoning their thrones for the monastic cowl, but that fortunately proved to be a passing fashion.

The Church introduced several contributions to the development of an English nation. In the first place, of course, it consolidated a unifying ideology, removing allegiance to regional or tribal inheritances, and after the decision to tie the new faith to the Roman centre the Church also assisted the total separation from the Celtic neighbours. Rome furthermore offered ready-made contacts beyond the limits of the island, and by the eighth century numbers of Anglo-Saxons – monks, emissaries, even aspiring kings – are found travelling the Continent. Merovingian and Carolingian ladies married into English royal houses, adding further talent to the formidable role played by women in that society. The Church also enlarged

[14] Ibid., 124–6.

and settled the intellectual horizon of the new converts: both vernacular and Latin literature benefited, to such a degree that the standards first set by Bede became sufficiently widespread to make England a source of intellectual inspiration for the continental monarchies. The outstanding example of Alcuin (*c.*755–804), who after 781 helped to civilize the court of Charlemagne, and whose edition of the Vulgate Bible became the standard text used in the Middle Ages, typifies the role that the learned men of England were playing abroad.

But what the Church did not do was to unify the island politically. At least, after the reorganization carried through by Theodore, the original structure which gave each kingdom its single diocese and each king his single attendant bishop (usually a monk of some kind) disappeared, and the two provinces of Canterbury and York, both looking to Rome, offered an alternative to the royal divisions. Nevertheless, round about the middle of the eighth century England contained its separate kingdoms, coexisting sometimes at peace and sometimes jostling for ascendancy, with the mini-power blocs of Northumbria, Mercia and Wessex seemingly in permanent command of the scene. No doubt Mercia in the days of Offa and his successors held a kind of leading position owing to its relative size and its occupation of the middle of the island, and one consequence of this would appear to have been the fact that the Midlands speech became the main source of the English language as it developed. But there was no English kingdom, no English people, no real English identity, inside the multiple structure. Then, just when a sort of settled permanency looked to have emerged from three centuries of conquest, settlement and warfare, everything was once again thrown into turmoil. The next wave of Germanic invaders struck, as the Vikings of Denmark and Norway decided that their home regions were too small to hold them.

Danes and Normans

After some hit-and-run raiding (mostly in the north) from 793 onwards, the real Danish attacks began with an assault on Sheppey in 835. Thereafter, the raids became just about annual.

In 850, a Danish army for the first time overwintered in England, and fifteen years later they started on the serious undertaking of a conquest of the island. Although they were by no means always victorious they had by 878 absorbed Mercia and the north and driven the remnant of the Wessex forces under their new king, Alfred, into refuge at Athelney. This, however, was as far as they got, for Alfred gathered his armies together and began the counterattack. In 886, he both secured the nominal allegiance of all the English and came to terms with the Danish king, Guthrun. In effect the country was now divided into an English south and west, and a Danish north and east – the region known as the Danelaw. Alfred's success by stages established a form of suzerainty over both parts, and when Athelstan roped in the Northumbrian regions in 927 a single kingdom of England was at last in existance – half a millennium after the disappearance of the single Roman region of Britannia.

Plate 4 King Alfred (870–899) depicted on one of his silver pennies. (Reproduced by courtesy of the Trustees of The British Museum, London.)

It was, however, an England greatly altered from the old Anglo-Saxon days. The Danish invaders, belated heathens, began as pirates and plunderers: the destruction they left wherever they alighted wiped out the monastic and royal civilizations so painfully built up, and left especially the north in that condition of backwardness and wilderness that contrasts so noticeably with its great days of Oswy and the Venerable Bede. True, in due course the Danes ceased their raiding and settled,

by stages accepting Christianity. They restored some prosperity
to East Anglia and the Vale of York, and they became a
permanent component of the English people. At this point they
did not, as some seem to think, form part of a true Danish
empire.[15] They had left their homeland as completely as the
earlier Germanic settlers had left theirs. When, after the failure
of the Wessex kings in the reign of Æthelred the Unready, the
Danish monarchs returned in the persons of Sweyn and Cnut,
they did make England part of a short-lived Danish empire but
did not seriously affect the separate structure and existence of
the island which offered them the valuable property of an
established royal crown. The first, chief and most lasting effect
of the Danish invasions was to consolidate England politically,
even if ethnically it may be said to have become more
complicated. The second effect, less enduring because of the
work put in by the house of Wessex, lay in the return of a dark
age of brutal warfare and mindless destruction. After the Danes
came, there was no Alcuin available to help educate the empire
of the Carolingians.

The restoration began with the heroic figure of Alfred and
culminated, rather oddly, in the pliant Edward the Confessor,
and it produced an England that was not only united but also
new in essentials. The most obvious product of this renewal was
a really strong monarchy. These kings were now true kings, not
glorified chieftains. The Danes had first shown up the military
deficiencies of the Anglo-Saxons, but the Wessex monarchs
altered this. They fully exploited the possibilities inherent in the
duty to serve when summoned by making an effective force of
the fyrd; they built defensive points (*burhs*) to withstand the
raids from the sea and up the rivers; they invested in a navy.
Loyalties to the monarch equipped them with a formidable
army of professional retainers, of their own and of their near-
feudal tenantry. Wherever they controlled, they organized the
localities into shires which only sometimes coincided with the
old kingdoms, and everywhere they introduced the subordinate
organization into hundreds: royal rule took over from the

[15] Hugh Kearney, *The British Isles: A History of Four Nations* (1989), a mixture of
shrewd insights and wildish fantasies, writes up the 'free' peasants and traders of the
alleged Danish empire at the expense of the narrowly militaristic and authoritarian
kingdom of Wessex. A case of Celtic revenge upon the self-satisfied English?

kindred, and the realm became governable. Shires might stand
under the hand of remnants of the earlier royal houses but
usually they were now governed by ealdormen (earls, in the
Danish set-up) under the king. Not all the kings were personally
successful, and before the end came with the Normans' arrival,
ealdormen could become overmighty subjects, but this did not
happen with the regularity found in the declining Carolingian
empire, which by the year 1000 had broken up into separate
entities only nominally subordinate to emperors and kings. The
English kingdom was held together by the dominance of
whatever royal house occupied the throne. Those kings had
achieved an authority that enshrined the rule of a realm, and the
days of a purely personal overlordship were gone.[16]

Control of the military affairs and the government of the
realm, though they owed something to the pre-Danish kings,
thus attained a position of power which endured independently
of the personalities of the rulers; though strong kings naturally
did better than weak and imposed themselves more noticeably,
kingship began to have a meaning apart from kings. High-flown
language might pretend even more, but such noise had no
meaning: the kings of England did not seriously think of
themselves as emperors even if now and again they used the
term.[17] They inherited and consolidated the role of the lawgiver
which had now grown into that of keeper and guardian of the
law; and they developed certain instruments of rule, especially
the formal charter and the remarkable Anglo-Saxon writ, a well
structured instrument for conveying their authority across the
realm. It would seem more likely now that they never created an
office deserving the name of a chancery,[18] but they manifestly

[16] H. R. Loyn, 'The King and the Structure of Society in Late Anglo-Saxon England',
History 42 (1957), 87–100.

[17] H. R. Loyn, 'The Imperial Style of the Tenth Century Anglo-Saxon Kings', *History*
40 (1955), 111–15. However, what was 'a stylistic flourish' in the tenth century became
a very useful discovery for the age of Henry VIII when Thomas Cromwell seriously set
about consolidating the 'empire' of England.

[18] This is the view of Pierre Chaplais, 'The Royal Anglo-Saxon Chancery of the
Tenth Century Revisited', in *Studies in Medieval History presented to R.H.C. Davis* (ed.
H. Mayr-Harting and R. I. Moore, 1985), 41–51, as against the opinion of Simon
Keynes, *The Diplomas of King Æthelred 'the Unready'* (1980), 14–19. It would be
interesting to know whether Chaplais persuaded the recipient of this *festschrift*, who
earlier had accepted the existence of a highly developed chancery and exchequer in the
eleventh-century Anglo-Saxon kingdom: R. H. C. Davis, 'The Norman Conquest',
History 51 (1966), 279–86.

employed expert scribes and local administrators – a nascent bureaucracy. The most solid and most impressive foundation of their rule lay in wealth. The consolidation of the kingdom greatly increased the crown estate which made possible an impressive lifestyle at the court, but more unusual was the novel power to extract taxes from the subject. Some contributions, of a modest sort, had commonly been available in times of emergency, but the Danish invasion created a taxing policy of remarkable size, virtually unknown elsewhere in western Europe. Before they settled, the Danish armies had developed a considered policy of financial blackmail: they demanded to be bought off if further destruction was to be avoided. The English thus built up a system for raising the cash that went into pirate pockets, and as taxes will, they continued to be raised after peace returned and the money went to the kings of England. The Anglo-Saxon geld – a tax laid upon the freeholders of land – was assessed and administered with an efficiency unusual in the Early Middle Ages and supported a crown that could by the standards of the time be called rich.[19]

Behind the taxing system stood the royal monopoly in the minting of coins. Earlier beginnings in this were very fully developed by the English monarchy before the Norman Conquest – so fully that even the intrusion of a continental power with little experience of a controlled coinage could not undermine the trustworthiness of the English silver penny, which retained its high standard of purity until the sixteenth century. This success rested on another astonishing administrative achievement already mentioned. Kings maintained their exclusive right to produce coins (which in turn by their design proclaimed the greatness of kings) by retaining a monopoly over the dies sent to local mints whenever required, and in the tenth and eleventh centuries it became practice to call in the whole of the coinage every few years for reminting. One way and another, the monarchy which took hold of the realm after overcoming the threat of a Danish conquest settled into a degree

[19] Cf. H. R. Loyn, *Anglo-Saxon England and the Norman Conquest* (1962), 305–14. The amounts raised are in dispute. J. Gillingham refuses to believe the traditional figures, while M. K. Lawson thinks them likely (*EHR* 104 [1989], 373–406, and 105 [1990], 939–61). For our purposes it is enough to know that even the lower figures are pretty remarkable by eleventh-century standards.

of effective rule not seen in the island since Roman days. Increasingly it mattered less whether the person holding the crown came from Anglo-Saxon stock or claimed Danish descent: the word that now counted was English. It also, somewhat surprisingly, did not matter all that much whether that person was himself a man of weight, a warrior or a lawgiver; kingship and its subordinate authorities in the local administration governed a settled realm. The point comes across very well in the two men – admittedly men of very real weight – who in effect created the folklore of English kingship. The two pre-Conquest kings entrenched in popular memory are Anglo-Saxon Alfred with his cakes and Danish Cnut with his tide. A word is necessary on King Alfred.

King Alfred the Great (849–99, ruled from 871) forms a sort of prototype – the kind of king that the English came especially to admire. After all, he is the only man in over a thousand years of monarchic history who has been granted that distinguished epithet. He was also the first English king to elicit a biography by a contemporary (Asser). And although we have been reminded that all we think we know about him – more especially from Asser and from the Anglo-Saxon Chronicle which Alfred refashioned – originated under his rule and guidance,[20] no one has yet taken scepticism to the point of destroying the image. Alfred's achievement consisted of three major triumphs. In the first place, he proved himself as a leader of men and of armies, reorganizing the fyrd, building his realm's defences, and winning a war that had seemed lost when he came to the throne. Secondly, he governed efficiently from his court,[21] involving the great men of his kingdom in the regular routines of government and meeting them benevolently in the great council called the *witenagemot*. And thirdly, he restored and revived the spritual and intellectual culture of his dominions. His own activity in translating Latin works into Anglo-Saxon was designed to return his people to the compass of European civilization and to bring back the standards set by

[20] R. H. C. Davis, 'Alfred the Great: Propaganda and Truth', *History* 56 (1971), 169–82. The article unquestionably demonstrates the presence of a well-promoted bias in the accounts.

[21] Alfred was responsible for adding the city of London to the West Saxon dominions, but the centre of the kingdom remained at Winchester until after the Norman Conquest.

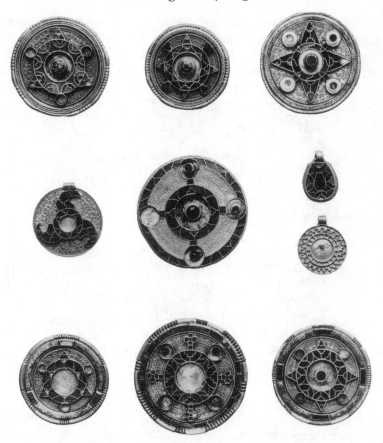

Plate 5 Group of Anglo-Saxon Kentish jewels from Faversham.
(Reproduced by courtesy of the Trustees of The British Museum, London.)

Bede's Northumbria some 200 years earlier. The works so made available included both Bede's *Ecclesiastical History* and Boethius' *Consolations of Philosophy*. Alfred set a standard for the future as a patron of learning, though it has to be admitted that he found few to follow his lead to make kings into men of learning themselves. In person, he seems to have been a decent man, as Anglo-Saxon kings went. Though one may doubt whether he would have recognized himself in the garb of an eminent Victorian – a sort of headmaster in his kingdom – in which the nineteenth century tended to clothe him, he does form an interesting and encouraging model for the kings of

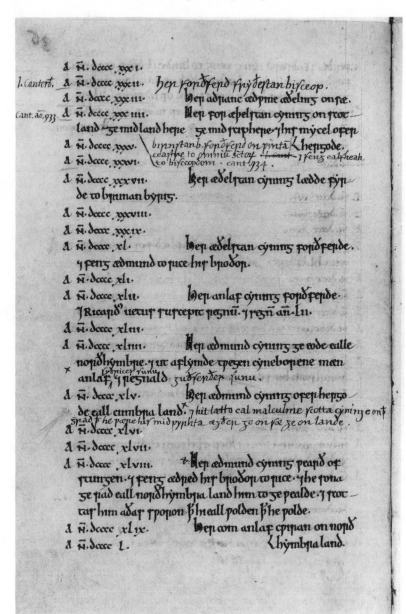

Plate 6 Page from the Anglo-Saxon Chronicle which tells of Athelstan's victory at Brunanburh in 937. (The Bodleian Library, Oxford, MS Laud, Misc. 636, fo. 35v.)

England: determined, highly competent, unshaken by adversity, and passionately devoted to learning. In actual fact, of course, he reached perfection in none of his attainments. The unification of England was mainly the work of his immediate successors Edward the Elder and Athelstan. The full shiring and the growth of local government under the ealdormen took place in the tenth century and was rounded off by the Danish kings. And his scholarly achievement was soon overtaken by the revival of Latin and literature coming from the Continent. But it was Alfred who by his example at a time of dire trouble made those later developments possible in England.

Alfred also renewed the alliance with the Church and with Rome (which he visited as a child) that had been created before the Danes rampaged over the country. The century and more of brutal assaults by wild and heathen conquerors had in effect set back both the faith and the organization of the Church in England to a condition not all that different from the early days of conversion. This was particularly so because that Church depended on the existence of monasteries; and monasteries unprotected by spiritual awe offered the most promising target to the invaders' search for portable booty. In the wake of the Danes, the centres of Christianity crumpled, especially in the north where by the end of the ninth century no religious house remained standing. The simultaneous assaults of Norsemen on Ireland, on the Isle of Man, and on the west coast of Scotland prevented regeneration from the old Celtic centres. The work was all to do again, though both the diocesan structure and contacts with the Christian Continent remained in sufficient repair to promise fairly quick results, and in the course of the century after Alfred's death the Church came back in strength – even converting the Danes. The main agent of this revival was once again the monastic order, but a monasticism different from the somewhat relaxed practice that had ruled in the past; promoted by such leaders as St Dunstan (intermittently falling out with his kings), the Benedictine rule, in the severe style imposed by the reforming movement of Cluny and other French centres, now took firm hold.[22] The Wessex dynasty dutifully followed this programme of renewal; one of them, a lesser

---

[22] David Knowles, *The Monastic Order in England* (2nd edn, 1963), chs 3 and 4.

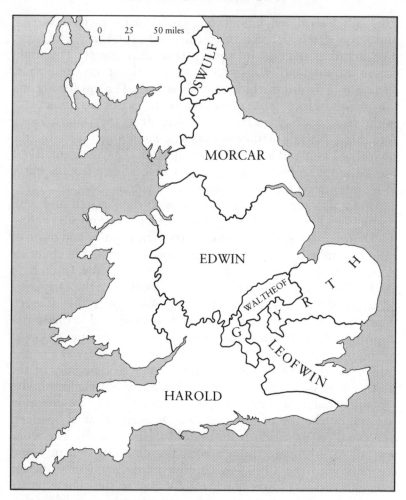

Figure 2 The English earldoms at the end of 1065 (after E. A. Freeman, The History of the Norman Conquest of England, *6 vols, Oxford, 1867–79).*

Edward, even returned to the curious habits of an earlier age which turned the victims of family quarrels into officially recognized saints. The renewed Church, however, also opened the way to the victory of Latin over the vernacular in both government and culture.

Altogether, the renewed Church, like up to a point the renewed monarchy, proved really less insular than the predecessors had been. The ruling house established links with princes elsewhere, so that Norman influence was strong at the court of the Confessor and Duke William could claim to have been chosen for the succession. And the Church was now more closely attached to the Roman pontiff and all his works, adding yet another element characteristic of medieval England until the Reformation. All this fitted in with yet another effect of the Danish intrusion and the settlement which followed upon it: the island came to be incorporated in a much wider network of trade and travel. The Danes certainly practised a freer form of peasant landholding than had prevailed in the Anglo-Saxon past, and in this last century before the Normans came slavery does seem to have been in retreat. But apart from influencing the agrarian scene the Danes also helped York, Norwich and even London to play active roles in international exchanges. They also set the example for a more advanced form of shipbuilding. None of this was entirely new, of course, but the scale was and the contacts ranged further afield.[23]

This was the country that fell to the Normans after the one decisive battle of Hastings in 1066: a realm of reasonably prosperous agriculture and trade, organized and ruled by just about the most advanced and richest monarchy of the West, united to a degree quite unknown at this time in either France or Germany. Of course, the defining seas and the relatively small area involved helped, as did the fact that the invasion of 1066 was also the last in the history of the English people. After some 600 years of constant incursions and frequent internal war, a high degree of internal peace and a high level of royal power, backed by a reformed Church, had achieved something like permanence and stability. This the Normans inherited; they did not create it.

The Norman Conquest was an accident. It really stemmed from the failure of King Alfred's line after the temporary interruption by somewhat out-of-date Danes; the Confessor somewhat unnecessarily proved his Christian virtue by failing to produce any offspring. This left two claimants for the succession: Anglo-Saxon Harold, son of Godwin, that ealdor-man who came nearest to setting up a separate power under the

---

[23] Loyn, *Anglo-Saxon England and the Norman Conquest*, esp. ch. 2.

crown (as the counts and dukes of continental Europe were doing), and Duke William of Normandy, a leading beneficiary of the break-up of the Carolingian empire. Harold was crowned, and if he had not been called upon at the crucial moment to beat off a Norwegian attack which had something very old-fashioned about it, he would not have had to face the Norman attack (a deal more modern-looking) with a worn-out and enfeebled army. So the victory of Stamford Bridge was followed by the disaster of Hastings. Though the outcome was an accident, that accident carried drastic enough consequences. However, the fact remains that what the Normans took over was an English kingdom peopled by an English nation.

2

Communitas Anglie

The Norman Conquest of 1066 may in its way have been an accident, but it unquestionably determined the history of England ever after. Immediately, it altered the setting within which the people recognizable as 'the English' had come to live, and in the short run it seemed to threaten the continued existence of that identifiable branch of the Germanic nations. In the long run, it vastly altered both the circumstances and the inner reality of the kingdom. It took just about two centuries for these effects, and the further effects stemming from the first effects, to work themselves out; only with the accession of Edward I in 1272 had the fact of an established realm of England, peculiar to itself, become assured. These 200 years witnessed many further transformations, many false starts and more significant changes of course, but they do form a coherent period of time during which the new structure emerged and became confirmed.

After the Conquest

The opening of this age of transformation – the Conquest and its immediate consequences – has become one of the most embattled areas of English history. At times one feels that only accident prevented the combatants from borrowing the swords, lances and battleaxes of the people about whose fortunes they were debating, and some of the things said have been quite as deadly as the thrust of steel. Some Old English fanatics directed

Plate 7 William the Conqueror. Genealogical history from Brutus to Edward I. English, end of the thirteenth century. (MS Bodley rolls 3. The Bodleian Library, Oxford.)

Plate 8 Detail from the Bayeux Tapestry depicting the Battle of Hastings. (Tapisserie de Bayeux et avec autorisation spéciale de la Ville de Bayeux.)

attention to the continuity of experience and reduced the
Conquest to a minor hiccup in the even flow of English history;
and since they received some support from F. W. Maitland there
was obviously quite a good case to be made that way, though
Maitland, as usual, was cautious and guarded himself diligently
against the danger of error springing from overstatement.[1]
Those splendid gladiators, H. G. Richardson and G. O. Sayles,
who always took much inspiration from Maitland, went
overboard and decided that everything after 1066 derived
directly and exclusively from what had gone before.[2] In a
somewhat surprising *jeu d'espirit*, Lewis Warren attacked the
problem from another angle with much the same result when he
argued that the Norman kings displayed only modest capacities
and little if any originality.[3] But the Normans have been able to
parade their champions, starting with J. H. Round, whose
formidable scholarship drew on a bitter fighting temperament –
or the other way round – to demonstrate the overwhelming
change that the Conquest brought,[4] and this stance re-emerged
in that of R. Allen Brown who, starting life as the historian of
castles and rider of horses, came to see little but drastic
innovation in the reigns of the Norman kings.[5] That line also
had the effective support of Sir Frank Stenton, the leading
Anglo-Saxon historian of a long generation.[6] Though some of
this conflict arose from the defects of the evidence which called
for much ingenious interpretation, it goes without saying that
those giants among scholars had good grounds for their diverse
views. By the same token, it also goes without saying that the
likely truth cannot be so definitely on one side or the other.[7]

Certainly, a first impression must be that 1066 marked a
major, indeed an enormous, break in continuity; it was

[1] *Domesday Book and Beyond* (1897).
[2] H. G. Richardson and G. O. Sayles, *The Governance of Medieval England from the Conquest to Magna Carta* (1963). This contains a memorable onslaught on William Stubbs.
[3] W. L. Warren, 'The Myth of Norman Administrative Efficiency', *TRHS* (1984), 113–32.
[4] J. H. Round, *Feudal England* (1895).
[5] E.g. R. Allen Brown, *The Normans and the Norman Conquest* (1969).
[6] F. M. Stenton, *The First Century of English Feudalism 1066–1166* (1932).
[7] As is most urbanely explained by H. R. Loyn, '1066: Should we have Celebrated it?' *Hist. Research* 63 (1990), 119–27.

manifestly not just a replay of 1042 and the arrival of a new king from abroad. It opened an age which called in doubt the very existence of an English nation. The Norman kings ruled from 1066 to 1154, to be followed by the Angevin dynasty and its Poitevin connection (1154–1272). Thus for some 200 years the throne was occupied by men whose chief concerns lay outside England.[8] Indeed, it looked as though that country had become merely an outlying part of one continental empire after another, though the current view among the experts disapproves of the idea that either Normans or Angevins (Henry II and his successors, descended from the counts of Anjou) presided over a genuine empire – a unified agglomerate of territories. Yet the fact cannot be overlooked that all the kings from William I to Henry III were always likely to spend less time in England than elsewhere, and certainly concentrated in the first place on the politics and warfare of their dominions in France. Even if England did not become simply a subordinate part of its ruler's extended territories, it became the chief supplier of the means that enabled him to retain his hold over Normandy or Maine or Anjou, not to mention Henry III's extravagant programme in Gascony and Sicily.[9] Thus the realm which the kings of Wessex had carved out in the British Isles, and which the Danish kings had treated as the centre of their loosely structured empire, looked down to the middle of the thirteenth century somewhat marginal in the accumulations built up by what were most definitely foreign kings. This could not but affect the self-awareness of the people of England as Englishmen.

   This basic problem was enormously increased by the most drastic effect of the Norman Conquest. Before the end of the Conqueror's reign the old top layer of English society – thegns and ealdormen – had been almost totally replaced by a new such layer consisting of Normans and men from other French regions such as Brittany and Flanders. The Danish invasions had led to the settlement of peasants – free peasants in general

---

[8] For the best summary account of those 200 years see M. T. Clanchy, *England and its Rulers, 1066–1272* (1983). I here acknowledge my general indebtedness to this excellent book.

[9] The arguments are rehearsed in David Bates, 'Normandy and England after 1066', *EHR* 104 (1989), 851–80, esp. 865–8.

but not people to drive out the existing governing sort. William's army also came in search of profit and landed wealth but it consisted of professional knights ready to turn into a baronage. It would appear that the real takeover of English manors and demesnes followed upon the abortive rebellions against the invaders of 1069–70 in the south and a little later in the north, but by 1086, when Domesday Book was put together to provide a register of the new tenurial set-up, there remained only two English landowners of quality south of the Tees. The rest were French and overwhelmingly Norman. This effect was enlarged by the fact that the Church in England also turned Norman; as episcopal sees fell vacant continental bishops took over – and took over the control of the episcopal lands as well. The numbers involved look small: a people of 1.5 to 2 millions was now dominated by some 12,000 foreigners many of whom, at least to begin with, also held often large estates in Normandy. Nevertheless, the effect was striking. The English, properly so called, became for several generations the subjects of a manifestly non-English ruling class who, to begin with, could not even talk with the occupiers of their lands; and the great cleft between the top and the mass emphasized the hierarchic structure of society well beyond what had been visible before the Conquest.

Norman Practice

Perhaps the most manifest exemplification of this change lay in what has been called the introduction of feudalism. It is worth remembering that the word itself was unknown before the seventeenth century: it has never been anything but a construct invented and used by historians. In consequence it is not surprising to find much learned debate about its meaning, a debate often misdirected by the Marxist identification of a feudal stage supposedly preceding the onset of capitalism. If by feudalism we understand a social structure in which wealth is mainly derived from the possession of land, in which landed ownership is in the hands of a ruling caste relying on the labour of a peasantry essentially unfree (that is, tied to the land – adscriptus glebae), and in which governing authority emanates

Plate 9 *The Four Horsemen of the Apocalypse depicted as medieval knights oppressing the downtrodden peasants. (MS Bodley rolls, English Life, The Bodleian Library, Oxford, MS Tanner Bod. 184, p. 58.)*

from a central ruler but comes to rest in the hands of lesser rulers throughout the realm, then it is clear that the Conquest at most confirmed and redefined a feudal system already current in

1066.[10] However, for that very reason so wide a concept is not very helpful: any society spread over a reasonably large territory, specializing in agriculture, lacking easy means of communication, and physically too extensive to be centralized by the means available at the time, is bound to display the features of this loose kind of feudalism. Of course, Anglo-Saxon England did look like that: how else could it have looked?

If, on the other hand, one takes the reality of a true feudal structure to lie in the military organization required to hold down a newly conquered kingdom and for the external warfare that followed after, an organization which then dictated the social and political relationships within that society, the Conquest did introduce an altogether new system by importing practices already visible in Normandy. This involved the formal relationships between lord and vassal expressed in the latter's oath of fealty and the former's promise of protection. It rested upon a definition of parcels of property as knight's fees (*feoda*) held on condition of military service if called out, and it produced a network of castles all over the country from which and by means of which the knightly order controlled a potentially rebellious people. The rapid production of these military measures has been called 'less the introduction of "the feudal system", and more the spontaneous reaction to immediate and urgent needs',[11] but at any rate it happened. The Normans brought in the essentials of an order which the fact of conquest and the transfer of landownership enabled them to develop more completely than it had existed in their continental duchy. And from the point of view of the English, the multitude of castles – whether rapid motte-and-bailey structures or in due course the stone keeps that housed the feudatory and his troop of knights – mattered more than the continuity of basic relationships within the manor. The accumulation of manors in fewer hands – the creation of large though scattered possessions called honours – reinforced this truly feudal innovation upon which for several generations the power of the conquering

[10] This was the view held by Maitland in *Domesday Book and Beyond* and also most influentially by Marc Bloch whose *La Société féodale* (2 vols, 1939–40) appeared in English in 1961.

[11] R. Allen Brown, *The Origin of English Feudalism* (1973), 86. This book presents the clearest exposition of the 'feudal revolution' argument.

Normans was to rest. Englishmen either accepted their inferior status, as most did though not without complaining, or tried to continue resistance as outlaws, becoming the material more influential in the romantic revival of the nineteenth century than in the reality of the eleventh.[12]

The reality of the change was further underlined by the great change that came over the languages of learning and of government. Anglo-Saxon England had provided the leading example of a vernacular culture worthy of the name in the whole of western Europe. French and German did not achieve a like status of literary quality and use till the twelfth century, whereas Old English had reigned for hundreds of years. The

Plate 10 A medieval engraving depicting the legend of Robin Hood and Little John. (The Bodleian Library, Oxford.)

[12] Cf. M. H. Keen, *The Outlaws of Medieval Legend* (1961), which really shows how marginal those allegedly heroic, really rather terrorist, resisters were in medieval society.

coming of a ruling class unable to speak that language inevitably reduced English to an inferior position, with French and Latin taking over. Latin in particular commanded a formidable monopoly in scholarship and administration. It made its mark on the former in the course of the so-called twelfth-century Renaissance when a number of Englishmen reached notable levels of attainment (especially John of Salisbury, perhaps the most interesting philosopher of that age) as members of an international learned community.[13] But they did so by accepting the self-appointed leadership of France: it was in this century that Francomania, that long-standing affliction, established itself as fashionable in England. And starting with the Norman kings, whose government relied in the main on members of the clergy, Latin became the language of official proceedings and documents, another long-lived change which still affected the running of affairs in the eighteenth century. (The law was to provide a specially interesting example of what was happening: its proper records were kept in Latin, but because court proceedings were at first conducted by word of mouth a debased species of French served counsel and judges until the 1730s.) Even those chroniclers like William of Malmesbury or Orderic Vitalis who were conscious of their English descent and bitter about the Conquest chose to write in the Latin which gave them access to an upper-class readership. A few old-fashioned monks continued to write a continuation of the Anglo-Saxon Chronicle started by King Alfred, but this piece of antiquarianism came to an end in 1154. English became the spoken language of the lower orders – of peasants and servants – and for several generations its career as a literary vernacular appeared to be over.

If the state – a term not unsuitable before the Conquest but probably less fitting thereafter in those collections of regions ruled by Norman and Angevin princes – turned Latin and continental, so even more so did the Church. Of course, the pre-Conquest Church had known and used Latin, and it had had close ties with papal Rome. These traditions received powerful reinforcement from the fact that leadership passed from Englishmen to men brought in from several parts of Europe.

---

[13] R. W. Southern, *Medieval Humanism and Other Studies* (1970), 135–80.

Both bishops and abbots tended after 1066 to come from abroad, and the difference this made is well illustrated by the one exception. Wulfstan, bishop of Worcester, appointed in 1062, lived in charge of his see until 1095 and in that time preserved the English traditions, until his death opened the door for a succession of Normans. The first two post-Conquest archbishops of Canterbury, Lanfranc and Anselm, were both Italians born who had made a career at the Norman abbey of Bec. They certainly differed greatly from each other in their preoccupations and fortunes: Lanfranc, the energetic adminis-trator always fully in William I's confidence, and Anselm the awkward philosopher who managed to quarrel with just about everybody. Lanfranc introduced the high priestly claims of the Gregorian reform, and though Anselm at intervals fell out not only with his kings but also with Rome he maintained these novel attitudes. It is from the rule of Pope Gregory VII rather than that of Pope Gregory I that we should date the character-istically friendly relationship between medieval England and the papacy. One result of this was to be the emergence of secular (beneficed) rather than regular (monastic) clergy in charge of the English Church: Lanfranc and Anselm were among the last spiritual leaders to be monks, and with the further reforms that settled the Benedictine houses and brought in the Cistercians the orders turned away from the virtually universal involvement in royal government that had characterized the Church of St Dunstan.

King, Army and Administration

Thus both at first sight and on closer inspection it does look as though 1066 marked a relentless watershed in the fortunes of the English. They became a subject people ruled by newly settled invaders; their realm became a lesser component in powerful accumulations of territories centred upon France; their Church became an instrument of French and Italian politics; and they had to learn Latin if they were to make any sort of career. But this is not the whole story: a closer look yet indicates that there was much continuity spanning the seeming chasm. Anglo-Saxon England, contrary to all

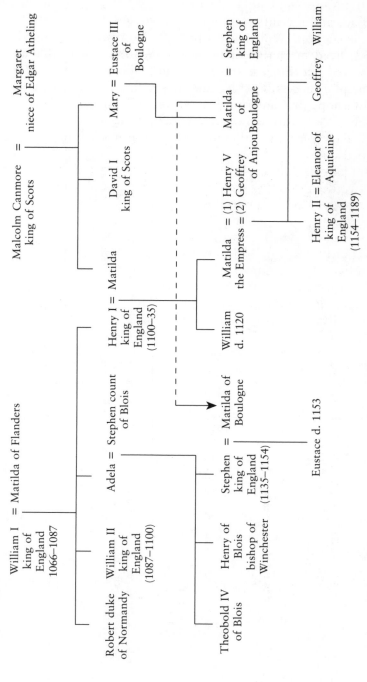

Figure 3 *The English succession from William I to Henry II.*

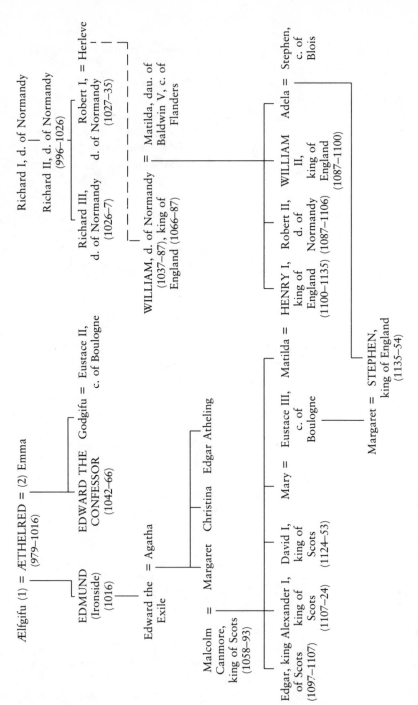

Figure 4 *Claimants to the English throne, 1066–1100.*

appearances, did not die; it lingered, and it left its mark upon
the new rulers.

The most obvious point, and in some way the point that
determined everything else, lies in the fact that those foreign
rulers who became kings of England held no other royal crown.
However many other regions they acquired and ruled, and no
matter that most of their days and concerns concentrated upon
the Continent, only England made them kings. And the royal
office implied more than mere dignity or standing. Dukes of
Normandy and counts of Anjou were vassals of the king of
France and swore fealty to him; kings of England knew only
liegemen and no superior lords. By the end of the twelfth
century this mattered greatly as the Capetian kings – especially
Philip Augustus (1180–1223) – settled down to the business of
imposing their authority on the great nobles who had hitherto,
as regional rulers, managed to ignore the implications of
vassalage. John lost Normandy to the French king in 1204 but
he remained king of England, and his son succeeded to the
throne despite the attempts of a French prince to wrest the
realm away from him. It might be noted that though John
regained control over a rebellious baronage by surrendering his
kingdom to the pope, receiving it back on conditions of nominal
dependence, this famous absurdity did little except to inflate the
sufficiently large ego of Pope Innocent III and during the
ineffectual years of Henry III to enable papal emissaries to help
rule the realm: by mid-century, any notion that the king of
England was anyone's feudatory would once again have been
regarded as absurd. After England broke with Rome, plays on
King John quite failed to mention this interlude.

Thus the dukes and counts who conquered or inherited the
throne of England gloried in the office which gave them truly
independent status and which in their title always came first.
The Norman kings called themselves *rex Anglorum*, using the
phrase employed by Danish Cnut or English Athelstan; Henry II
occasionally, and his sons regularly, changed this to *rex Anglie*,
king of England, thus testifying to the essential unity of a realm
in which Englishmen and Frenchmen, and others (including
Jews) all acknowledged the authority of one king. For Henry II,
the title and the possession were to form the basis of wider
claims: this king meant to extend the realm of England over all

Plate 11 King John. (MS Bodley Rolls 3. The Bodleian Library, Oxford.)

the British Isles. The Normans had already managed to bring much of Wales under royal control, directly as in Henry I's penetration of Pembroke,[14] or indirectly through the powerful lordships which they established around the east and south of that part of the island that the Anglo-Saxons had never incorporated. After the turmoil of Stephen's so-called reign, the first Angevin king not only re-established control over England and much of Wales but claimed overlordship over Scotland (a

[14] R. R. Davies, 'Henry I and Wales', in *Studies in Medieval History presented to R.H.C. Davis*, ed. H. Mayr-Harting and R. I. Moore (1985), 133–47.

claim without positive content) and extended his reach over Ireland, gradually and never wholly conquered from 1155 onwards (ostensibly under papal licence). Even if these claims contained a high measure of make-believe and hope, they did underline the primacy of the English kingdom in the hierarchy of dominions subjected to their continentally based monarchs.

More than title came to the Normans and Angevins from their kingship in England. The kingdom conquered in 1066 had been in many ways the most advanced region of royal authority and government in western Europe, and the new kings quickly realized the advantages to be gained from this inheritance. This included even forms of military organization useful both in holding down England and in waging the frequent wars on the Continent, even though the most obvious break with the past appeared in the Norman baron with his mounted knights and private castle.[15] The Anglo-Saxon fyrd survived the Conquest. The great fyrd – the general obligation of all free men to bear arms and obey a royal summons – continued to be available through the Middle Ages though it was rarely called out; as warfare became more and more professionalized the services of the generality proved increasingly useless. Even so, the principle survived to form the basis of the raising of armies by commissions of array introduced from the fourteenth century onwards. What has been dubbed the select fyrd – the armies relying on the thegn and his retainers – fitted quite well with the Norman practice of enfeoffing militant landowners possessed of what were in effect private armies, and on several occasions the Norman kings called upon their English subjects to come to their aid. They did not call in vain; facing the occasional rebellion from their greater barons, all those kings found their English troops more reliably loyal than their Norman feuda-tories.[16] The English soldiers did not have to face the problems of dual loyalties that could affect Normans holding lands in both Normandy and England and troubled to know which contestant in those family quarrels they ought to obey. In any case, above other considerations the habit of obeying the call of the king was already entrenched, and was to remain so into the twentieth century. So while the select fyrd disappeared in the

[15] C. Warren Hollister, *The Military Organisation of Norman England* (1965).
[16] Ibid., 118–19, 222.

takeover of its identity and functions by the Norman feudal army, the great fyrd endured and was by stages incorporated and reorganized by the monarchy, a process beginning with the assize of arms of 1181 and culminating in Edward I's Statute of Winchester of 1285 which defined the duties and equipment of various ranks of able-bodied men in a structured nation in arms.

However, by the later twelfth century both the knightly cavalry of William I and the English infantry inherited from the Anglo-Saxons had ceased to form the effective hard core of royal armies. From early on, much reliance had been placed on mercenary forces – on soldiers fighting not as a public duty or even in response to obligations connected with landholding but at first for plunder and ultimately for pay. By the time of Henry III at the latest, wage service had almost entirely superseded tenurial service,[17] and the effective organization of the king's armies centred not upon the 'feudal' contingents brought along by magnates but upon the royal household and entourage that supplied the leadership to manage and command troops serving for pay.[18] This development also benefited from two things taken over from the Anglo-Saxon kings. From the start, the Norman rulers succeeded in asserting a first claim on the loyalties even of the tenants of their own tenants, a claim markedly more positive than anything found in the dismembered Carolingian empire where greater lords ignored kings and lesser lords fought their private wars. Private wars were unknown in Norman and Angevin England, except now and again in the special conditions of the Welsh Marches, and in this the authority of the king of England owed quite as much to the traditions of pre-Conquest England as to the practices of the Norman baronage. And secondly, the new dynasties inherited a power to tax their subjects – or a traditional willingness on the part of their subjects to pay taxes – upon which their ability to pay for armies largely depended. Once the idea that troops served in return for awards of land had ceased to be workable – once lands had been settled and rampaging knights had turned into landowners – the king needed to

[17] Ibid., 166–9.
[18] J. O. Prestwich, 'The Military Household of the Norman Kings', *EHR* 96 (1981), 1–35.

convert feudal obligations into hard cash if he was to be able to fight his wars efficiently. And this stage had been reached when Henry II restored peace and order. The professional and mercenary troops continued to be recruited from the entourages of lesser lords (household knights and sub-knightly serjeants) but they had to be paid for. So, not surprisingly, the ability to collect money from the people turned out to be the most important inheritance enjoyed by the kings of England.

Duke William had known no such opportunities in Normandy where his government relied in part on services in kind (food renders and military duties) enshrined in the feudal relationship, but in great part on such wealth as the ducal lands (demesnes) might proffer. Like his subjects, the new king found both these resources greatly augmented by the Conquest with its vast additions of land to the demesne and the even vaster enlargement of the feudal potential embodied in the enfeoffment of the new nobility. One of those assets, however, turned out to be a wasting one as time passed: Henry I found his personal demesne much diminished by the sizeable grants to potential dissidents that his brother and he himself had had to make in their efforts to maintain themselves on their thrones on both sides of the Channel. To some extent, these grants compensated the kings by enlarging the income from the so-called feudal incidents – payments for the right to enter upon one's inheritance and increasingly valuable rights of wardship over heirs succeeding as minors. There were also somewhat haphazard yields to be gathered from the royal administration of justice, from the income of episcopal sees kept briefly vacant, and from the sale of offices and privileges.[19] But the main refreshment of the royal finances stemmed from the methods inherited from the pre-Conquest monarchy, more especially the annual contributions from the counties, converted into regular payments collected by the sheriffs, and from national taxation. The general tax known as Danegeld had long been accepted as leviable even when it was no longer devoted to buying off the Danish raiders, and until the reign of Henry II it was imposed with some regularity. One purpose served by the inquiry which produced Domesday Book lay in ascertaining what might be

---

[19] Judith Green, 'William Rufus, Henry I and the Royal Demesne', *History* 64 (1979), 337–52.

due in this fashion,[20] and Henry I appears to have succeeded in raising an annual contribution of 2s. per hide. However, the collapse of effective government in the reign of Stephen put an end to this system, and Henry II found it impossible to return to the raising of geld. But he maintained the ancient royal right to tax: he promoted the yield of the county farms, turned to demanding special levies (aids) on given occasions when he could plead specific needs, and converted military obligations into money payments (scutage) used for raising paid armies instead.[21] This change in the details of taxation did not alter the fundamental fact that kings of England had long before the Conquest established their right to tax to a degree quite unknown in other dominions at that time: one of the most agreeable consequences of moving into the command of a rich and reasonably well governed realm.

Of course, success in this taxing policy depended precisely on this relatively high degree of effective government, and here too the Norman kings, though they added their own contribution, exploited what they took over from Anglo-Saxon England. That inheritance included two particulars that turned out to be both essential and very much available. The bane of princely government in western Europe during what is usually called the High Middle Ages lay in its inability to control the members of the realm. Every such dominion tended to fall apart as local magnates, often in the first place installed by princely favour, set up subordinate rulerships in defiance of central authority. After all, that was what the Norman dukes had exploited in France when in the eleventh century the Capetian kings' effective rule had shrunk into a small region around Paris. Oddly enough, the Anglo-Saxon monarchy had managed to prevent the emergence of provincial lordships, even though those provinces represented what had been separate kingdoms until the Danes overwhelmed them and Wessex reorganized things. Even before the Conquest, a few ealdormen claiming royal blood had shown signs of becoming overmighty subjects, but all such beginnings had fizzled out. The Conquest enabled the new kings to exploit their inherited powers by imposing

---

[20] Sally Harvey, 'Domesday Book and Anglo-Norman Governance', *TRHS* 25 (1975), 175–93.

[21] Judith Green, 'The Last Century of Danegeld', *EHR* 96 (1981), 241–58.

their authority throughout the kingdom. Ealdormen became earls and earls became the top rank of the nobility with no territorial rule attached; the shire structure remained intact and the old shire-reeve, now sheriff or in French viscount (vice-earl) exercised power in that locality very much as the king's agent. Sheriffs needed watching, and the kings of England were to find that at times they sat uneasily on top of a heaving mass of very powerful subjects, but they always recovered control. Even the existence of large franchises possessed of a measure of self-government never produced the fissiparous effect of normal behaviour in a feudal kingdom. England remained very definitely one realm, as it had been before 1066.[22]

The shire was more than a convenient division of the realm; it was a genuine administrative unit. 'The Normans', it has been said, 'inherited from the Anglo-Saxons an administration at shire level that was literate, active and continuous.'[23] Since the assessment and collection of the geld was organized by shires on the basis of the land they contained, headquarters held something like a land-register worked out by inquiry – the germ from which Domesday Book grew. The sheriff was responsible for receiving, executing and reporting back on orders from the king's government, and his court represented the most important regular centre for settling disputes, pursuing criminals, and ensuring the co-operation of local men of weight. This court 'best explains the success of the Norman settlement', the more so because the transfer of landownership altered only people, not entities.[24] It was not that the Normans adapted the shire to their use but rather that they adapted themselves to an existing system which by the standards of the day was exceptionally effective.

The other instrument inherited from the Anglo-Saxons was a remarkable and highly flexible means for keeping in touch with this kingdom-wide organization, a means for conveying the royal will and instructions to regions and individuals. This was the king's writ, authenticated by his seal. All the rulerships that

---

[22] Franchises could have become serious obstacles to unity if they had not either fallen quickly into royal hands (Cornwall, Lancaster) or remained in the control of bishops appointed by royal patronage (Durham, Isle of Ely).

[23] H. R. Loyn in *Domesday Studies*, ed. J. C. Holt (1987), 2–3.

[24] Ibid., 11–12. And cf. J. C. Holt, ibid., 41–64 on Domesday Book as the product of an agreement between the king and the great men, to establish rights and duties.

emerged from the Carolingian empire used written documents, of course, though they also relied heavily on personal messengers equipped with authority, but none had worked out anything like the writ – brief, concise, exact and highly authoritative. The writ could readily be changed from the vernacular into Latin, and the whole central organization built up by the Norman and Angevin kings – and by them bequeathed to later ages – grew upon those little scraps of parchment with their pendant seals. The great offices of state, more especially Chancery and Exchequer, the central courts which produced and administered the common law of England, and the central body of administrators in the royal Council and Household, all effectively depended on their power to issue writs which commanded obedience and initiated action. In due course, Parliament too came into existence on the back of the royal writ. It may well be true that the Anglo-Saxon monarchy lacked the settled central offices which post-Conquest bureaucracies organized by stages, but it had invented and passed on the one essential means towards the building up of a sophisticated system of government.

However, all that development owed a great deal also to means not available before 1066 and introduced by the strong personal rulership of men like William I, Henry I and Henry II. That rulership could remain personal despite the frequent absences of those kings because they could and did appoint effective deputies – justiciars – usually clerics who, like Ranulf Flambard under William II or William Longchamps under Richard I, might be widely hated but caused that hatred more by efficient government than by self-promotion. The royal entourage supplied both the men and the offices which turned kingly rule into reality. Here was found the central organization both for conducting war and for overseeing peace, and though royal household knights can be looked at as the successors of Anglo-Danish housecarls their military effectiveness was markedly greater and prepared the ground for a far more efficient army. The ordinary administration in the king's Household (those who managed the maintenance of his court and travels) and his Chamber (the financial centre) not only gave those kings the means to make their rule real but also, interestingly enough, laid down the lines which royal administration was to follow throughout the Middle Ages. Work that at first was carried out by Household officers by stages became concentrated in specialized departments settled 'out of court'. The first such department was the Exchequer, which originated in the need to keep tight control over the king's income and expenditure.[25] It would appear now that this institution owed little to Norman practice or example; it was an English growth promoted by officers confined to the king's English dominions.[26] From the regular sessions for auditing the accounts of collecting officers (especially sheriffs) and spending officers there grew that highly sophisticated separate office described by its boss, Richard FitzNeal, in the *Dialogue of the Exchequer*, written in about 1179. It was the first central office to keep a regular record in the pipe roll which registered sheriffs' returns of the farms of the counties; the earliest example exists for 1130–1, and the continuous series survives from 1155 to 1833. In its outline and in much of its detail that office underwent little change before its abolition in the latter year.

The other administrative development of note concerned the function of issuing and registering royal missives, whether orders or grants of land and office – the function of the Chancery. Just when the body of scribes employed in this business can be said to have turned into the identifiable institution remains disputed, the more so because for most of the Angevin time the Chancery and at least some of its records continued to accompany the king on his travels. Reliance on the royal seal for authentication naturally called for an officer to look after it, and keepers of the seal were known back in pre-Conquest days. But it was in the twelfth century that the title of chancellor came to be reserved for the keeper of the great seal, and several notable king's servants built their careers on that office – men like Roger of Salisbury, first organizer of the Exchequer and ultimately bishop of Ely, or Thomas Becket,

[25] For the early history of the Exchequer see R. L. Poole, *The Exchequer in the Twelfth Century* (1912); T. F. Tout, *Chapters in Medieval Administrative History*, I (1937), 74–88. Neither is perfect. For the *Dialogue* see the edition and translation by Charles Johnson in the Nelson Medieval Classics (1950). There is, of course, a vast amount of reliable information in Thomas Madox's famous *History and Antiquities of the Exchequer* (1711), but it takes years of study to excavate and absorb it.

[26] C. Warren Hollister, 'The Origin of the English Treasury', *EHR* 93 (1978), 262–75.

archbishop of Canterbury and ultimately martyr. But in some ways the most important man to hold the office was Hubert Walter (another archbishop of Canterbury) who in 1198 moved over from the unpopular office of justiciar to set about organizing the royal writing office. It was Hubert who in that year initiated the Chancery Rolls, the record of instruments issued under the great seal, and as those rolls grew massive and enormous in number a permanent establishment separate from the Household became a necessity. The king's writing clerks and chancellors were naturally mostly clerics, the people who could write, and had originally been closely associated with the royal Chapel, but throughout the thirteenth century they formed an identifiable body, though positive separation from the Household cannot be vouched for until late in the reign of Edward I. Whereas the Exchequer was a definite department by about 1170, the Chancery reached that position only in the 1290s.[27]

The Englishing of Normans

Thus the era of Norman and Angevin kingship produced a high-grade system of royal government which guided the affairs of the people of England, but from above. However, the existence of this system affected the people through all its ranks, not least because it called for men to operate it. The emergence of Exchequer and Chancery produced therefore a distinct royal bureaucracy, with career structures for clerks at several levels and endowed very quickly with that determined preservation of existing methods which is the hallmark of the bureaucratic mind. Those not on the inside soon enough expressed their disgust at the promotion of men from supposedly very low classes in the service of the crown where they could lord it over honest knights and gentlemen, and where they could add the powers of government to the Church's claims over faith and morals. In fact, the professional bureaucracy which developed from Henry II's reign onwards drew more on the lower ranks of

[27] For the history of the Chancery see H. Maxwell-Lyte, *The Great Seal* (1926), an effectively unreadable depository of the Public Record Office's corporate knowledge of what had been the chief medieval royal record office.

the knighthood than on the plebeians – lower ranks where younger sons especially needed to find means of livelihood outside landowning from which the rules of inheritance by primogeniture increasingly barred them. The Church stood ready to receive, and the crown eagerly exploited the increasing reservoir of men able to write records, keep accounts, and run a steadily more complicated structure of government.[28]

When the Exchequer and the Chancery separated from the royal Household they did not terminate that body's central role in government. On the contrary, departmental institutions within the Household of necessity reproduced the lost original departments. The kings continued to rule from within their court and entourage, served there by Household specialists under the oversight of the king's steward. The Chamber under a chamberlain looked after the money, even after the original chamberlains had become Exchequer officers out of court. When the great seal ceased to travel around with the king, he needed a new seal kept within the Household; thus a privy seal is vouched for under John, remaining thereafter in the Household and from 1307 at the latest held in a department headed by a keeper until in the fifteenth century it too went out of court. The Household officials were quite as much bureaucrats as were their brethren in those departments 'of state' that had separated from the king's court. By modern standards, the total numbers involved remained very modest, but by the standards of those first bureaucratic centuries they formed a sizeable body of professionals, recruited from people of English descent for the simple reason that there were far too few Normans around to fill the need. In any case, time did its work of removing the distinction. Right at the top of the social order, great men continued to have property and interests in both England and on continental territory, and many found wives for themselves or their sons in Normandy or Anjou. But the knighthood and baronage of England by stages accepted their English origins and even learned the language. Richard FitzNeal remarked in

[28] Ralph V. Turner, 'Changing Perceptions of the New Administrative Class in Anglo-Norman and Angevin England: The *Curiales* and their Conservative Critics', *JBS* 29 (1990), 93–117. A review article by Scott L. Waugh, ibid., 386–92, suggests that in this era the simplicities of the original knightly society gave way to a complex structure in which lordship and patronage rather than birth and military prowess determined fortunes.

his *Dialogue of the Exchequer* that he could no longer see any difference between Englishmen and Normans, and by the middle of the thirteenth century the mother tongue of the feudal classes had become English. A knowledge of French was expected from both men and women, but as a matter of culture and education, not of birth.[29] The northern barons who initiated the confrontation with King John in 1215 expressly refused to get involved in Norman affairs, and though the protest of 1258 was led by a Frenchman (Simon de Montfort) it was borne up by English resentment at Henry III's Poitevin advisers and resulted in the avowed recognition that there was a community of England. By the time that Edward I came to the throne ancestry mattered inasmuch as it underpinned claims to social status, but racial origin had ceased to signify. The greater baronage had become English magnates, and the lesser ranks of knights and esquires had become English gentry – all of them members of a landed class with possessions and with duties in the community, but no longer, except in the fantasies of romance, a warrior caste at all.

However, did this Englishing of the nation extend below the ranks of the landowners? Of course it did: there it had never ceased to exist. One consequence of the Conquest was that slavery disappeared. Anglo-Saxon society and law had to the end confronted criminals or even those failing to pay the wergild due to the victims with the possibility of genuine enslavement. The Normans, devoid of finer feelings, firmly believed in execution or at least serious mutilation, and since they also put an end to warfare within the kingdom they turned off the chief source of slaves – captives in battle. But they did at first reduce the bulk of the native English to a status of dependency which in law was expressed as serfdom. The peasantry of the Anglo-Saxon parts had not been truly free before, even though personal freedom prevailed within the Danelaw, but they had not been tied irrevocably to one piece of land and service to one lord. This they became quickly enough after the Norman barons replaced the Anglo-Saxon thegns: for some two or three generations, being English implied being a serf *adscriptus glebae*. The full growth of the principle and the

---

[29] M. T. Clanchy, *From Memory to Written Record* (1979), ch. 6.

Plate 12 Magna Carta, 1217. (MS Ch. Glos. 8. Bod. The Bodleian Library, Oxford.)

means to enforce it at law limped behind the reality: until Henry II came to restore order after the confusion of Stephen's reign it would appear that serfs could still leave their bit of land if they felt overexploited. But after 1155 the king began to assist lords to recover such fugitives with writs that addressed themselves to enforcing the subjection of the 'natives' (the action of naifty). And though such measures often led to disputes in court over the status of the alleged 'native' or villein, the bulk of the English peasantry now stood in a state of serfdom.[30] True, escape routes were available, more especially the Church: secular clergy and religious orders recruited from unfree men whom ordination or reception made free. And there were the towns, about which more in a moment. But the steady increase in population and the favourable economic conditions which prevailed into the early fourteenth century penalized the peasant whose lord could afford to enforce his legal rights. The end of serfdom came only with the collapse of the economy and the population after the Black Death from 1348 onwards: thereafter rarity value gave the peasant an upper hand. I should add that the term 'peasant' was unknown to medieval English: there is a good deal to be said for the view that, as far back as we have evidence, the English even at the bottom of the social scale practised a noticeably individualistic attitude to property and personal status which made emancipation easy in due course; they did not think in terms of kin or (as Marxism would insist) of class.[31]

The temporary social depression of the real English did, however, have a profound effect upon the English language. As we have seen, before the Conquest, English was the main Germanic vernacular that had achieved the status of a literary medium: it was a written language used by administrators, chroniclers, thinkers and poets. And though the Conquest did not altogether terminate these uses, Latin and French overwhelmingly took over the role of the written language in England, until English re-emerged in the course of the thirteenth century. The fallow time proved to have been truly beneficial.

[30] Paul R. Hyams, *Kings, Lords and Peasants in Medieval England: The Common Law of Villeinage in the Twelfth and Thirteenth Centuries* (1980), esp. Part IV.
[31] Alan Macfarlane, *The Origins of English Individualism: The Family, Property and Social Transition* (1978).

Middle English is a distinctly more flexible language than Anglo-Saxon, grammatically simpler and with a markedly richer vocabulary including much borrowing from the temporary ascendancy languages. In this period the English language began its remarkable career as easily the most adaptable and most varied means of communication ever put together by man – much superior, it should be said, to Latin or even Greek, and far less hampered by rules than either French or German. The effects of the subterranean years became manifest in the age of Chaucer, who demonstrated the extraordinary variety of uses to which English could be put. It seems to me that the language owed its escape from the ossification inherent in scholarly control to its temporary disappearance from the mouths of scholars.[32]

The Development of Law

Nothing better demonstrates the continuity combined with innovation that prevailed in England after the Norman Conquest than the development of the king's law. True, matters of the law most readily survive in the record, making it appear even more important than it was, but that does not alter the essential point. If ink and parchment offer to the law a special advantage, it must be remembered that that special advantage presents the historian with the best chance of understanding what happened to the English people after their throne fell to French-speaking foreigners.

As we have seen, the late Anglo-Saxon and Anglo-Danish monarchies regularly attended to the laying down of regulations enforceable in various courts, and we have also seen that in the progress of time what had been general (and varied) custom increasingly became law made by and for kings. The Normans in Normandy knew of no such legislative activity but they quickly picked up the idea, and codes of little originality appeared occasionally into the reign of Henry I. The treatises called 'Quadripartitus' and 'Leges Henrici Primi' were a lawyer's somewhat primitive commentary on the traditional

---

[32] Cf. Clanchy, *From Memory*, esp. 165–74; Janet Coleman, 'English Culture in the Fourteenth Century', in *Chaucer and the Italian Trecento*, ed. P. Boitani (1983), 33–63.

customs of the realm, and like the so-called laws of William I
they did little more than reiterate the peace-keeping principles
inherited from the past. Two kinds of innovation did occur.
William I found it necessary to protect 'Frenchmen' against
native fury and revenge by special penalties, and the curious
Anglo-Saxon belief in money fines did not altogether withstand
the savage habits brought over by the Normans. Mutilations
and ultimately death increasingly became the sanctions enforced upon criminals, pursued at the instance of the ruler
rather than the local community; felonies emerged specially
defined as pleas of the crown. More confusing was the need to
incorporate in the public law the relationships and obligations
involved in the strictly feudal settlement of lands. The enforcement of the contracts upon which the fief rested demanded
clarification in law of such things as lawful possession and rules
of inheritance that had not been called for in pre-Conquest
days. Then the terms of charters granting 'bookland' governed
each case specifically; what was now needed were general rules
recognized and supported by the king's courts.

Well into the middle of the twelfth century, the law and its
application remained remarkably conservative. Henry I's cor-
onation charter – the first formal summary of a king's
acknowledgement that the law had binding force upon his
actions – embodied strictly traditional terms; its chief concern
was to disavow the alleged ill dealings of his predecessor in his
relations with the lay and clerical landowners in the feudal
pyramid.[33] It was only the impossibility of keeping peace and
order in the anarchic days of Stephen that set the stage for a
major transformation of the scene in the reign of Henry II. That
king faced the complaints of men deprived of their rights by
superior force, and he responded by ordering sheriffs to enforce
just claims or else, if that proved impossible, to bring the
contending parties before the king's justices. This got over the
problem of making lords in their baronial courts behave fairly,
a difficulty tenants could not overcome without help. Thus
there developed the so-called possessory assizes embodied in
writs sorting out recent disputes: *novel disseisin* (had the
plaintiff been recently ejected from land he was occupying?),

---

[33] W. Stubbs, *Select Charters* (rev. edn, 1913), 117–19.

mort d'ancester (who held the disputed land at the death of the last previous possessor?), *utrum* (was the matter properly the concern of a Church court?). Behind such immediate remedies, the writs of right offered to sort out claims more permanently. There is still much argument whether Henry II deliberately worked to concentrate all justice in royal hands, thus superseding the role of feudal and even regional courts, or whether in the first instance he was only trying to assist claimants in their local courts.[34] What cannot be doubted is that within a few decades of these judicial remedies first appearing the king's justice was replacing the justice administered by inferior lords in their courts baron. Thus the century after 1150 witnessed the birth of the common law of England, a law derived from three roots – local custom, the feudal relationship and the royal duty to see justice done – but coalescing quickly into one custom of the realm dispensed by the judicial officers of the crown. The fact was made plain very convincingly by the sudden appearance of textbooks of the law, summarizing and systematizing what had been coming into existence under pressure of need. The treatises called Glanville (*c.*1180) and Bracton (completed *c.*1270) were the work of professional judges even if not of Ranulph Glanville and Henry Bracton alone. They benefited from the revival in Italy of Roman law, and in their work they laid out the beginnings of the only other system that ever was to rival the law of Rome. In the course of time, the common law of England was to serve far vaster areas of population and litigation than Rome could ever have considered.[35]

From the point of view of the people – plaintiffs and defendants in litigation – the immediate impact was felt not in the esoteric details of the law so much as through the realities of courts and judges.[36] Even before the reforms of Henry II, the Exchequer had begun to offer reasonably regular answers to problems for those who came seeking the king's justice.

[34] S. F. C. Milson, *The Legal Framework of English Feudalism* (1976) in effect defends the second notion against F. W. Maitland's picture of a king deliberately legislating for a centralized system.

[35] For a clear outline of this history see J. H. Baker, *An Introduction to English Legal History* (2nd edn, 1979).

[36] Alan Harding, *The Courts of Medieval England* (1973), offers a useful introduction, though I cannot quite agree with his inclination to tie changes in the law to changes in class structure which I do not think mirror reality.

However, for a century after the Conquest the practice of dealing with disputes and breaches of the peace (civil and criminal issues) in the local courts inherited from the Anglo-Saxon past, with the addition of the feudal courts tied to the creation of the fief, continued to dominate the scene. The sheriff's court of the shire, meeting at least twice a year, and the hundred courts held by leading local men several times more often, received energetic endorsement from the Norman kings. From their point of view they had the advantage of spreading law-enforcement throughout the realm, but they posed the problems of uncontrolled power in the hands of local men, landowners and magnates capable of abusing their position for private profit and tyranny. Sometimes sheriffs ceased to be the king's officers and became agents of magnates, even if the office was not simply taken over by such men of great local power. The same people as sat in judgement were too often bringing the accusations in the first place. Predictably, in Stephen's reign these local tyrants escaped from central supervision, so that Henry II began his restoration of good order by cutting these local judges out of the system. Of necessity, therefore, another set of judges had to be put up.

The ensuing development owed much to the long-standing power of the English monarchy, but a great deal also to the fact that England was now part of a territorial complex and moreover was the part which least required the regular presence of the king himself. Henry I spent much time in Normandy, even after he regained control over it at the battles of Tinchebrai (1106) and Brémule (1119). Henry II visited his English kingdom quite rarely by comparison with his stays in Anjou and Aquitaine. Richard I managed to stay away through virtually all his reign, first by going on the crusade and then by getting himself captured in the Alps on his journey home. (The raising of his ransom money set useful precedents for the king's right to demand aids, but it also undermined the entrenched English willingness to pay taxes.) Only John, deprived of Normandy, infested England throughout, and little good it did his general reputation, at the time and among historians. But absentee kings needed to attend to their government by proxy, which is why the twelfth century was the great age of the justiciar. Government by deputy favoured an increase in bureaucratic

practices at the expense of personal intervention, and the
Norman kings' Exchequer showed the way to the Angevin
exploitation of the royal entourage as a breeding-ground for
departments both in general government and in the administration of justice. Though Henry II and his ministers first chose
to bring the king's law to the parts of the realm by means of the
general eyre – regular visits by royal judges travelling through
the regions – by the end of the twelfth century the pleas of the
subject began to come to a regular court, soon called the Court
of Common Pleas and settled in a fixed place under the terms of
Magna Carta. The enforcement of good order against criminal
offenders continued to be handled in the counties, but by the
reign of John the work was no longer discharged in the old
courts of shire and hundred but by royal commissioners.

Royal justice benefited from an unexpected advantage. The
king alone could demand the bringing together of local people
sworn to report and decide upon the truths of accusations; the
jury, even in its primitive pre-Conquest guise, was a royal
instrument which Henry II expanded massively. Local knowledge in the guise of juries of presentment told the king's judges
what offences needed trial; trial juries brought their local
knowledge to the establishment of the truth. When the Lateran
Council of 1215 outlawed the old trial by the ordeal of fire or
water, the jury took over decisions on the facts of a case. (Trial
by battle, though not formally abolished until 1828, was
becoming rare as ever fewer contending parties felt able to
engage in duels or trust that they might win their case that way.)
Since crime continued to be triable only in the shire in which it
was committed (where alone the necessary knowledge might be
found), criminal jurisdiction did not for a long time settle in a
fixed court (the Court of King's Bench, permanently at
Westminster from about the 1380s onwards). What really
matters in this history of law and jurisdiction was the
systematization carried out centrally and locally by incrasingly
professional experts – judges making and applying general rules
by means of the royal instrument of the writ, and advocates
arguing their way to new definitions. The years of the Angevin
monarchy thus witnessed the settlement of the common law and
the organization serving it; change thereafter was to take place
only along the lines opened up under Henry II until a new kind

of society swept away the Middle Ages in the reign of Queen
Victoria. It is worth notice that all these developments grew out
of old English practice, even though what emerged was
manifestly transformed into novel ideas and institutions. The
common law was English rather than Norman or Angevin.

One of the really new developments produced the professional body of lawyers practising in the courts and supplying
at the king's choice truly professional judges. The men who
administered the law in Henry I's day had been great men both
lay and ecclesiastical, magnates and bishops who used their
social position to bring order to the realm and resolve disputes.
The men who did this in the reign of Henry III were specialists,
and few of them came from established great families. The law
now offered a career to poor men's sons, and with that career
came wealth. The common lawyers of England constituted the
only profession in medieval Europe which had nothing to do
with the Church – a profession of laymen. Of necessity they
developed their means of instruction and mutual contact,
practices which in the course of the fourteenth century settled in
the Inns of Court in London. Such law as was taught at the
universities (which came into existence by stages from the later
thirteenth century) was the revived and recast law of ancient
Rome called the civil law.[37] The universities remained the
preserve of the clergy, while the common law turned out laymen
of learning and distinction. This separation of roots and
functions was to persist till the nineteenth century.

Church and King

The Church itself remained in very much the traditional
relationship to both the rulers and the ruled in the realm of
England. In pre-Conquest times ecclesiastics had been responsible for giving the realm an ordered structure by means of the
episcopal dioceses, and kings had always relied on their clergy
for both the advance of civilization and much of their

[37] Cf. Ralph V. Turner, 'Roman Law in England before the Time of Bracton', *JBS* 15
(1975), 1–25, a useful summary which emphasizes the role of Roman lawyers in
assisting the codification of the laws current in England and the consequences of the fact
that the work was done before the university-trained lawyers could take charge of
English justice.

government. The Conquest by stages replaced the English bishops by French-speaking feudatories and administrators, but the really big change occurred not in England but at Rome. The twelfth century witnessed the establishment of the papal monarchy, and English kings soon found that their leading clergy followed Rome. What had been territorial Churches well integrated with princely rule turned all over Europe into more or less obedient sectors of the Universal Church ruled by the successors of St Peter. And that Universal Church demanded special status and treatment for its clergy. Priests ever more visibly distanced themselves from the laity, most particularly in the supposed enforcement of strict celibacy and most tiresomely in refusing to accept royal jurisdiction over all offences committed by tonsured clergy.

In England, this demand led notoriously to the epic battle between Henry II and his archbishop of Canterbury, Thomas Becket, murdered in 1170 and therefore sainted soon after. Becket, once the king's friend and loyal servant, had as archbishop chosen to represent the clerical demand for independence from royal control, and after a series of clashes, exile and return lost his life spectacularly in Canterbury Cathedral. The pope, knowing how to reward such loyalties, rapidly bestowed the saintly halo. Though Henry had to submit to a humiliating penance, and though many people since have regarded Becket's fate as a victory for the Church, in actual fact the episode made no real dent in the power and ascendancy of the crown.[38] England had been and continued to be a faithful follower of the Church that looked to Rome, a tendency reinforced by the proliferation of new monastic orders (Cistercian houses redeeming the waste lands of the north and of Wales, Austin canons settling in the towns, knights Templar following in the wake of the Crusades),[39] but in fact the king and his

[38] For a review see James W. Alexander, 'The Becket Controversy in Recent Historiography', *JBS* 9 (1970), 1–26. This argues that Henry II failed to establish the kind of control which he sought to exercise over the Church, but the argument seems to me to underrate the degree to which kings of England used the Church and its seeming independence to their own advantage.

[39] A very inadequate summary. The foundations are listed in *Medieval Religious Houses in England and Wales*, ed. D. Knowles and R. N. Hadcock (1953); and cf. D. Knowles, *The Monastic Order in England* (2nd edn, 1963), esp. chs 13 and 14; *The Religious Orders in England*, I (1950), ch. 3.

government avoided conflict with the spiritualty and ran affairs in conjunction with it. When the crown got into difficulties it fell back upon the Church. John did so in 1215 when he tried to escape the consequences of baronial rebellion and French invasion by turning himself into a vassal of Rome, and Henry III likewise after the baronial victory of 1258 relied on a papal legate to help him undo the work of the late Simon de Montfort. Despite Becket, the strains in the body politic were practically never between spiritualty and temporalty; they occurred within the hierarchy of the laity's social order.

King and Barons

The two centuries after the Norman Conquest were on the whole prosperous for the people. Everything expanded.[40] More and more waste lands and forests were brought under the plough to employ and feed a growing population. Towns that had been founded as bulwarks of defence became centres of industrial production, and old Roman towns like York, Lincoln or Winchester flourished. London especially grew in size and influence; with the assistance of royal charters it reorganized its administration; in 1191 it achieved the status of a commune, a privileged and self-governing body of merchants structured in gilds or companies. The growing towns absorbed a part of the excess population of peasants, the more conveniently because admission to the freedom of a town terminated villein status. But the main beneficiaries of the expansion were the land-owners. Too many peasants pressed upon the holdings available, giving to the manorial lords an unfailing whiphand, and as demand grew for bread grain at home and for sheeps' wool abroad, the military rentier class of barons and knights turned into magnates and gentry operating as entrepreneurs in trade and manufacture. In this period England became the chief source of wool for European manufacturing centres in Flanders and Italy, creating a regular export trade which in turn brought in the special products (wine!) and luxuries of France and its neighbours. None of this was entirely new but the new scale and

[40] Cf. the careful account in E. Miller and J. Hatcher, *Medieval England: Rural Society and Economic Change 1086–1348* (1978).

Plate 13 An engraving of The North East View of Warwick Castle. (The Royal Commission on the Historical Monuments of England.)

extent brought about a real transformation from the relative simplicity of Anglo-Saxon days to the marked proliferation of visible wealth that erected cathedrals and monastic buildings all over England. Henry III spent much money on building the palace of Westminster. The property-owning, landed sector dominated society, and the age of the gentry, which lasted until the end of the nineteenth century, opened in the twelfth as old thegns and new knights settled to their possessions, paying their duty to their feudal lord, the king, in money rather than with the sword. By the end of Henry II's reign we are dealing with an English people differentiated less by origin and descent than by wealth reflected in the social hierarchy. From this time onwards, claims for regard as well as discharge of duties all operated within a single nation conscious of both nationhood and pyramidal structure – rising from a peasantry which contained both freemen and serfs up to the universal landowner, the king.

The king, as we have seen, continued to be responsible for maintaining the peace in the realm, and ordinarily this meant no more than seeking out and punishing crimes, as well as settling civil disputes which might lead to loss of peace. Occasionally, however, major ruptures threatened the social order, and in this there happened an important and interesting change of venue. The Norman kings and Henry II encountered rebellions that arose essentially from divisions within the royal family – struggles over the succession to the various parts of the higgledy-piggledy dominions that they claimed, or troubles with disobedient sons. As a rule the kings won fairly easily because they retained the loyal service of their vassals and because great barons looked to them for advantages. The situation was profoundly altered by two things. The baronage became specifically English while kings remained determined to strut on a wider European stage, and King John's aggressive policy against his nobility united an internal opposition against himself. The crisis of 1215 began in the north where the barons refused to obey the demand for military assistance in the attempt to reconquer Normandy, and it culminated in the overwhelming alliance of feudatories and bishops that extorted Magna Carta from a most reluctant king. The Great Charter was a concession, not a gift, as John proved when he cancelled it (with papal help), but it was restored early in Henry III's reign and remained as a foundation charter of liberties and rights available to an ever-increasing part of the nation as growing wealth and growing law swept in layers of society well below the ranks that had first promoted it. The real significance of that famous confrontation at Runnymede where John surrendered to the pressures of barons and prelates could not be long evaded: it put an end to the despotic potential within Anglo-Norman kingship, anchored the principle of co-operation, and instituted a relationship between king and baronage marked by a mutual and watchful suspiciousness which endured for the rest of the Middle Ages.

The fact was brought home very plainly in the crisis of 1258–65. The baronial rebellion stemmed from the incompetence of Henry III but it demonstrated a kind of class loyalty within the magnate body, all thinking of themselves as English now even though the ultimate leader of resistance, Simon de Montfort, earl of Leicester, was a Frenchman who had earlier made his mark in feudal warfare around Toulouse.[41] In its particulars, the revolt proved a failure. The Provisions of Oxford (1258) attempted to subject the king to the iron control of a magnate committee in charge of all policy, and when Henry III tried to wriggle out of this reduction to impotence with the assistance of Louis IX of France (Mise of Amiens, 1262) he was taken prisoner in Simon's victory at Lewes in 1264. By this time magnate unanimity had broken down, but the rebels' support reached down into the people to include knights and burgesses: the magnate republic threatened to become a demagogic mêlée. But next year, at Evesham, Henry's son Edward terminated Simon and rebellion both, and the highly premature attempt to erect a Venetian republic in England fell apart – as on the whole it deserved to do. England was a kingdom of very ancient standing, and so it remained.

However, the crisis also left some permanent effects. For one thing, Henry III had found himself facing a set of opponents expressly speaking for the whole realm – the *communitas Anglie* – and that community, embodying a nation, was and remained a reality. For another, the rebels' insistence that the king must seek advice and co-operation from the great men of

[41] D. A. Carpenter, 'Simon de Montford, the First Leader of a Political Movement in English History', *History* 76 (1991), 3–23.

the realm laid the foundations of an institution expressing in action the old feudal principle that a lord should take counsel with his vassals. The Parliament envisaged by the Provisions, with its three meetings every year, was never broadly based and was also bound to fail in its ostensible purpose of giving the baronial council its opportunity to control the king; like the restoration of the justiciar as controller of the crown, it was a somewhat pointless dream. Yet the idea of such meetings around the king's Council, to consider problems of government and society, opened the road to the most efficient machinery for bringing together rulers and ruled that was to emerge in medieval Europe. The real history of the English Parliament does not begin in 1258,[42] but its prehistory does – though it is also true that that prehistory can be tracked back to the Anglo-Saxon assembly in which kings associated themselves with their great men in the occasional gatherings of the wise men (*witenagemot*). Like so much else in post-Conquest England, earlier traces were preserved and developed: continuity was as plain as was drastic change hiding under the cloak of continuity. The work had been done by kings, and though governing the community of England differed greatly from governing a conquered kingdom from bases on the Continent, yet government was and remained the king's.

The *communitas Anglie* triumphed in effect over two potentially rival royal theories, both entertained in those Angevin years but neither as effective as the identification of a specifically English realm. The more obvious and more extravagant moved English kings to continue their empire-building on the Continent. In retrospect we can see that by the end of the twelfth century the Capetian kings of France, striking out from the region of Paris, had taken over from the overambitious Plantagenets as the dominant power in western Europe. John, desperate to recover Normandy, and Henry III, wrapped in the dreams of a feeble man looking for glory, thought otherwise. Henry was encouraged in his follies by the Poitevin ministers he favoured; they in their turn hoped to use the Anjou connection and the uncertain hold over Aquitaine to resist the Capetians. Out of this mêlée sprang such extravagances as the promotion

[42] For Parliament see below, p. 103 ff.; a good introduction to current thought is found in G. O. Sayles, *The King's Parliament of England* (1974).

of Henry's brother, Richard of Cornwall, for the succession to
the throne of the Holy Roman Empire and the absurd attempt
to gain the crown of Sicily for his younger son, Edmund.
Henry's three sisters married the Emperor Frederick II, a king of
Scotland, and Simon de Montfort, achievements which rather
pitifully highlighted the pretence of great power and influence in
a Europe that actually was changing character drastically.
Several times Henry III got involved in unsuccessful wars with
France. All these pursuits of glory a long way from England
infuriated the real power base upon which he should have
relied: the *communitas Anglie* asserted itself.[43] In the king's
minority the realm had been kept contented under the guidance
of William Marshal earl of Pembroke (d. 1219) and Hubert de
Burgh (d. 1243); when Henry took over in person he got rid of
such tutors and called in the likes of Peter de Rivaux and Peter
des Roches (bishop of Winchester since 1205) – men from
Poitou who used England for the benefit of now distant parts.
The result was 1258 and the collapse, for a time, of the Angevin
monarchy.

These far-flung ambitions in the wake of Henry II's greatness
contrasted rather strikingly with the effective failure to complete that king's endeavour to establish the English king as
positive ruler of all the British Isles.[44] As we have seen, those
kings advanced their claims and took armies to Wales and
Ireland, though in the main those penetrations beyond the
boundaries of England were carried out by baronial private
enterprise. Henry II in effect confined himself to asserting his
suzerainty over such potentially overmighty subjects. In this, he
in Wales and John in Ireland were on the whole successful, and
they even managed to promote new men more firmly attached
to themselves in the place of the earlier Norman barons. 'Even
in the remarkably autonomous and fragmented aristocratic
world of the Welsh March it was the king of England who had
the last – as indeed he often had the first – word.'[45] Scotland
posed a different problem because it was recognized as a
kingdom in its own right. All that could be attempted here was

---

[43] Cf. Hans-Peter Geh, *Insulare Politik in England vor den Tudors* (1964), 20–54.
[44] R. R. Davies, *Domination and Conquest: the Experience of Ireland, Scotland and
Wales 1100–1300* (1990), ch. 4.
[45] Ibid., 75.

the imposition of a feudal suzerainty over those lesser kings who nevertheless retained their independent control in Lothian and Galloway; it was in the twelfth century that the frontier between the two kingdoms became a reality. That reality survived even the discomfiture of William the Lion, captured in battle and forced to agree to the humiliating treaty of Falaise (1174). While it may well be true to say that the Angevin kings asserted a genuine domination over those outlying parts, it also remains true that no formal conquest took place and that therefore the strong internal government which developed in England was not extended even into Wales, let alone into Ireland or the Scottish kingdom. Dreams of empire on the Continent took precedence over genuine rule in the Isles. What did exist when Henry III died in 1272 was the community of England embodying a people that was very definitely English and no longer Saxon or Norman or French. Here the work of the kings both before and since 1066 had built up a structure of law, taxation, administration and ecclesiastical control which made England the most advanced polity of the age, even if its culture owed most to French and Italian influences. This polity was built to last, and last it did, very much within the terms already visible by the middle of the thirteenth century. King, magnates, gentry, trading towns and labouring peasants: that was the pyramid. An English nation, aware of itself through all these layers, was the reality.

3

The First English Empire[1]

The Expansion of England

Edward I was Henry III's son, but there is a good reason why one should speak of the end of Angevin and beginning of Plantagenet rule in 1272. In many ways, the new reign marked a decisive break with the past. The long years during which the kingdom of England stood on the margins of a power structure centred upon the Continent of Europe were over; for both its rulers and its people, the realm once again occupied the middle point. Moreover, its people now very definitely thought of themselves as one and as English. The English nation, speaking English throughout its social ranks, had unquestionably arrived, and the Poitevins and Savoyards thrown out by the rebellion against Henry III were the last foreigners to claim power within the land. Even the Church ceased to import Frenchmen and Italians to fill bishoprics, though the popes continued to try using English sees as provision for their entourages (a system known as provisors). Before long, the rapidly increasing self-consciousness of the nation produced a characteristic mixture of tolerant superiority and grim xenophobia, both nourished by experiences in war and politics. While in the twelfth and thirteenth centuries the people of England had generally looked to France for civilization,

[1] For outline and background I have relied on three books: Anthony Tuck, *Crown and Nobility 1272–1461: Political Conflict in Late Medieval England* (1985); Peter Heath, *Church and Realm 1272–1461: Conflict and Collaboration in an Age of Crisis* (1988); R. L. Storey, *The End of the House of Lancaster* (1966).

learning and the good life, by the middle of the fourteenth they knew that all things were done best in England. The University of Oxford could claim equal status with that of Paris. The order of the Garter (1348) symbolized a triumph of chivalry which even secured the honour of mere imitation when in 1430 the dukes of Burgundy created the order of the Golden Fleece. And as everybody knew, both personal freedom and personal well-being were much better served in England than anywhere else. That much of this was mere illusion signifies nothing. By the middle of the fifteenth century, when Sir John Fortescue wrote his book on *The Governance of England*, he was able to give lasting currency to two English convictions: that every other realm groaned under despots and that everywhere else the peasantry had to live on mere vegetables, while in England kings governed with the active consent of their subjects and people ate good red meat.[2] Moreover, the Plantagenet kings, their theologians and their propaganda enshrined English nationalism in a confident doctrine which made the English God's favourite children – an elect nation well meriting special divine regard.[3] This nationalism rested on a powerful streak of chauvinism – of hatred for all foreigners who, it was repeatedly asserted, were battening on the wealth and welfare of the English.[4]

And yet the first impression that any casual reading of the Later Middle Ages must leave highlights the misery, uncertainty and agony of constant domestic disturbance, aggravated by the demands of foreign war and the ravages of devastating disease. War, of course, had been around much of the time, ever since the Anglo-Saxons first came to settle in the island, but the reign of Edward I opened a new phase – the phase of deliberate and unrelenting empire-building. True, these activities rested on and benefited from earlier enterprise, and the crown of England

[2] Cf. F. R. H. Du Boulay, *An Age of Ambition: English Society in the Later Middle Ages* (1970), ch. 2.

[3] J. W. McKenna, 'How God became an Englishman', in *Tudor Rule and Revolution*, ed. D. L. Guth and J. W. McKenna (1982), 25–43.

[4] E.g. in the 1370s: G. A. Holmes, *The Good Parliament* (1975), ch. 1. Papal fiscal exactions often rested on continued appeals for crusades against the infidel, but while individual Englishmen still wasted lives and substance in such enterprises no king, despite frequent promises, ever again engaged in them (C. Tyerman, *England and the Crusades 1095–1558* [1988]).

even after the loss of Normandy, Maine and Anjou still held
Gascony (Guyenne, Aquitaine), but now its centre of gravity
lay unmistakably in England. And from this centre the
Plantagenet kings first set about establishing a firm and
unchallenged hold over the British Isles. In this, success proved
variable and the consequences were by no means always
propitious.

Edward I managed to conquer Wales by 1282, where a kind
of national revival had created the principality of the north
under Llewellyn the Great (d. 1240). That principality, guarded
by massive castle-building at Caernarvon, Conway, Harlech
and Beaumaris, became part of the royal patrimony, while the
eastern and southern regions settled firmly into English lordships. Wales was organized by royal decree (the Statute of
Rhuddlan, 1284), and though unrest and warfare continued for
about another decade the Celtic west was by the end of the
thirteenth century effectively attached to England. The laws and
customs of Wales continued to govern affairs there and full
incorporation had to await the reign of Henry VIII, but the
Welsh gentry became increasingly anglicized and movement
from one part of the realm to the other became commonplace.
Ireland, as usual, posed greater problems, partly because
controlling it across the sea always caused difficulties and partly
because the Anglo-Norman conquest had never completely
overcome Gaelic independence. Indeed, in the fourteenth
century a Gaelic revival pressed hard upon the English who, in
addition, began to divide into old settlers and newcomers often
at odds over territorial possession; the regime of justiciars and
lieutenants trying to rule from Dublin found itself frequently
under severe pressure. Special measures, summed up in the
Statute of Kilkenny (1366), endeavoured to preserve English
law, language and habits against the resurgence of native
practices. Edward III tried to settle a country riven by feuds and
ambitions by means of deputies, and Richard II twice took an
army over, but Ireland remained in a state of habitual
confusion, even though large parts of it supported English
noblemen – among them Richard, duke of York, who was to
claim the throne from Henry VI. Ireland continued to be
divided into Gaelic and English parts, a situation further
confused by Scottish invasions in the north, and those parts in

their turn remained in a state of fluid confusion as various leaders of both communities pursued their personal and family ambitions. It appears that the part controlled by Dublin was at the end of the fifteenth century reasonably well ordered,[5] but it must be said that the lordship of Ireland was never in the Middle Ages reduced to general normalcy. On the other hand, it also caused no problems in England, except occasionally by providing the wealth and (more rarely) the manpower that enabled some of the English nobility to advance their interests at home.

The real disaster occurred in Scotland, where Edward I attempted to turn the formal overlordship he inherited into a reality by making the Scottish king a vassal of England. For a while he succeeded, and when defeat in battle forced John Balliol to surrender his kingdom to his English suzerain (1296) Edward appeared at long last to have united all parts of the island under one crown. Success proved to be remarkably short-lived, and the real effect of the English aggression north of the Tweed turned out quite disastrous for the English. Temporary defeat led only to national uprisings under William Wallace and Robert Bruce; before Edward I died he could see that things had gone wrong; and in 1314 a comprehensive defeat in the battle of Bannockburn disposed of Edward II's efforts to emulate his father. Though a kind of war continued into the reign of Edward III, Bannockburn really secured the independence of Scotland. In fact, continued warfare led only to frequent Scottish incursions into northern England. Those raids left behind general devastation and produced the reconstruction of the north as a frontier region always prepared for battle and far too often involved in it. This in turn led to the emergence of great feudatories among the baronage – especially the Percies but by the fifteenth century also Nevilles and Dacres – equipped with emergency powers and backed by what were in effect standing armies. In their turn, they became a source of potential disruption in England which throughout the era of the Lancastrian kings was to make itself felt in national politics and provided the support that Richard III needed when he robbed his nephew of the crown. By this time, the memory of Northumbria as the cradle of Anglo-Saxon civilization had

[5] S. G. Ellis, *Reform and Revival: English Government in Ireland 1470–1534* (1986).

turned into a bleak joke. All this conquering, by force of arms, only produced standing insecurities like the major Welsh uprisings under Owen Glendower (1399–1413) or the need to subdue the northern levies at Shrewsbury in 1403; even though in the end the kings won everywhere south of the Scottish march, they ruled a kingdom never at the sort of peace that had been manifest in the days of Henry II.

Or rather, they succeeded in gaining spells of internal peace only by promoting war abroad. Not that they always had a free choice in the matter: England's past history as part of a territorial complex centring upon France left trailing commitments and needs. The restoration of royal ascendancy in France had still left the English king possessed of Gascony (or Aquitaine), though he was supposedly obliged to do homage for it to the Capetian king; moreover, Bordeaux and its hinterland depended overwhelmingly on the wine trade with England and did not seek to sever the connection. Both Edward I in the 1290s and Edward II in 1324 thus found themselves briefly involved in war with France, but the real war opened in 1327 when the death of the last descendant of Hugh Capet left the French succession in doubt. Edward III claimed that throne, and thus began a war which lasted some 120 years and formally did not end until France recovered Calais in 1558. That war with its changing fortunes dominated the fourteenth and fifteenth centuries. It started badly for England, but victories at Crécy (1346) and Poitiers (1356) led to a triumphant English ascendancy in the south and west of France, though Edward in effect put by his claim to the throne. Between about 1370 and 1415 the French recovered and the English failed to maintain their military superiority. Then followed Henry V's rapid and total conquest of France, his marriage to a French princess and his creation of a dual kingdom – all of it put at great risk by his early death. However, English rule continued for some years especially in Normandy, which received settlers from the island, until Joan of Arc reversed everything by lifting the siege of Orleans (1429). Thereafter, by stages, the English lost all their conquests except Calais, and France became the most powerful kingdom in western Europe. All these ups and downs had their effects on the history of a nation which more than once shifted from arrogant exaltation to deeply resentful despondency and

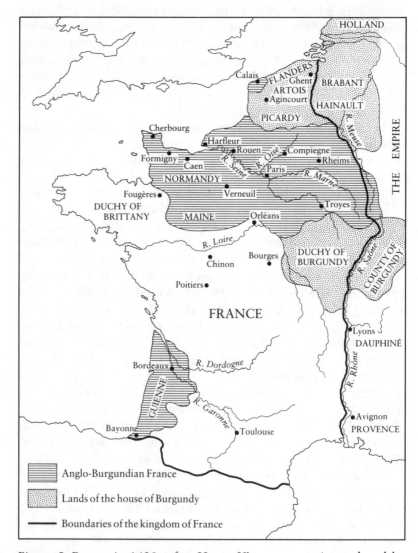

Figure 5 France in 1429, after Henry V's conquests (reproduced by kind permission, from M. Keen, England in the Later Middle Ages, *London, Methuen & Co., 1973).*

back again. The one continuous effect lay in the confirmation of national self-identification: the English, through all their social ranks, knew that they were wonderful, and to the annoyance of visitors from abroad kept saying so. More especially, their soldiers etched their formidable image upon the minds of their enemies, so much so that it took a century or more after the victory at Agincourt in 1415 for their reputation as fighting men to evaporate – and this even though by about 1475 it was quite plain that there would be no reconquest of the lands lost so rapidly after the even more rapid conquests registered by Henry V.

The Crown's Troubles

One important element in these violent ups and downs was the occupant of the throne: personal monarchy called for persons with special qualities if it was to work. The situation at heart favoured it: other things being equal, the English, including magnates and baronage, inclined to the service of the monarchy. After all, kingship had already had an effective history reaching back to the eighth century. By one of those strange dispensations which make one wonder about the ways of providence, the succession of kings in England seemed always to introduce a disastrous occupant just as monarchy looked likely to become despotic, and a rather competent person just as it looked likely to disintegrate. Edward I displayed both high skill and solid determination in restoring his kingship after his father's collapse in the face of a baronial opposition which he had needlessly provoked, and down to the 1290s Edward's rule worked well. In his last years, however, he lost his touch and showed every sign of that sort of overweening ruthlessness that caused rebelliousness among the baronage.[6] The predictable trouble resulted, and in 1297, in the so-called confirmation of the charters (Magna Carta and the Charter of the Forests) Edward in effect returned to a more accommodating policy. However, he handed the realm on to his fairly dreadful son, burdened with heavy debts and devoted to trouble-making favourites. Edward II's reign in effect experienced two civil wars, and while the king won the first when he defeated Thomas earl of Lancaster at Boroughbridge in 1322, he lost

[6] Cf. K. B. McFarlane, 'Had Edward I a "Policy" towards the Earls?' in *The Nobility in Later Medieval England* (1973), 248–67.

throne and life in the rising managed by his estranged queen, Isabella, and her lover Roger Mortimer (1326–7). It took Edward III some three years to restore monarchical control and another ten to create a government of men loyal to himself, but he then displayed all the right skills both to control the realm and to lead it to triumphs in foreign war.[7]

However, he lived too long and in his last decade (the 1370s) that formidable king collapsed into a sad caricature of himself, ruled and exploited by his mistress, Alice Perrers, and some determined self-seekers, supposedly his ministers. His heir, Edward the Black Prince, predeceased his father, so that there succeeded in 1377 a child, Richard II, barely ten years old. Richard in his turn managed to restore a measure of royal rule, but after surviving a powerful opposition overstepped the mark and was in his turn deposed and murdered (1399), making way for Henry of Lancaster, who showed every sign of being a king of quality until struck down by disabling disease. Kingship was preserved and enormously strengthened by the highly successful and entirely skilful rule of Henry V, but just as the situation looked ready-made for a powerfully dominant monarchy that king died on campaign and the throne fell to an infant not yet one year old. Henry VI's monarchy drifted from disaster to disaster – from a minority dominated by noble faction through the king's mental and physical collapse into a civil war from which the Yorkist dynasty emerged in the quite impressive person of Edward IV. He too managed to die before his time in 1483, only forty-one years old, and he too left an infant heir, a situation ready-made for his brother Richard to turn usurper. Both the Yorkists made the mistake of allowing faction to revive in strength. Even so, Richard III's defeat and death at Bosworth (1485) might easily have fallen out the other way, and Henry VII, first of the Tudor dynasty, had to fend off the revival of rebellion through part of his reign. Then, however, the extraordinarily disturbed and agonizing history of England's kings entered a haven of some peace and continuity. Shakespeare's panorama of events from the fall of Richard II

---

[7] For the rehabilitation of the third Edward see May McKisack, 'Edward III and the Historians', *History* 45 (1966), 1–15; Natalie Fryde, 'Edward III's Removal of his Ministers and Judges, 1340–1', *BIHS* 48 (1975), 149–61; W. M. Ormrod, 'Edward III and the Recovery of Royal Authority', *History* 72 (1987), 4–17.

onwards may not now satisfy the understanding of historians, but there was a pretty good case for seeing the fifteenth century in the light he threw.

In those two centuries four kings had been deposed and murdered, and a fifth had died in war. Two had died much too soon and three had lived too long. It was a tribute to the institution of monarchy that it survived this record. One reason for that survival must be sought in the equally extraordinary history of baronial deaths that accompanied the misfortunes of kings. The Wars of the Roses (Lancaster and York battling for the crown in the second half of the fifteenth century), which at one time were falsely reckoned to have destroyed the nobility, merely continued established practice. Every turn of the wheel disposed of leading figures, from the execution of Thomas of Lancaster in 1322, through the executions of two earls of Arundel by their furious monarchs in 1326 and 1397, to the judicial murder of William lord Hastings in 1483. Headless corpses constantly clutter up the stage. In 1330, Roger Mortimer (who had already seen to the disposal of King Edward II) took care of the execution of the then earl of Kent, and a few weeks later that earl's nephew, King Edward III, had Mortimer consigned to the same fate. To be a king's favourite came to be equal to a death warrant: Piers Gaveston, Hugh Despenser, Michael duke of Suffolk, Richard Woodville lord Rivers, and so on and so forth. The high death rate among the peers was accompanied by constant ups and downs in titles and possessions. Yet at the same time the peerage, regularly replenished, emerged as an established order of the realm, defined most obviously by the receipt of personal summons to the king's Parliaments but also distinguished from the next noble rank (the knights) by wealth and influence. The Welsh and northern marches provided on occasion the means for creating the sort of provincial power which had never before made an appearance in feudal England, but rivalry never led to anarchy.

These developments were much assisted by the proliferation of the blood royal.[8] Most of Edward I's children died young,

---

[8] Cf. R. A. Griffiths, 'The Crown and the Royal Family in Later Medieval England', in *Kings and Nobles in the Late Middle Ages*, ed. R. A. Griffiths and James Sherborne (1986), 15–26.

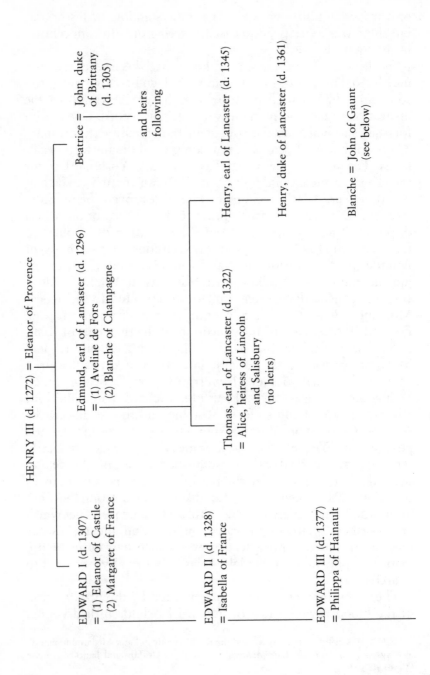

HENRY III (d. 1272) = Eleanor of Provence

EDWARD I (d. 1307)
= (1) Eleanor of Castile
  (2) Margaret of France

Edmund, earl of Lancaster (d. 1296)
= (1) Aveline de Fors
  (2) Blanche of Champagne

Beatrice = John, duke
           of Brittany
           (d. 1305)

and heirs
following

EDWARD II (d. 1328)
= Isabella of France

Thomas, earl of Lancaster (d. 1322)
= Alice, heiress of Lincoln
  and Salisbury
  (no heirs)

Henry, earl of Lancaster (d. 1345)

EDWARD III (d. 1377)
= Philippa of Hainault

Henry, duke of Lancaster (d. 1361)

Blanche = John of Gaunt
          (see below)

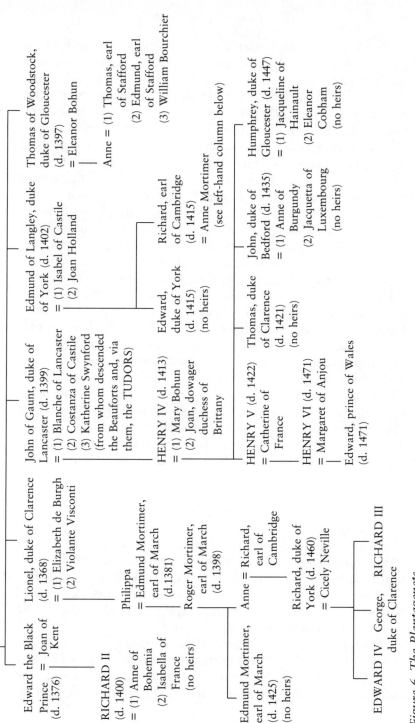

Figure 6 The Plantagenets.

but even so his second marriage yielded earls of Norfolk and of Kent. Edward II, possibly homosexual in his tastes, at least produced a successor, and it was this long-lived king who filled the realm with Plantagenet offspring, several of them made dukes, that were to infest the centres of power and politics for a long time. This was, of course, especially true of his third son, John of Gaunt, duke of Lancaster, from whose marriage there sprang King Henry IV, while the legitimized Beaufort offspring of his liaison with Katherine Swynford peopled the power structure of Lancastrian England. Henry VI's minority was troubled by the feud between his uncle Humphrey, duke of Gloucester, and his great-uncle Henry Beaufort, cardinal and bishop of Winchester. Both died in 1447, leaving the road clear for other Beaufort descendants (dukes of Somerset), for the earls of March and Cambridge descended from John of Gaunt's elder brother, Lionel duke of Clarence, and the Nevilles who intermarried with all this royalty. Edward III used to be blamed for promoting and endowing his family above all other nobility, but he really had very little choice. At least he provided for a safe and known succession, or he would have done if Richard II and Henry VI in their different ways had not provoked the rebellions which put the crown up for sale. Late-medieval kingship never lacked aspirants from the many branches of the Plantagenet tree, and it retained its hold on the nation; but that abudance of offspring direct or by marriage provided a kind of family matrix for the quarrels exploited by the nobility.

Taxation

The most immediate effects of these continuous states of war within and outside the realm arose from the primary demands which such conditions make on a society. What was needed all the time and beyond any earlier experience was money and soldiers. Edward I's temporary conquest of Scotland and defence of Gascony produced the crises of the 1290s: in 1296 there began a prolonged battle with the papacy over the king's right to tax the clergy, and in the following year he had to give way before the first real signs of magnate opposition since the collapse of the mid-century rebellions. He left a vast debt to his successor, and the steps taken to remedy this, though highly profitable to the royal Exchequer, contributed massively to the overthrow of Edward II. Edward III at least entered upon the French wars with a reasonable balance in hand, and the victorious phase of that war down to 1360 was managed quite well – quite well in the sense that victories could make a war pay for itself and also encouraged the nation to contribute. Thus the long-disputed tax on the export of wool (the maltolt) finally came to be accepted as a regular imposition round about 1350, a decision which initiated the regular reliance on a customs revenue, but only on condition that that revenue was expressly conceded to each monarch in Parliament. Meanwhile direct taxation in aids and tallages continued to be asked for and granted, so much so that the property tax called the tenth and fifteenth could in 1334 be converted into fixed contributions from the local communities. But with the collapse of Edward III's reign the nation's willingness to pay also collapsed. A series of poll taxes on both laity and clergy heralded an ever increasing resistance, and a crown that had once been exceptionally wealthy became a poor relation among such European *nouveaux riches* as France and Burgundy. Henry V's renewal of victory briefly renewed a readiness to pay taxes, but after that the descendants of the Danegeld payers of old learned to dread and resist all direct taxation. Even the clergy, hitherto fleeced most successfully, ceased to cough up the expected cash.

In fact, from the last decade of the fourteenth century onwards a new cry made itself heard: the king, it came to be said again and again, should live of his own.[9] This slogan started as a protest against purveyance – buying provisions for king and court at artificial prices – but in the face of ever repeated taxation it became in Richard II's reign a general demand. The king's own included the profits of justice and of feudal rights, but its chief component, and the only element that made a reality of the whole idea, was the crown estate: the lands retained in royal hands and yielding an income in kind and in rents. The crown estate benefited from every royal triumph in the conflicts with the nobility, and it was confiscations that

[9] That this was an innovation was proved by B. P. Wolffe, *The Royal Demesne in English History* (1971).

enabled Edward II to hand on a sizeable reserve. But the crown estate suffered from the need to keep the nobility peacefully loyal by means of gifts and endowments; more particularly it suffered greatly from Edward III's necessary policy of setting up his family in a manner suitable to their station. Besides, greedy favourites like the Despensers under Edward II or the dukes of Suffolk and Somerset under Henry VI always made inroads on the royal means of livelihood. When in 1399 Henry of Lancaster took the crown, he returned to the king's coffers the largest accumulation of property built up in the fourteenth century, a fact which made the call for financing the monarchy without recourse to taxation seem feasible. Uprisings in Wales and the north, followed by the renewal of war, soon proved such hopes to be futile, and in Henry VI's reign Parliament became ever more determined to refuse money grants. Instead the king was urged to restore his own by resuming lands previously granted away, and by the 1450s acts of resumption made a pretty regular appearance. However, exemptions granted to claimants prevented them from taking serious effect until Edward IV initiated a determined policy and transferred the exploitation of the crown estate to the king's Chamber, directly under the royal eye. Even so, it was only Henry VII who faced the unpopularity resulting from energetic resumption and exploitation sufficiently to create, for a time, a secure financial basis for the king's government without constant calls for tax money.

The chief reason for these financial stringencies was, of course, the war. The wars in France created a constant need for soldiers. The general feudal levy, successor to the fyrd, was summoned for the last time in 1327, after which, since it could not be made to serve continuously and abroad, it ceased to be used. The armies of the Hundred Years War were contract armies, negotiated for with magnates and lesser nobility who raised forces committed to them by indenture but relied on the king to pay. The happy theory that the war would pay for itself in booty and ransom money seems to have worked down to 1360 but never thereafter; instead the king waged his war on whatever wealth he could extract from his realm. At the same time, those retinues began to be a problem in times of external peace; for the first time since the Conquest, private armies and private warfare made their appearance in England.

Until recently it was held that these facts produced a major change in the social structure of England and in the relationship between crown and subject, a change summed up in the concept of 'bastard feudalism'. It was held that whereas in the age of feudalism proper the social ties consisted of personal loyalties embodied in the knightly fief and the duty of service attaching to it, from about the second quarter of the fourteenth century money took the place of fealty and the *milites* of the old dispensation became the retainers of the new. The individual entities comprising such retinues extended similar paid relationships beyond the military needs of the realm into tightly-knit systems of lords and followers, the latter doing whatever work the running of the lord's affairs involved: administering estates, dealing with legal problems, maintaining the state of the boss especially by riding escort on formal occasions. Every major landowner relied on an organized council of servants and at need could raise an armed force to overawe, or beat down, adversaries; more particularly he could and did use retainers to twist the law to his own advantage. In this age of bastard feudalism England, once united under the crown, was thought to have become an uneasy patchwork of rival powers in noble hands.

Lately, however, it has come to be recognized that this interpretation misleads somewhat: bastard feudalism would appear to be dead.[10] It is clear that both the central role of noble households and the use of contractual forces are to be found all the way back to the Norman Conquest; magnates had started retaining legal specialists by the 1230s at the latest; ever since kings had moved to limit seigneurial independence and jurisdiction, the nobility had tried to preserve some freedom of action by the evasive devices that used to be thought of as peculiar to bastard feudalism. What we see happening is the struggle for a measure of independence among the socially ascendant classes against the consolidation of a kingship that had been exceptionally strong even before 1066. The apparent crisis of an apparent bastard feudalism sprang rather from two aspects of royal policy. The great wars forced kings to let feudal retainers get better armed, better organized and more entrenched in

[10] See P. R. Coss, 'Bastard Feudalism Revised', *PP* 125 (1989), 27–64; J. M. W. Bean, *From Lord to Patron: Lordship in Medieval England* (1989).

society. At the same time, a royal policy (pursued by both Richard II and Henry IV) designed to establish direct contacts with and control over the ranks below the nobility enhanced the threat to magnate power even in the localities and encouraged a more intensive tying together of the lord's political following.[11] Yet what was most remarkable – and entirely contrary to the concept of bastard feudalism – was the continued and even increasing ascendancy of the crown when it was in the hands of a competent king. Edward III had no difficulty in undoing the aristocratic achievements of his father's reign; Richard II, temporarily forced into circumspection, demolished with ease the noble opposition who thought they had him in bonds, until he threw his victory away by breaking faith and trust; Henry IV, usurper though he was, overcame a series of real rebellions until his health failed him; Henry V could prepare for an invasion of France while brushing aside a conspiracy involving some quite powerful-seeming nobles.[12] A measure of loyalty to kings, overriding obligations to noble patrons, time and again made itself felt among the gentry. It was only when the monarchy fell into virtual abeyance, under Henry VI, that the fissiparous effects of retaining dominated English politics. And even then kingship kept some of its hold on sentiment: when the duke of York in 1450 claimed the crown he surprised and shocked the bulk of the aristocracy, who gathered round the useless king in possession. The civil wars that ended the house of Lancaster, promoted York and finally left England in the hands of the Tudors would not have been possible without the organizations controlled by such noblemen as Richard, earl of Warwick and alleged 'kingmaker', but it was not the nobility and its retainers who caused the wars. For this, entirely personal accidents were responsible, and – as both Edward IV and Henry VII showed soon enough – not even those wars had really weakened the power of the monarchy to exercise rule.[13]

[11] C. Given-Wilson, 'The King and the Gentry in Fourteenth-Century England', *TRHS* (1987), 87–102.

[12] T. B. Pugh, 'The Southampton Plot of 1415', in *Kings and Nobles in the Later Middle Ages*, ed. R. A. Griffiths and James Sherborne (1986), 62–89.

[13] J. R. Lander's introduction to his collected essays (*Crown and Nobility 1450–1509* [1976], 1–56) seems to me to play down the disruptive activities of the nobility a little too much, but he provides a convincing antidote to earlier notions of total lawlessness and ungovernability.

Plague and Population

War was one of the decisive influences on the people of England in the Later Middle Ages; the other was devastating disease. In 1348–9, bubonic plague – the Black Death – which had been spreading north from the Mediterranean reached England and killed at least a third of the population. Some estimates speak of half or more. Plague recurred at intervals for some two centuries (the Great Plague of London in 1665 was in fact the last fling of that rat-and-flea-borne disease), and though both its reach and its virulence tended to decline it succeeded in keeping the population below its thirteenth-century peak of about seven million until the beginning of the eighteenth. Just as plague began to be less destructive, in about the 1480s, a mysterious new killer called the sweating sickness made its appearance, and though it vanished in the reign of Elizabeth it had by then contributed noticeably to the impact of death.[14] The effects of those killing diseases were rendered more fearsome and lasting by a change in the climate which came to England in the early fourteenth century as mean temperatures dropped by several degrees. This put an end to the production of wine in such places as Gloucestershire, but its most widespread effect was to reduce productivity in general: in 1313–15, England experienced the worst famines ever recorded in the island. But for the reduction of the population in the wake of disease it seems likely that famine or near-famine conditions might have become as endemic in England as they were in late-medieval France, at least until agriculture rallied in the sixteenth century to meet the calls made upon the production of bread grains and meat.

Climatic change and epidemic disease put an end to the agrarian boom of the twelfth and thirteenth centuries, but the consequences differed with the sectors affected. Landlords suffered because they lost much of the labour tied by serfdom to their lands; the peasants, on the other hand, found themselves able to exploit a new rarity value. Despite attempts to freeze the situation by law (Statute of Labourers, 1351), the wages of

---

[14] R. C. Gottfried, 'Population, Plague and the Sweating Sickness: Demographic Movements in Late Fifteenth Century England', *JBS* 17 (1977), 12–37.

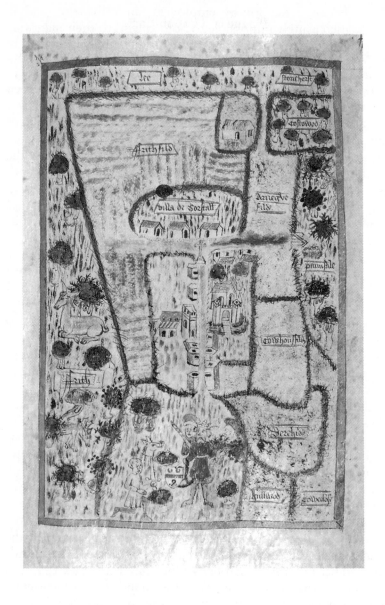

Plate 14 The village of Boarstall, Buckinghamshire, from a map of 1444, showing the church, the moated manor, peasant houses and open-field strips. Buckinghamshire County Record Office.

labourers competed for by employers naturally rose, and it
proved increasingly impossible to hold villeins to their manorial
ties. In effect, serfdom disappeared from England, where it was
never formally abolished. It is true that its disadvantages at
times of agrarian stability can be overstated. Labour services
had never been really oppressive; the lords' formal rights over
bodies, inheritances and marriages had never been enforced
with the legal rigidity that the system pretended; manorial
courts had protected peasant holdings, whether free or unfree;
and peasants who managed to acquire some wealth had more
commonly employed it in adding to their holdings than in
buying themselves out of villeinage.[15] Memories of Marxist
laments about the exploitation of labour mixed with over-
simplified ideas concerning freedom and viewed through the
distorting lens of the serfdom introduced in eastern Europe
from the sixteenth century onwards have habitually misled
liberal opinion among English historians. It is important to
remember that villages and manors depended on their inmates
for their organization, for the settlement of rights and the
solving of disputes; and though before the late-medieval
changes unfree men could not seek redress in the king's courts
they found it in the courts of lords who knew well that their
exploitation of their lands depended on a reasonably contented
peasantry. It is not an accident that the first signs of peasant
unrest appeared only after the disruption caused by the Black
Death and the misplaced efforts on the part of the lords to
retain a social structure that had died in the plague pits.

For the collapse of the population after 1348 did transform
the scene as it gave a powerful negotiating position to the
people who did the digging, sowing and harvesting, while
rendering all production for the market less profitable. Lords
came to value their lands less for the yield of saleable produce
than as a source of rents. Edward I's legislation against
subinfeudation prevented the creation of new rungs in the
feudal ladder, and while the original idea had been to extend the
feudal profits of the king, the effects of the law, combined with
the agrarian crisis, were to swell the ranks of the independent
middling landowner, the gentry. Especially ecclesiastical institu-

[15] J. Hatcher, 'English Serfdom and Villeinage: Towards a Reassessment', *PP* 90
(1981), 3–39.

tions increasingly deserted demesne farming and leased out their lands to occupiers; supposedly unfree lands (copyholds) with their fixed burdens were bought up and converted into leaseholds with rents adjustable to circumstances. This development was assisted by the willingness of the king's new court of Chancery[16] to offer protection to copyhold tenants, so that once more the distinctions between free and unfree status became altogether blurred. By the sixteenth century villeinage still existed and could on occasion be enforced in the courts, but in fact it had for all practical purposes disappeared; a social structure of lords, free peasants and serfs had been quietly transformed into one of freeholders and leaseholders of varying wealth and rank, but all of them, below the nobility, running rural England. The men who really called the tune were no longer military knights and clerical administrators, but lay gentry and yeomanry, often lawyers, who sat on baronial councils and served as stewards on the estates.

However, none of this means that the people recognized the improvement in their situation and were ready to be governed. Early in the reign of Henry IV, the French historian Jean Froissart recorded his impression of the English nation.[17] He thought that the English were 'of a haughty disposition, hot-tempered and quickly moved to anger ... Moved by envy and greed they were incapable by nature of joining in friendship or alliance with a foreign nation.' More especially, their middling sort formed the most 'untrustworthy people under the sun', but their nobility were quite different – 'noble and loyal' where the common people were 'cruel, perfidious, proud and disloyal'. The people would give their nobles nothing for free; everything, even an egg or a chicken, had to be paid for. And kings had the greatest difficulties in levying taxes.

In these last points we may discern the grounds for this categoric opinion: what we hear are the complaints of the English upper classes with whom Froissart was personally acquainted, perhaps reinforced by the laments of the French at those invading hordes of marauders who for three generations had been spoiling parts of their kingdom. It is the reverse view of that self-satisfied picture of the sturdy yeoman, the confident

---

[16] See below, p. 102.
[17] Quoted in Janet Coleman, *English Literature in History 1350–1400* (1981), 13.

individualist, who formed the English self-image.[18] There was truth in this view from both ends. The English were hard to govern, and they proved it frequently in minor riots, or in lynchings like the murder by London mobs of Bishop Walter Stapledon in 1326 and of Archbishop Simon Sudbury in 1381. Royal demands for money too often lay behind the really violent outbursts. It was a third poll tax in half-a-dozen years that led to the worst disturbances of the age – the so-called Peasants' Rebellion of 1381 under the leadership of Wat Tyler and a hedge-priest, John Ball, in the course of which London was occupied by rebels from Kent and Essex. Financial exactions similarly called forth the rebellion of Jack Cade (socially a bit more elevated than those rioters of Richard II's reign) in 1450. Both these outbursts, which involved a good deal of killing, were put down by the established order with reasonable promptitude. It is therefore important to remember that they were but the most violent manifestations of a potential for unrest which simmered throughout the realm and throughout the age. The people willing to resort to violence in this manner included, of course, those who took their capacity to kill and destroy to the French wars, but they also formed the bands led by disaffected or plainly criminal members of the lesser nobility who practised their marauding in England itself. The freedom-loving commons of England included a sizeable number of straightforward hooligans, and when defeat in France terminated what may be called a legitimate use of such tastes the king's government in the reign of Henry VI proved incapable of keeping the peace at home.[19]

However, it would be wrong to see nothing but crime and violence in those generations. Much of the country much of the time enjoyed reasonable peace and augmenting wealth. After all, it was in the fifteenth century that the wool towns of East Anglia built their splendid churches, that the most remarkable architectural skill came to be displayed in the perpendicular style of cathedral and college buildings, and that the nobility began to turn its formidable but uncomfortable castles into

[18] Alan Macfarlane, *The Origins of English Individualism* (1978).
[19] Organized crime occurred repeatedly before and during the Hundred Years War: J. Bellamy, *Crime and Public Order in England in the Later Middle Ages* (1973), chs 2 and 3. Storey, *End of the House of Lancaster* gives a vivid enough picture of public disorder in the fifteenth century.

agreeable residences. The wealth of England grew less in fields of wheat and barley than on the backs of sheep. English wool had for centuries been the staple material for cloth production in such Flemish centres as Bruges and Ghent, and the lasting occupation of Calais made possible the establishment of a settled centre for its export in the hands of the Company of Staplers who after trying various other places came to rest there in the 1390s. However, the really important development by-passed the Staple. As has been said, the needs of war finance led to the imposition of a heavy export duty on wool. On the other hand, the rather backward state of English cloth exports justified only a light duty on the manufactured product. This discrepancy produced in the fifteenth century the characteristic trade of unfinished English cloth sold to the highly developed finishing industries of the Continent, and after 1440 this concentrated on the convenient route between London and Antwerp. The Company of Merchant Adventurers controlled the London end and had its permanent representatives in the newly dominant port and mart on the Scheldt, an arrangement which in effect lasted into the 1620s.[20] Between them, Staplers and Adventurers also began to accumulate sufficient surplus money to start replacing the foreign financiers who had supplied the needs of the three Edwards: by the end of the fifteenth century, London was as much a financial centre as a manufacturing one.

In fact, cloth manufacture, once resident in such towns as Lincoln and Gloucester, in the course of the century moved out of those gild-regulated locations into the relative freedom of the countryside, with East Anglia and the West Riding of Yorkshire especially prominent. London apart, English towns in general underwent a period of decline, at least partly caused by the plague which was most devastating in densely populated areas. Town walls were allowed to decay and serious building ceased in the second half of the fifteenth century; even gild and chantry foundations, used by many historians as indicators of popular attitude to feelings both of religion and of the community,

---

[20] For the beginning of this see R. Davis, 'The Rise of Antwerp and the English Connection, 1406–1500', in *Trade, Government and Economy in Pre-Industrial England*, ed. D. C. Coleman and A. H. John (1976), 2–20.

began to lose their endowments.[21] It would be wrong to over-emphasize these difficulties. By continental standards, all English towns except London had always been small; the people and their rulers lived on the land. But declining towns reflected the loss of market facilities in an age of population decline and therefore constitute a significant measure of the general economic problems of the time which the dominance of the European market in wool and unfinished cloth tended to disguise. As for London, it had by the late fourteenth century become what it remained thereafter: the undisputed capital of England, run by trade gilds (livery companies) and well organized under the rule of mayor and aldermen. The fact that the king's government settled in the neighbouring city of Westminster demonstrated where the national centre of gravity lay. Occasionally London reminded kings and their favourites that it was not to be taken for granted,[22] but by the time of Henry VII it had become one of the mainstays of royal government.

The Church

Not surprisingly, the fortunes of faith and Church in this age also depended on war and plague. Like the laity, the clergy met ever-increasing tax demands with ever-increasing resistance, but unlike the laity it could inadvertently contribute when the moneys supposedly raised for the support of the papacy were raided by the king. Edward II, refused grants by his clergy, secured some 90 per cent of the papal tenth, no doubt a fair retribution for Boniface VIII's endeavour (with the bull *Clericis Laicos* of 1296) to prevent that king's father from getting money at all from the Church in England. The plague reduced the number of clergy available in England, though vacant livings were filled surprisingly quickly: it looks as though before 1348 there had been rather a surplus of priests in the realm.

---

[21] R. B. Dobson, 'Urban Decline in Late Medieval England', *TRHS* (1977), 1–22.

[22] May McKisack, 'London and the Succession to the Crown during the Middle Ages', in *Studies in Medieval History presented to F. M. Powicke*, ed. R. W. Hunt et al. (1948), 78–89; Caroline Barron, 'London and Parliament in the Lancastrian Period', *Parliamentary History* 9 (1990), 343–67.

Opinions differ on the question whether the experience of God-created devastation led to a collapse of faith, but it does seem clear that a degree of apocalyptic apprehension came to people in the wake of the Black Death. England did not experience the worst forms of such reactions that were found elsewhere. The English could not blame the Jews for supposedly poisoning wells and massacre them in revenge: they had driven all Jews out of the realm in 1290. But they also did not produce other kinds of fanatics (like the bands of flagellants) and could show but few mystics. The chief reaction in the Lollard movement, about which more in a moment, was sober rather than enthusiastic, and even the spreading orders of friars – the most active part of the Church – behaved more circumspectly in England than elsewhere.

Thus, generally speaking, the official religion looked reasonably quiescent and increasingly national. Bishops, even when provided by the papacy, were now mostly English and in the main served as ministers of the crown. More and more of them had trained as lawyers; even though the number of university-trained theologians grew rapidly few of them made it to the top. For a short spell England followed the continental practice of finding bishops among the offspring of the aristocracy. Courtenays and Arundels made it to Canterbury, and most notoriously a Beaufort to Winchester, but these remained rarities. Leading administrators like Adam Moleyns, clerk of the king's Council and bishop of Chichester when he was murdered by mutinous sailors in 1450, were more usual, though it should be noted that the body of king's servants who administered the realm increasingly drew on the laity, especially trained common lawyers. The national convictions of the clergy became very plain when they were roped in by both Edward III and Henry V to stir the nation's passion in support of the king's wars: sermons and days of prayers abounded, all carefully organized from above.[23] The effects of all this assaulting cannot be properly measured; while it is true that national support at times reached high levels of fervour it does look as though this was so only during years of high success; the efforts of the

[23] A. K. McHardy, 'The English Clergy and the Hundred Years War', *SCH* 20 (1983), 171–8; 'Liturgy and Propaganda in the Diocese of Lincoln during the Hundred Years War', *SCH* 18 (1982), 215–27.

clergy could not maintain such ardour when things went wrong – that is, when they were most needed.

The main feature of the history of the Church in England during these two centuries, however, stemmed from events outside the realm. By the beginning of the fourteenth century, the great age of papal power was manifestly ending. The universal rule which Gregory VII had initiated, and which had reached its height in the reign of Innocent III, the pope who accepted King John's offer of vassalage, looked pretty tatty in the hands of Boniface VIII (1294–1303) who specialized in vast claims of clerical independence from secular powers that he could not enforce. Edward I restored a degree of amity when he compelled the pope to allow the English clergy to be taxed, but in the next reign the troubles of the papacy became very manifest. The popes had left Rome, taking up residence at Avignon and becoming in effect clients of the crown of France; the office was monopolized by Frenchmen who abandoned all efforts at universal impartiality, and with the outbreak of the Hundred Years War the popes in effect became champions of England's enemies. King and Parliament joined hands in attacks on papal rights and in defence of national independence. More particularly, attention concentrated on the elimination of papal appointments in the English Church, known as provisors; this produced the powerfully anti-papal Statute of Provisors (1351) augmented by legislation to limit papal interference to the detriment of the king's courts in England (Statutes of Prae-munire, 1353 and 1393). On the face of it, England in the fourteenth century turned hostile to a papacy with which it had hitherto worked in general harmony; even though the weapons so created were used rather to gain a sullen acceptance by the popes of the king's claims over his clergy and their wealth than to mount a general attack, the new relationship was adverse to the notion of a Church standing above national boundaries.

Even the clergy of England showed signs of national aspirations so very different from the days of Thomas Becket or even the loyally popish Robert Winchelsea, archbishop of Canterbury from 1293 to 1313, who had given Edward I a lot of trouble. William of Ockham, Oxford's most famous alumnus in the first half of the century, wrote an attack on the Avignonese papacy on behalf of the English monarchy, before he transferred his person and his labours to the court of the Emperor Lewis of Bavaria, another enemy to French popes.[24] The situation worsened after 1378 with the so-called Great Schism – with rival popes claiming the allegiance of the faithful from Avignon and Rome respectively. The second hero of the Oxford schools, John Wyclif, cherished an unrelenting hatred of the papacy, and he for a time commanded valuable political support from John of Gaunt. When a leading churchman and philosopher backed the strident lay demand for the disendowment of the allegedly overfed clergy he presented claims of spiritual welfare of much use to a monarchy, nobility and gentry looking for new wealth in difficult times. Wyclif made the mistake of extending his violent criticism from these well-received broadsides into heretical attacks on the central tenets of the faith (transubstantiation and the mass), for which reason he was condemned,[25] forced to leave Oxford, and after his death (1384) treated as a heretic who had managed to escape excommunication and the stake but not posthumous degradation. But Wyclif had sown seeds, and if some of those seeds produced a growth that the monarchy abominated, the general attack on papal claims to rule in the Church met wide acceptance in those three decades when rival popes appealed for support.

The unwelcome growth from Wyclif's sowing was the heresy of the Lollards.[26] It spread sporadically but widely, and though it never developed into a clear-cut or consistent set of beliefs it was marked out by certain general characteristics. In the first place, it believed in the vernacular as the instrument of faith and instruction: its tracts were written in English and it promoted an English translation of the Bible. This gave it a wide appeal in circles that had no acquaintance with the standard forms of education or discourse: it was a popular heresy and more especially could make a real impression on women, whose role in the official Church was virtually null. Secondly, Lollards rejected the claims of the priesthood and emphasized the direct

[24] M. Wilks, 'Royal Patronage and Anti-Papalism from Ockham to Wyclif', in *From Ockham to Wyclif*, ed. A. Hudson and M. Wilks (1987), 135–63.

[25] A. Kenny, 'Wyclif', *Proc. of the British Academy* 72 (1986), 91–113.

[26] See esp. Margaret Aston's collected papers: *Lollards and Reformers: Images and Literacy in Late Medieval Religion* (1984). Also J. A. F. Thomson, *The Later Lollards* (1965).

Plate 15 The genealogy of Geoffrey Chaucer. (The Mansell Collection, London.)

relationship between the believer and his God. This followed from, as well as promoted, a general rejection of the formal aspects of religion, from the mass to the worship of saints and images. The Great Schism gave the Lollards their chance: they could exploit a widespread contempt for schismatic popes in a general denunciation of papal claims as both hostile to the concerns of the English and adverse to the basic principles of the Christian Scriptures.[27] Thus Lollard heresy spread far and fast around the turn of the fourteenth century, attracting support not only from the commons but also among the gentry and the king's knights.[28] This turned out to be a mistake. Neither Richard II nor Henry IV were eager supporters of the papacy, but neither also favoured a movement which looked likely to become subversive; episcopal moves against those heretics regularly gained royal favour in the 1390s. In 1401 clerical representations secured the passage of a statute which committed the secular power to carry out sentences of death passed by ecclesiastical tribunals (*De haeretico comburendo*), and burnings for heresy for the first time made their appearance in England. Persecution produced its predictable result in the rebellion of Sir John Oldcastle in 1414, but the defeat of that rising also put an end to the political potential of Lollardy. The movement did not disappear, but it played no further part in the general unrest of the time, which in fact owed nothing to religious dissent. Lollardy revived in numbers in the early sixteenth century, provoking some more persecution, and surviving Lollard attitudes contributed to that fall of the old Church which we call the Reformation. But those proto-sectaries were not themselves rebels.

Lollard teaching anticipated some of the essentials of the sixteenth-century turmoil, more especially the rejection of clerical exclusiveness, the emphasis on personal piety, and the use of the English language. It is, however, worth notice that it also avoided some of the characteristics which marked the continental Reformation at the popular level: Lollards were sober and restrained in their beliefs and behaviour. They did not go in for mystic experiences, did not foam in ecstasy, and

---

[27] Margaret Harvey, 'Lollardy and the Great Schism: Some Contemporary Perceptions', *History* 62 (1977), 385–96.

[28] K. B. McFarlane, *Lancastrian Kings and Lollard Knights* (1972), Part II.

restricted their attacks on the things they disliked to com-
monsensical utterances.[29] They were not the ancestors of
seventeenth-century puritanism (or indeed twentieth-century
pentecostalism): they were much more sensible, much nicer,
than that. But of course such self-restraint still exposed them to
the power of their enemies in the official Church. The odd thing
is that they really missed their best chance of gaining power in
the early days of their existence. Wyclif had denied the need for
a separate ecclesiastical rulership in the English Church; he
spoke of a national Church-cum-state under the rule of the
monarchy. The Great Schism seemed to offer the English crown
the chance to turn this national and nationalist concept into
reality.[30] Instead, Henry V accepted the restoration of formal
papal power at the Council of Constance (1414) and established reasonable relations with Pope Martin V (1417–31).
That pope tried in vain to secure the repeal of the legislation
against provisors which limited his patronage in England,[31] but
the ultimate outcome of all that politicking was a peaceable
compromise which denied any hostile potential to the papacy
while accepting the formality of Roman rule over the English
Church. Yet the papacy of the fifteenth century had simply
replaced its earlier obedience to France by the role of an Italian
prince: the late-medieval papacy was universal only in name
and claim, a name and claim accepted virtually only in England.
The Lancastrian kings quite deliberately avoided the radical
implications of the anti-papal agitation because they found it
easier to control and exploit the clergy in partnership with
Rome. Between the healing of the Schism and Henry VIII's
change of heart (1417–1534) nothing was further from the
minds of English kings than any break with Rome; from
Rome's point of view, they were the only reliably faithful sons
among the rulers of Europe. And Lollardy retreated into the

[29] England, like Europe, had its late-medieval mystics, but they were markedly more
marginal in influence and contributed nothing to Lollard heresy. D. Knowles, *The
English Mystical Tradition* (1961), vainly tried to give content to the last word of his
title.

[30] Margaret Harvey, 'The Power of the Crown in the English Church during the
Great Schism', *SCH* 18 (1982), 229–41.

[31] R. G. Davies, 'Martin V and the English Episcopate, with particular reference to
his Campaign for the Repeal of the Statute of Provisors', *EHR* 92 (1977), 309–44.

Plate 16 The aisle and nave of Durham Cathedral depicting Romanesque style. (The Royal Commission on the Historical Monuments of England.)

villages of Essex, Kent and the Cotswolds, cherishing its English Bible and English tracts in a spirit of sober piety.

Royal Justice

We have seen that in both the secular sphere and the sphere of religion the fourteenth and fifteenth centuries were remarkably full of noise and upheaval. We have also seen that despite everything the king retained ultimate control and even a measure of obedience until the potential of disaster finally crystallized in the civil wars of Lancaster and York. That is to say, the high degree, repute, power and political control which the Norman kings had inherited from their Anglo-Saxon predecessors, and which had been so energetically augmented by Henry I and Henry II, survived the follies of some kings and the arrogance of others to remain the chief feature of English politics and of their national organization. And despite that age of ever-renewed disturbance, the monarchy also continued to build up both its means of rule and the organized state of England.

Much of this was achieved in the first part of Edward I's reign, before imperial ambitions diverted that king's attentions once again to continental war and the conquest of Scotland. The list of major statutes is impressive, and they were strictly the work of the king and his lawyers. Those laws dealt with rights in land, prohibiting grants to the 'dead hand' of the Church (Mortmain, 1279) and continuous subinfeudation (*Quia Emptores*, 1290), practices which had deprived the crown of rights due upon the death of a tenant-in-chief, though the reform also protected great lords against losses further down the scale. The Statutes of Acton Burnell (1283) and of Merchants (1285) protected trade and efficient debt-collecting. Multi-purpose edicts like those of Winchester (1285), Westminster I (1275) and Westminster II (1290) attended in the main to problems of law enforcement, and *Quo Warranto* (1290) established a procedure for ascertaining and thereafter protecting rights of franchise claimed by feudatories. All these measures responded to particular needs and sometimes particular complaints; they codified and settled the practices of the developing common law rather than creating them; and they became the hard core of education at the Inns of Court and the points of reference in 200 years of litigation. Round about 1300 there also began the series of Year Books, annual collections of cases tried in the central courts; the work of student lawyers, they offered guidance in the technicalities of the law to future generations. The age thus witnessed a striking growth in the legal profession, briefly interrupted in 1289 by a major scandal when the king, returning from Gascony, was confronted with a flood of complaints against corrupt judges and administrators. Edward acted with his usual mixture of clear-sighted energy and unprincipled ruthlessness, but the ultimate effect of dismissals, imprisonments and heavy fines was good: at the top of the legal machinery behaviour thereafter remained respectable and proper. And the profession also produced intelligent reflection and progressive thinking, most notably in the work of John Fortescue (1394–1476), chief justice to Henry VI and adviser to Edward IV, whose writings on law and politics reflect an ability to get down to fundamentals which was rare among the practitioners of the law; these rather tended to promote pettifoggery and involvement in detail.

Thus the common custom of England became the elaborate structure of the common law, relying on precedent and decisions, and operated by highly trained professionals. At least that was the situation at the centre, in the king's courts. Disseminating law and law-enforcement through the realm posed less well-handled problems, especially as the General Eyre of Angevin times had lapsed. The old communal courts of shire and hundred by stages largely ceased to deal with cases either civil or criminal; the shire court in particular became an instrument for agreeing and forwarding the petitions of the locality to the king's courts (especially the early Parliament).[32] One of the inescapable consequences of concentrating law-making and law-enforcement in the king's hands was the need for new machinery throughout the realm to give reality to those central claims. The king, of course, had at his disposal the sheriffs in their counties, and they continued to act as chief links between centre and localities. But earlier experience had

---

[32] J. R. Maddicott, 'The County Community and Public Opinion in the Fourteenth Century', *TRHS* (1978), 27–41.

underlined the dangers lying in wait for kings who left all local power to sheriffs, and the policy to prevent them from becoming the rulers of the shires was continued. In the early thirteenth century a new county officer had been created – the coroner, responsible for superintending the enforcement of the law against evil-doers, a role that he shared with the sheriff. But reliance on such officers had its political drawback, inasmuch as it could easily offend those members of the active gentry who did not hold office, and by the middle of the fourteenth century reliance had shifted to a novel institution, the justices of the peace empowered by royal commission to investigate and deal with crime and misdemeanour. Thus, although the kings of England never attempted to set up bureaucratic systems in the country, they commanded the services of quite a considerable body of men who were qualified to superintend the scene not by training and not for pay, but as a function of their social standing controlled by dependence on and obedience to the king's central administration.

Such a system, of course, worked well only if dependence and obedience were real. The affinities gathered around noble and knightly patrons could thus prove troublesome, especially as they began to contain armed retainers: this is how 'livery and maintenance' disrupted good order. Livery meant the wearing of identifying marks or clothing, and although by statute confined to the higher ranks within the nation was difficult to control: a lord's following, visibly identifiable, often threatened the peace. Maintenance meant using force and influence to bias the administration of justice in favour of members of the affinity, contrary to the truth of a case. As the preservation of order and enforcement of the law came to rest in the hands of exactly those people who either controlled or belonged to the organization of a patron's clients, the risks materialized and the normal processes of the law became liable to frequent subversion. This happened especially in the sadly disturbed middle years of the fifteenth century as opposition to the king's hated favourites undermined traditions of obedience. One possibly surprising consequence of these uncertainties was the growth of alternative ways of settling disputes. The king's government led the way by responding to petitions, first in Parliament but in the fifteenth century mainly through the lord chancellor. The

Chancery became a regular court resolving disagreements by
methods outside the common law and called equity, that is,
supposedly by principles of natural justice. The example was
followed by baronial councils which also heard and decided
complaints on a quite regular basis;[33] furthermore, private
arbitration rather than suits at law proliferated into settlements
provided by individuals by whose decisions disputants had
agreed to abide.[34]

However, though such arbitration, whether organized or
casual, did good service in preventing disputes from regularly
escalating into violence, it also underlined an important fact
insufficiently recognized by historians. By the middle of the
fifteenth century the system of the common law could no longer
satisfy the lawful needs of Englishmen: law and life had grown
apart. The burgeoning jurisdiction of Chancery rested more
especially on two aspects of landownership which the law did
not recognize. The chancellor began to protect copyhold, in
effect the old unfree tenure which the king's courts had always
remitted to manorial jurisdiction but which after the demographic upheavals of the age had ceased to be connected with
servile status. And the chancellor enforced the testamentary
device known as enfeoffment to uses, or in short the use. The
use separated the legal ownership in land from the receipt of its
benefits by conveying the estate to a trust enjoined to channel
the income to a named person. Since the trust could be
maintained in permanent existence, landholding tenants-in-
chief never died, so that the so-called feudal profits (death duties
and especially rights of wardship over minors) ceased to come
to the lord (especially the king); also, in this way it proved
possible to evade the rules of primogeniture and provide for
offspring, male and female, who by the common law would
have been left without inheritance. But the common law did not
recognize the use, and since someone had to make sure that the
foeffees (trustees) did as instructed, the chancellor found
himself appealed to. The fact is that social arrangements,

---

[33] Carole Rawcliffe, 'Baronial Councils in the Later Middle Ages', in *Patronage,
Pedigree and Power in the Later Middle Ages*, ed. C. Ross (1979), 87–108.
[34] E. Powell, 'Arbitration and the Law in England in the Later Middle Ages', *TRHS*
1983, 49–67; 'Settlement of Disputes by Arbitration in Fifteenth-Century England',
Law and History Review 2 (1984), 14–22.

political interests, family commitments and the lawful desires of Englishmen increasingly failed to find their answers in the courts of the common law. From about 1490 onwards, the law – that is to say, judges and advocates – came to recognize this fact, and the half-century that followed witnessed a major renewal from within, by decision and opinion ultimately codified in statute, which very largely replaced the medieval system of remedies by new machinery and new devices; but this was done so quietly, without the sound of trumpets, that this silent revolution has only recently been discovered and analysed.[35]

Parliament

The monarchy thus survived. It even improved the machinery of government. In the 1320s, Bishop Stapledon thoroughly reformed the Exchequer (thereby arousing the hatred of the Londoners which caused him to be lynched), and all kings increasingly organized their household departments of the Wardrobe and the Chamber to secure a firmer and more immediate hold on their resources. The Yorkists and Henry VII made the treasurer of the Chamber, directly under their eye and put in charge of the crown lands, their chief officer of finance. As the great seal controlled by the chancellor 'went out of court' and became separated from itinerant monarchs, lesser seals – first the privy seal with its keeper and lastly the signet kept by the king's secretary – became organized departments with staffs of clerks. One way and another, royal government remained in touch with the nation and survived the upheavals of politics. The king's Council wobbled between being the king's government and the target of dissatisfied subjects seeking to reform it, but none of those attempts took root. However, the chief instrument of both contact and upheaval was the king's Parliament which in these two centuries became an established institution.

No theme in English history has provoked more confused and confusing reflections than the origin, purpose and fortunes of Parliament, but fortunately the more extravagant misrepresen-

[35] See below, p. 135.

tations, begotten by the conflicts of the seventeenth century and the self-satisfaction of the nineteenth, need not trouble us any longer.[36] The Parliament did not start as a body representing the English people in their various ranks or estates; it was not an instrument designed to limit or at least control the power of the monarchy; but it nevertheless fulfilled perfectly visible and sensible functions in the running of affairs. The first official use of the term so far discovered dates from 1236,[37] a fact which usefully demonstrates that the old notion which linked the 'origin of Parliament' to Simon de Montfort and the Provisions of Oxford was mistaken. On the contrary, the rebellious barons of Henry III's reign were trying to adapt a part of the royal machinery of government to their endeavour to impose conciliar control on the king. They were not the last people to try this, always in vain; the Parliament remained one of the king's courts, intermittent and specially summoned because not regularly needed, and serving a purpose special to itself. That purpose concerned the effective contact between the ruler and the ruled, the centre and the parts of the realm. Royal government had for long possessed means for finding out what was troubling people, even as it had always had means to convey decisions and intentions to those concerned, and the most effective method had always consisted in summoning up men from the localities to attend upon the king and his councillors; men chosen by the shire courts had occasionally served this function long before there was a Parliament. The barons of the mid-thirteenth century tried to regularize the practice, and their example moved Edward I to do so more efficiently. Throughout his reign he frequently called for representatives to meet him, to hear and carry back information of what was required of the English in the service of their king; and they in their turn found those occasions ideal for bringing up the problems hanging in the locality (often unfinished business at law) to put before councillors for their advice and the king's decision. As it has been well put, 'representation was

[36] For a good introduction to the late-medieval Parliament see *The English Parliament in the Middle Ages*, ed. R. G. Davies and J. H. Denton (1981); the earlier part of the story is idiosyncratically illumined in G. O. Sayles, *The King's Parliament of England* (1975).
[37] Cf. *EHR* 82 (1967), 747–50.

an extension of, not an antithesis to, royal and conciliar government.'[38] Who was called to those meetings – meetings that were in effect enlarged sessions of the king's regular council – depended on the needs of the moment. The great men – earls, for instance and leading bishops – were always wanted, but elected knights or burgesses were at first rare. So far Parliament was a very flexible and variable instrument: most manifestly not an institution but a familiar occasion of very fluid composition.

Institutional structuring came about between 1307 and 1340, between Edward II's accession and Edward III's explosion into the cosy scene of mutual back-scratching which characterized the king's government when the king left England to claim the crown of France. The baronial opponents of Edward II found in their king's Parliament a convenient stage on which to pursue their political ends, but they also discovered that there was profit in calling the representatives of the communities in order to broaden support in the nation. When the king won this conflict at Boroughbridge he and the Despensers in their turn appealed to the shires, and by 1340 it was settled that for a Parliament to deserve the name it had to include the Commons. At the same time, the diocesan clergy evinced a preference for its own representative bodies – the Convocations of the two provinces – and ceased to be summoned to Parliament, though the bishops remained, being called (so the argument went) as tenants-in-chief equal to barons. Thus there emerged the Parliament of two Chambers, early in Edward III's reign: the afforced king's Council which in due course became the House of Lords, and the House of Commons elected by shires and boroughs. By the middle of the fifteenth century the business machinery of Parliament was well developed in the hands of expert bureaucrats trained in the Chancery; they provided these intermittent and always newly formed assemblies with an element of continuity.

At this time, too, the Parliament acquired special functions not dischargeable anywhere else. The financial pressures of the French wars compelled Edward III to seek taxation by consent, and he soon realized that he would most visibly gain this from a body that exemplified the political and tax-paying nation. At the same time, it came to be recognized that laws promulgated

[38] J. C. Holt in Davies and Denton, *The English Parliament*, 22.

on the occasion of a meeting of Parliament had the most publicity and therefore authority. Thus by 1350 Parliament's chief functions of authorizing money grants and making laws on the basis of initiatives from either king, or judges, or the Commons were settled. The flood of private petitions which had bothered Edward I's Council in Parliament abated as Council and Chancery worked out machinery for dealing with them outside the parliamentary meetings; even so, the flood left behind the private bill for a legislative settlement of the affairs of individuals and localities, a thing unknown in other late-medieval parliamentary institutions. The English Parliament remained a part of the king's government, not a representative of the nation against the monarch. Taxes were agreed to especially by the Commons, and the king made his statutes with the advice and consent of Lords and Commons; the idea that the authority behind these laws was not solely the king's but included the Parliament was first expressed in 1433 and did not become a standard piece of phrasing until the reign of Edward IV. At the same time, since the Parliament was called to consider affairs it remained available for raising matters of dispute and protest, as when the Commons attacked Edward III's government in the Good Parliament of 1376 or when the duke of York stated his claim to the crown in 1450 and again in 1460. Yet at heart the Lords and Commons, depending as they did on a royal decision to call them, served the needs of a royal government working by consent.

One aspect of activity in Parliament, already alluded to, deserves further brief notice. Time and again, meetings were used to press upon the king a reform of his Council, and this call became particularly strident in the reign of Henry IV when the Commons several times demanded that councillors be appointed in Parliament. Behind this repeated assault lay the conviction that bad government arose from the use of bad councillors, or rather from the convention which disguised disapproval of the king as dislike of those he favoured. No king ever really accepted such demands, whatever soothing talk he might use. On the face of it, the Commons demanded a Council composed of specified nobles and faction leaders appointed under their eye. The worth of all this came out clearly at the start of Henry VI's reign when the regency Council was put

Plate 17 The Dance of Death, from a fifteenth-century Book of Hours.
(Reproduced by courtesy of the Trustees of The British Museum, London.)

together without a word from or in Parliament: the noble
leadership could act directly and did so. No king ever
surrendered his right to choose the men through whom he
governed, and nothing better describes the political insignifi-

Plate 18 The Battle of Tewkesbury, depicting English longbowmen from the Wars of the Roses. (The Mansell Collection, London.)

cance of the Parliament, and especially of the Commons, than those pompous and fruitless efforts at interference.

After the Civil Wars

Thus when the troubles of the fifteenth century finally threw up an effective and lasting monarchy in the hands of the Tudors the realm and its monarchic structure proved to have survived remarkably well. The end of civil war called for no more than putting the inherited system into operation, a thing that Henry VII did with skill, determination and a degree of ruthlessness. The idea once current that he deliberately eliminated the nobility – those supposedly overmighty subjects – and used men of the alleged middle classes for his service has had to be abandoned in the face of the facts. The same sort of people worked for Henry VII as had worked for Henry V and Edward I. The first Tudor king was concerned to assert the rightful claims of the crown, especially in the fundamental problem of finance: a king's authority depended in great measure on his ability to survive without forever seeking to tax his subjects. It also depended on his securing the consent and respect of all men of power in his realm, and Henry VII deliberately put an end to the reliance on factions which had destroyed the unanimity of the nation under the Yorkists. By about 1500, England was manifestly again that realm of one nation (the Welsh now in

Plate 19 *Allegory of the Tudor succession, attributed to Lucas de Heere, c.1572, oil on panel, 1295 × 1803 mm. (By kind permission of Sudeley Castle, Winchcombe.)*

effect incorporated with a Tudor on the throne) living under a strong but law-abiding king and a system of law promulgated and enforced by royal government. The one thing that had gone was the imperial pretensions that had led to the troubles with Scotland and the disastrous wars with France. Or, to be more exact, the pretensions were not forgotten but Henry VII had no intention of pursuing them actively. He would settle with Scotland by marrying his elder daughter to the king of the Scots, with France by a peace treaty (1492) which paid him compensation for claims given up, and with Ireland by allowing the Fitzgerald dynasty of Kildare to guide the Anglo-Irish parts into order and peace. As for the Church and religion, Henry VII responded to the preferences of his people when he ruled with the help of an episcopal civil service, worshipped in the most traditional way possible, and maintained cordial relations with the pope. In essence, nothing much had altered since the days of Edward I or even Henry II, except that England had become beyond doubt or limitation the realm of the English nation. Kingship was strong, but so was the independence of the subject pursuing his rights at law. Kings governed most successfully when they recognized their people and called on them to share the work of social and political advancement. Below the king, the hierarchies of peerage, gentry, merchants and yeomen fitted well together: national interest might yield before regional concerns, but there was no battle of the classes. Nor indeed of the sexes either.

4

From Cromwell to Cromwell[1]

The English thus emerged from the Middle Ages very definitely
as a nation, self-consciously aware of that identity and always
ready to assert it across a spectrum of behaviour that ranged
from kindly superiority to embittered chauvinism. Despite the
long experience of rulers from elsewhere and constant involvement in parts over the sea, despite even the contributory streams
of Welsh, Danish, Norman and Gascon blood, they manifestly
and recognizably differed from their neighbours in the islands
and beyond them. Unfreedom existed, technically, though
slavery did not, but the serfs of England, unlike the peasantry of
France or of the eastern fringes of Europe, already looked so
like free men that the servile conditions were never to be ended
by formal manumission.[2] The people of England believed
themselves to be better off than people anywhere else, and in
this were by and large correct; by comparison with other
Europeans, the English, through their various social ranks, were
relatively prosperous and safe from famine. Nothing existed
that could be called a class structure, but the social scene and
understanding recognized gradations ranging from the ascendant nobility (aristocracy and gentry) through the independent
yeomanry to the commons farming their lands, all of them to a
surprising degree willing and able to assert themselves. Though

[1] For introductory surveys of this period see D. M. Loades, *Politics and the Nation
1450–1660* (3rd edn, 1986); Claire Cross, *Church and People 1450–1660* (1976); J. A.
Guy, *Tudor England* (1988). While I have learned much from these and others, I must
adhere to my own views on occasion.

[2] Cf. D. J. N. MacCulloch, 'Bondmen under the Tudors', in *Law and Government
under the Tudors*, ed. C. Cross et al. (1988), 91–109.

this state of affairs was increasingly being ascribed to the special beneficence of a God who valued the English, a measure of independence high by the standards of the time sprang surprisingly enough from the strength and weight of the monarchy. Kings of England commanded a range of power and control over all subjects which outdistanced supposedly greater monarchs on the Continent, and the recent agonies of kingship proved this in the ease with which the monarchy resumed the seat of power with the arrival of the Tudor dynasty. And kings could rule because the law of England, the common law, was both their creature and their guide. A realm which harboured no provincial powers but only great men looking for advantage to the royal court possessed a remarkable degree of unity even when its peace was most disturbed. Compared with a France where Burgundy and Brittany and Navarre still formed semi-independent enclaves needing to be overcome by force of arms and diplomacy, or with a Holy Roman Empire composed of separate principalities often at odds with one another, the petty scale of the fifteenth-century civil wars in England emphasized the essentially national identity of that realm.

However, the wars had also shown that that identity might easily be threatened, more easily than had seemed likely, for instance, in the reign of Henry V: the English nation-state was by no means yet safely constructed, and the memories of Henry VI's reign were to play their part in assisting the Tudor monarchs to tighten the strings of control. The century and a half that followed upon the accession of Henry VIII in 1509 was to witness a series of developments which, though they drew upon the medieval experience of the English polity, amounted to a whole bundle of transformations the sum of which produced an unfailingly united and centralized kingdom with its own national civilization, so well centralized that it could afford to allow diversity and liberties, and in the end even real civil war, to endure without ever threatening the fundamental fact of national identity. Henry VII made his contribution with no thought of introducing change; his achievement lay in the firm reassertion of a monarchy backed by financial security and visibly the dominant focus of power within the realm and the ultimate dispenser of patronage. The possibility that magnate courts and councils might rival the king's disappeared as Henry asserted his function as the one source of rule and of favour; great men became his clients, bound as a rule in recognizances that threatened ruin to any lord that might try to stand out for himself. Henry VIII, who inherited a safe crown, never had the slightest doubt that he ruled everything. But in fact this was not quite true, as he discovered when he decided to rid himself of his first wife.

The Reformation

The authority of king and common law in England was always potentially rivalled by the claims of the Universal Church – the claims of papacy and canon law. The two powers had by Henry VII's time arrived at a quite comfortable *modus vivendi*. The Statute of Praemunire safeguarded the interests of the crown against papal ambitions, but it lay in effect dormant; Lollard heresy had been contained; the king's piety was formally correct to a degree that few European monarchs achieved; patronage was comfortably shared, and the interests of England were further safeguarded by cardinals at Rome who acted as the king's resident ambassadors.[3] Early in his reign, Henry VIII backed the papacy in the Italian wars that threatened Rome with either French or Spanish domination. A minor crisis arose in 1514 with the death in the episcopal prison of London of Richard Hunne, posthumously charged with heresy, which revealed strong anticlerical feelings in the capital, and the crisis was worsened by a surprising revival of Thomas Becket's attitude to the subjection of the clergy to secular jurisdiction, which led to an uproar in the Parliament of 1515. Henry forced the clergy to make peace by submission and declared himself free of any superior on earth, and this minor turmoil settled back into a peaceful coexistence personified in the rise to power of Cardinal Thomas Wolsey, archbishop of York, lord chancellor, and papal legate *a latere* who provided his king with a cobbled-together rule over both state and Church in England for close on fifteen years (1514–29). The next crisis should have followed much the same line: when in 1527 Henry sought a papal annulment of his marriage to Catherine of Aragon (on the

---

[3] W. E. Wilkie, *The Cardinal Protectors of England* (1974).

grounds that her earlier union to his late brother should by the law of Scripture have barred him from marrying her) he confidently expected to have his loyalty to Rome rewarded. Had he not even turned author to defend the papacy against the Lutheran assault?[4] Pope Clement VII would gladly have complied, but since 1525 Rome had stood under the power of the Emperor Charles V, Catherine's nephew, and Henry's reasonable request met the totally unexpected shock of a rebuff.

The consequences are well known. Henry chose to assert the independent rights and powers of the Church in England. Wolsey's fall and the legislation of the Reformation Parliament (1529–36) ended England's links with the Universal Church, undoing close on a thousand years and creating – officially recognizing – the Royal Supremacy over the two provinces of Canterbury and York. This 'break with Rome' in the end turned out to be permanent, but it need not have done; quarrels of this kind had before this been settled by treaty between the pope and this or that secular power.[5] Throughout the rest of Henry's reign Charles V's diplomats expected that the rift would be healed; there were sufficient people in England hoping for the same solution; and in the reign of Henry's daughter Mary (1553–8) that peace was in fact achieved, only for the break to be renewed with the accession of Elizabeth in 1558. It must therefore be stressed that all these efforts to bring England back to the universal fold were in fact doomed: the break that began in 1532–4 was from the first so very different from any disputes that had occurred in earlier centuries that medieval experiences only misled (as they still continue to mislead some historians). The two decisive elements new to the brew were the anti-papal revolution known as the European Reformation, and the person and policy of Thomas Cromwell. The spread of Protestant views in England began in the 1520s and benefited somewhat from a revival of Lollard anti-papalism which episcopal repression failed to extinguish. When England broke with Rome it for the first time possessed a not insignificant

[4] *Assertio Septem Sacramentorum* (1521), which granted the papacy the full traditional ascendancy in the Church and gained for Henry the title 'Defender of the Faith'.

[5] In 1514, long-standing disputes between the papacy and the crown of France had come to an end with a Concordat which left the French Church under the spiritual headship of Rome.

Plate 20 Hans Holbein, Thomas Cromwell. *(The Frick Collection, New York.)*

complement of clergy who sought to escape from the papal connection and supported the king with policies of revolutionary reform. And Cromwell, the man who showed Henry the way out of the dilemma created by the pope's refusal to end that first marriage, brought to the task his vision of a strictly independent, unitary realm, organized entirely within its own borders and dedicated to reform in both the spiritual and the secular sphere. These two elements came together in Cromwell's short but explosive career in power (1532–40). Cromwell, who in four years effortlessly swept some 800 monastic houses off the map of England, came to incline quite sincerely to the Protestant brand of the Christian religion, and with the assistance of Thomas Cranmer at Canterbury as well as other radical bishops initiated the gradual transformation of the theology of a Church whose total subjection to the authority of king and Parliament he had achieved by 1536.

It is, however, perfectly true that this ultimate transformation into a Protestant England took its time, though it is less certain that the arguments recently advanced for seeing the English people adhering to their Catholic past long after the Church had become officially Reformed will really stand up.[6] Not turning Protestant obediently at the king's command does not equal adhering to Catholic orthodoxy. On the face of it, the nature of the Church of England and its doctrine were certainly dictated from above. In 1539 a Catholic reaction procured the restoration of orthodoxy in the Act of Six Articles, and in 1540 Cromwell fell to Henry's search for a scapegoat and the axe, without a trial. Although reform and reformers survived the last years of Henry VIII, officially the faith remained traditional. Then the Reformation came in with a bang in the short reign of Edward VI (with the two Prayer Books of 1549 and 1552, backed by the advice of foreign Protestant refugees), only to be totally reversed under Mary who tried with considerable outward success to step back to the time before 1529. But that the Marian Counter-Reformation lacked inward strength was well proven by the possessing classes' refusal to give back the monastic lands and by the dismal failure of virtually all attempts to bring the monks themselves back.

The Elizabethan Settlement with its Acts of Supremacy and Uniformity in 1559 restored Henrician politics and Edwardian religion, and from that date the only question came to be whether the Church would stop at that point or undergo further

---

[6] Cf. J. J. Scarisbrick, *The Reformation and the English People* (1984); C. A. Haigh, *The English Reformation Revised* (1987).

reform by accepting first Zwinglian and then Calvinist Protestantism. Doctrine, in fact, adopted largely Calvinist principles, especially the fairly devastating notion of double
predestination – God's decision before the beginning of time to
save or damn hand-picked human souls who could do nothing
to affect that decree – but the Church remained unique in that it
preserved the organization of bishops and courts it had
inherited from pre-Reformation times. This outward structure
prevented a full surrender to Geneva. An anti-episcopalian
movement called the Presbyterian platform briefly made a lot of
noise, but by the end of the 1580s the queen and her bishops
had suppressed it. Differences remained, but they were differences within one ecclesiological system, and the only effective
dissent came not from Church puritans or the minuscule
separatist sects but from the surviving and reviving remnant of
Roman Catholics who faced ever-increasing severities of the
law. Even here effective persecution really concentrated on the
battle against seminary priests and Jesuit missionaries who
infiltrated the realm in support of their religion and of an
increasingly hated papacy. Indeed, the existence of Catholics
potentially supporting the hostile power of Rome (which had
declared Elizabeth no queen in 1570) provided an element of
unity for an English nation by now somewhat divided over
religious issues, in a manner that might have threatened the self-
conscious and national unity otherwise so well cultivated by the
Tudors.

How Protestant were the English by the later sixteenth
century? The evidence commonly used to measure this comes
virtually all from the pens and minds of deeply involved parties,
mostly divines sufficiently fanatic to know the truths of the faith
and to lament the failure of the generality – even the generality
of clerics – to believe and practise them. Their writings have
created an image of an insufficiently godly people, an image
from which it may be inferred that the people were insufficiently
Reformed and remained attached to their traditional religion.
The fact that some parishes failed to remove rood-lofts (site and
symbol of pre-Reformation ceremonial) seems to support this,
though the Edwardian Reformation also witnessed a good deal
of spontaneous image-breaking which worried authorities both
clerical and lay. Just what all this amounts to remains highly

debatable. There is no dispute over certain facts. By the 1580s
England was regarded abroad and at home as the foremost
Protestant power. The official religion of the late-Elizabethan
Church was Calvinist in doctrine and traditional in structure. A
body of ardent reformers, those we used to call puritans until it
became clear that the term was too precise for the muddles of
reality, laboured to improve the faith and behaviour of a nation
that did not meet their ideal; they received much support from
bishops anxious to set up a better-qualified ministry; and they
kept the printing presses active.

However, by the side of these official and reformist lines
other convictions – quite apart from surviving popery –
continued to exist. A tradition of believers in man's free will,
rejecting Calvinist predestination, descended from Lollardy and
humanism; it displayed sectarian strength in the Marian
persecution, and it re-emerged in some of the Protestant sects
which separated from the single Church of England towards the
end of the century. Within the Church itself, no single faith ever
prevailed unchallenged. The independent Church which Cranmer and Cromwell had projected in the reign of Henry VIII
professed to believe in a middle way between the extremes of
Catholicism and Genevan Protestantism, a stance which called
for a measure of latitude and tolerance adverse to the elevation
of any trend towards a sole authority. By the 1590s, anti-
Calvinist ideas made their appearance, especially at Cambridge
where Calvinist purity was also proclaimed, especially by
William Perkins. The variety of beliefs included such things as
the Covenant theology of some Protestant divines which
allowed something to the free will of men in seeking God's
grace and salvation; alternatively, a distinctly un-Calvinist
doctrine, derived at some remove from Cranmer, emerged for
instance in the work of Lancelot Andrewes, favourite preacher
and highly esteemed bishop in the reign of James I. These
deviations from Geneva are often called Arminianism, a term
derived from a Dutch theologian, but this fairly meaningless
classification obscures the real source of their inspiration, which
was English. James himself hoped to work towards an
ecumenical reunion, but he could not even end the quarrels
within his own Church, and throughout his reign both
Calvinism and anti-Calvinist belief shared Church and nation,

with neither side ever gaining victory or sole power. Typically enough, the Thirty-Nine Articles of 1563, while supposedly defining the faith, left room for a good variety of interpretations.[7]

What was the laity, in all its ranks, to do in such a mêlée of beliefs, all confidently advertised as the sole truth of God and Christ? Some, of course, espoused the cause preached by the radicals, who commanded strong support in Privy Council and Parliament. Some found the moderate, the middle-of-the-road, line attractive not only because Elizabeth preferred it but also because it favoured peace and tolerance; men as diverse as Lord Burghley and John Foxe, one a statesman and the other the influential recorder of the fortunes of the faithful, tended that way. But a large number, especially below the governing sort and blessed with obscurity, offended their eager pastors by refusing to follow the godly line, and their numbers were still considerable in the reign of James I, when even those who question the quick success of the Reformation accept that England was Protestant.[8] These less than passionate Christians were not, and even in the earlier days of the Reform had not been, true adherents to the old faith; they were moderate men and women who liked to think that God would be kind to them if they behaved well, attended Church (before adjourning to the ale house), and did their duty in the commonwealth and the family. In short, they were people governed by good sense. The greater part of the nation remained Christian in a vague way, undoctrinaire and somewhat indifferent to exhortations that flowed from the pulpits, set in their ways, accepting the forms of worship laid down by the law, but unwilling to become instruments of an intolerant persecution. They thought that Zeal-of-the-Land Busy was a rather dubious joke. Unquestionably the number of the truly godly increased with time and under the pressure of the preachers, and their increasing strength created one of the problems that were to face Charles I. But the godly never converted the main part of the English people especially in the villages of the shires; that part knew

[7] Cf. Sheila Lambert, 'Richard Montague, Arminianism and Censorship', *PP* 124 (1989), 36–68, as against the absolutes of N. Tyacke's *Anti-Calvinists: The Rise of English Arminianism* (1987).

[8] P. Collinson, *The Religion of Protestants* (1982), ch. 5.

that so long as they hated Rome, obeyed the king, and trusted in God they were treading the right path.

Episodes of Unrest

It was, in a way, just as well that the English nation contained fanatics but did not consist of them, for as a people they remained quite hard to govern and given to riot and revolt. The years between 1509 and 1640 witnessed quite a number of such manifestations of unrest – enough to remind one of the state of England in the fifteenth century and to make the rebellions of the seventeenth less surprising than some would seem to think them.[9] True, after Henry VII had beaten off some bogus pretenders to a Yorkist claim to the throne there were only two occasions on which the risings expressly attacked the reigning monarch: the attempt to pervert the succession by putting Lady Jane Grey in place of Mary Tudor, and the rebellion against the latter led by Thomas Wyatt, son of the poet and champion of the English identity against a Spanish marriage for Mary. Both adversaries collapsed ignominiously. Some well-known riots expressed a momentary and local fury, as did the London apprentices' attack on foreigners on Evil May Day 1517 or the failed peasants' conspiracy at Walsingham in Norfolk in 1537. The growing divisions in religion played their part in the major rebellions in the north in 1536 and 1569, and they helped to fuel the troubles of 1549, which sprang mainly from resentment at inflation and the deteriorating conditions of the commons. That year witnessed rumblings and explosions in many parts of the country, but real trouble arose in two very different regions: in Cornwall agrarian unrest drew strength from dislike of the Reformation, whereas in East Anglia the rebellious commons favoured the new faith.

The two great rebellions of the century, which occurred in the north, claimed to be in defence of the old order, claims which have led to a degree of glorification for those supposed

[9] P. H. Williams, *The Tudor Regime* (1979), ch. 10, gives a useful run-down. Dr Williams takes the unrest more seriously than I feel able to do. For a discussion of the problems (with not all of which I find myself in agreement) see A. J. Fletcher and J. Stevenson (eds), *Order and Disorder in Early Modern England* (1985), especially the introductory essay by the editors.

champions of the faith. Certainly, the Lincolnshire rising and the Pilgrimage of Grace, which between them convulsed seven counties north of the Trent in October–December 1536, drew some strength from resistance to Cromwell's administration and its policy of nation-wide interference and religious change, more especially the extinction of the monasteries, though in fact this had barely begun when the troubles broke out. Certainly, Robert Aske of Yorkshire managed to dress the Pilgrimage in a double halo of spiritual protest and the cause of the common man. Similarly, the rebellious earls of Northumberland and Westmorland in 1569 could profess that what moved them was the danger to the true faith. However, in both cases the reality was a good deal less exalted than the pretence; the real grievances concerned fear of financial exactions and threats of political decline for the ruling order of those northern shires. The risings really expressed the feelings of dissatisfied members of the aristocracy who mobilized their tenantry – rather successfully in 1536 and without much success in 1569. On both occasions also political infighting at the centre stirred up local discontent, in a manner quite reminiscent of the political warfare of the previous century.[10] Yet in some way the most significant aspect of those major crises was the easy victory of the central government – of a monarchy using its general power and the image of kingship. Henry VIII's agents used mostly the ordinary law to exact his revenge, whereas those of Elizabeth employed the law martial; this meant more victims in the less serious rising. But both upheavals seem to have had remarkably little permanent after-effect. That good Catholic Pilgrimage was followed by ready submission to the new order in the Church, and the rising of the earls has justly been called a last fling. The supposed dividing-line of the Trent was shown up as no longer existent in the united realm of England. Individuals and some families lost out, but the general order of Yorkshire or Durham looked very much like that of Wiltshire or Staffordshire: gentry government under the direction of king and Council.

The more general unrest provoked by economic distress posed more insidious problems, even when it fell short of the

[10] G. R. Elton, 'Politics and the Pilgrimage of Grace', *Studies in Tudor and Stuart Politics and Government*, 3 (1983), 183–215.

rather extraordinary protest strike in the south and east which Wolsey's financial demands provoked in 1525. At the heart of the problem stood the steady, almost inexorable, increase in population. The most conservative calculation takes the number of people trying to live in England from just under three million in 1540 to 5.1 million a century later,[11] and this despite the continued attacks of killing diseases like bubonic plague. The only reduction occurred just before the accession of Elizabeth when a combination of sweating sickness and influenza lowered the total by some 5 per cent. These figures do not constitute a population explosion, and even by the end of the period it seems that the level attained before the Black Death had not yet been reached again. But in a mainly agrarian country, accustomed for two centuries to low numbers of people especially below the gentry, this increase raised serious problems touching food supply and employment. The first was more or less solved by intensified production,[12] but that itself aggravated the second because the better use of land involved the enclosing of both arable and waste, reducing the number of people employed and taken care of by the traditional mode of farming. Enclosure was further encouraged by the boom in the export of cloth which favoured the conversion of arable into sheep pasture especially in the Midlands, and into cattle-rearing especially in East Anglia. This was what became known as depopulating enclosure, as parcels were combined into larger units and occupiers driven from the land. Enclosure and the more intensive use of agricultural resources really represented progress in potential wealth, but they did so at the expense of part of the people, quite a few of whom were driven off the land to join the wandering bands of vagrants. Enclosure therefore became the conventional complaint, for instance in Thomas More's *Utopia* (1516), and the first determined act against it was passed in 1489, an indication that this form of rural progress was well under way before the accession of the Tudors and long before the redistribution of land in the wake of the Dissolution of the Monasteries supposedly put the commons at the mercy of capitalist landowners. Wolsey tried hard to make a

[11] E. A. Wrigley and R. S. Schofield, *The Population History of England 1541–1871* (1981), 208.
[12] Cf. E. I. Kerridge, *The Agricultural Revolution* (1967).

reality of the legislation, and some rather reckless enclosing and emparking was punished with fines in the Court of Chancery, but the grievance continued to be used as an explanation of all distress long after it had become plain that in the main enclosing benefited efficient agriculture.

Two real crises did occur in the sixteenth century, followed by another in the 1620s. The first (in the 1540s and 1550s) sprang from a massive inflation of prices, provoked by a repeated debasement of the coinage. This was designed to finance the warlike policies of Henry VIII and the Protector Somerset against France and Scotland, as well as the enormous building programme in which Henry VIII was engaged in the second half of his reign. The new income from monastic lands, whether sold or retained, in the end did not suffice, and the unrestrained greed of the governing order with neither an effective king nor a Thomas Cromwell to control things produced the economic collapse of the mid-century. It was aggravated by a temporary but serious slump in the export of cloth, the market having been saturated before. The rebellions of 1549 arose from this complex of difficulties and distress, but things improved quite rapidly as the governments of Mary and Elizabeth, heeding the advice of Sir Thomas Smith's *Discourse of the Common Weal* (1549), restored the coinage and with it confidence. While prices remained pretty much at the newly inflated levels, wages and incomes at the bottom of the scale did not increase in proportion, a fact which has led some to speak of the pauperization of the English commons. As a building boom right through the nation indicates, this is an exaggeration; rather an exceptional prosperity resulting from a population collapse had come to an end.[13] Comparative prosperity prevailed until the next agrarian crisis struck in the 1590s, in the wake of several years of harvest failure and the pressures of the wars with Spain and in Ireland. Once again, unrest stirred in many parts of the country (though without leading to real rebellion), and the ruling sort decided to blame the holders of monopoly rights in trade and manufacture, granted by the

[13] For the extreme opinion concerning poverty see A. L. Beier, *The Problem of the Poor in Tudor and Stuart England* (1983); this depends a good deal on arithmetical conjectures. A more judicious account is found in D. M. Palliser, *The Age of Elizabeth* (1983), 118–29.

crown, which supposedly once more drove up prices. The next serious trouble in the 1620s was mainly the product of the trade-cycle's adverse effect on the export trade, aggravated by the spread of war on the Continent and mistaken schemes for finishing cloth in England at a time when the continental customer still really wanted only the unfinished white cloth. The English economy remained shaky into the era of the civil wars, but the sort of trouble that had stirred the north in 1536 or taken Wyatt's armed Kentishmen into London in 1554 did not recur.

While the bulk of the English nation continued to live on the land – in villages and manors – the towns too underwent various developments. In the main, they continued to suffer from the decline that had begun with the Black Death. Those towns that had decayed in the Later Middle Ages continued to do so; church building ceased and many edifices disappeared with the closing down of the friaries; the woollen industry drifted into the countryside to be organized by entrepreneurs who employed the domestic labours of weavers and fullers. However, there were two major exceptions to this rather sorry tale. Bristol was to take a great leap forward as overseas exploration and enterprise found this port in the west of the country most convenient; and London embarked on its extraordinary rise to metropolitan status in the European world.[14] Despite several devastating outbreaks of plague the city grew in population from about 50,000 in 1500 to about 200,000 by the middle of the seventeenth century – twice the overall increase in the national numbers. Much of this resulted from immigration rather than a rising birth rate: London became the major centre of attraction for rich and poor alike. Territorially it expanded in all directions, both north of the river and south; much of Middlesex became part of London, though not of the city, which remained confined to the old square mile within the walls. The city of Westminster became in effect part of London, and the road from one to the other

[14] A sunny view of these developments is presented by S. Rappaport, *Worlds within Worlds: Structures of Life in Sixteenth-Century London* (1989), and in F. F. Foster, *The Politics of Stability: a Portrait of the Rulers in Elizabethan London* (1979). For a markedly more sombre assessment see A. L. Beier and R. Findley, *London 1500–1700: The Making of the Metropolis* (1986), and Ian Archer, *The Pursuit of Stability: Social Relations in Elizabethan London* (1991).

blossomed forth in dense building around the Savoy, Essex House, Somerset House and their like; in another direction the growth of Holborn and Ely House near Smithfield added to the transformation of hitherto rural scenes. The attraction of London stemmed from several facts. As the seat of the royal government and courts of law, it offered employment and advantage to an increasing number of people involved in the running of the country. As the residence of the leading trading company, the Merchant Adventurers who effectively monopolized the export of cloth, it brought in large financial resources and offered a banking service independent of foreign operators; as the location for the new and vital industry of printing (the Stationers' Company was incorporated in 1557) it attracted the publishing concerns of the promoters of news-sheets and of policy in Church and state. All this expansion produced administrative problems. London was hard to keep even moderately clean, and the swelling ranks of apprentices and young migrants often threatened public order, though remarkably little real trouble occurred. In effect, the govern-ment of the city, continuing as before, became absorbed into the national structure: king and Council needed to keep on good terms with mayor and aldermen and with the livery companies which offered the freedom of London to anyone who would pay for the right to practise various trades. A good many foreign visitors testified to what had happened when in effect they talked of London as though it equalled England.

But though the capital's peace was rarely broken in any serious way – the second earl of Essex too late learned his lesson in 1601 when he failed to rouse support in the city for his rebellion – the English remained a nation hard to control and potentially given to unrest, though compared with their ancestors – not to mention Irishmen and Scotsmen – they really appeared to value law and order. Of course, there were always plenty of individuals willing to play with the law and upset good order: the possibility of major trouble remained alive and now and again it kicked.

Royal Control

Tudor government recognized these circumambient difficulties and from the first attempted to equip itself with the means of control, but in these respects too the real breakthrough came with the administration of Thomas Cromwell. Cromwell did not invent measures out of nothing, and was indeed well aware of the earlier efforts, but he instilled so novel a force and concentrated purpose into government that something like a major transformation took place in the relations between rulers and ruled. In the main, he tackled the problems along two lines: he provided a more efficient central government for the centralized state, and he used that government for the promotion of reforms in the common weal.

Cromwell's reform of the king's government was designed to provide a more secure financial foundation and to exploit this for the better control of the realm at large. Hitherto the restoration of the royal finances had concentrated on the enlargement of the crown lands and had administered the resources so obtained from within the king's private entourage under the treasurer of the Chamber and the chief gentleman of the Privy Chamber, made responsible for the cost of government under the personal supervision of the king. This worked well enough when the king was a conscientious accountant and reader of balance sheets, which Henry VII had been. Henry VIII did not copy his father in this, and the control of the national finances clearly could not remain in a state so dependent on the whims of the monarch. Cromwell first of all expanded the national fisc, mainly by expropriating the Church; the crown acquired the clerical payments (first fruits and tenths) hitherto levied by the papacy, as well as the massive landed estates of the monasteries dissolved in 1536–40. In addition Cromwell also cautiously initiated a policy of calling for parliamentary taxation for the purposes of ordinary peacetime government, so that the traditional principle – subsidies were raised for defence only – gradually disappeared. The administration of these moneys was removed from the Chamber and handed over to what were in effect financial ministries by the side of the Exchequer, and the Privy Chamber was reorganized into the regular pay office for the king's personal expenses, though it could also be used for holding reserves if there were any. This worked well under Cromwell's control; more especially, the Court of Augmentations, which administered the new land revenue, proved so extraordinarily efficient that even the heavy selling of lands in the 1540s (mainly to finance Henry's passion for war) did not reduce the annual income, while adding the profits from sales. Two things undermined this happy state of affairs. The disappearance of Cromwell greatly reduced general control, and the death of Henry VIII in 1547 opened the road to the private exploitation of the ex-monastic lands. By 1553, the royal finances, in any case threatened by inflation, were once again in a far from satisfactory state, but the revival of Cromwellian principles especially in the hands of William Cecil restored a fair measure of efficiency. The new machinery was incorporated in the Exchequer (1554–7) and until war broke out in 1587 Elizabethan government rested on a sound enough financial basis.

What, however, had altered was the main source of money. Income from lands at last ceased to be the chief pillar of national government, its place being taken by revenue from customs (augmented under Mary) and taxation: Elizabeth called for taxes in twelve of her thirteen parliamentary sessions. And although efficiency declined markedly as tax assessments increasingly failed to reflect the true wealth of the taxed population, government remained solvent in England while much richer monarchies in Spain and France repeatedly defaulted on their obligations. The Stuarts inherited a monarchy which was reasonably well funded, though penury (as it turned out) lurked round the corner. Further reforms of both sources of income and the instruments for controlling them were called for, until an enormous expansion of international trade made England rich towards the end of the seventeenth century. Though the measures taken often looked new and very different from what had gone before, they always rested on the principle that the running of the kingdom depended on the existence of a national administrative structure independent of the king's court and Household, the focus of politics. Such a structure had, of course, been in a sort of existence since the days of Henry II, but it had always depended on co-operation with, indeed on subservience to, the personal system of Household government until the reforms of the 1530s.

Cromwell also worked out the methods which would provide the continuous and preferably efficient management of national affairs at home and abroad when he invented the secretary of state, the characteristic functionary in English administration down to the present day, though under Cromwell and down to the eighteenth century the offices that backed the secretaries mixed aspects of the minister's private service with aspects of a national system. And Cromwell either witnessed or organized – the latter, in my view – the really decisive instrument for the successful government of England: the small, tightly organized Privy Council, with universal competence, regular meetings, and power to act independently of the monarch though always regarding itself as his agent. Tudor government, under the Privy Council with the secretaries of state as executive officers, proved to be generally effective, though much, of course, depended on the quality and application of the people involved. Lord Burghley was very good indeed, and slightly lesser lights like Sir Francis Walsingham did well enough, even if none of them quite matched Thomas Cromwell who combined genuine creativity with a willingness to attend conscientiously to routine.

This, then, was one half of the instrument shaped by Cromwell for the running and improvement of the commonwealth.

In addition, from the 1530s onwards, legislation intended to improve as well as control the conditions of the people of England proliferated. As Cromwell's office archive and correspondence testify, he rested his planning on close co-operation with intellectuals and visionaries – another aspect of his activities that set a standard followed by his successors. Legislation attended to the major problems threatening good order, such as poverty and vagrancy; it encouraged the towns to arrest decay by raising rates to rebuild; it assisted in the management of all sorts of trades and manufactures – fisheries, ale houses, cloth, leather goods, foodstuffs, and so forth. Here again the beginnings made under Cromwell found imitation and development throughout the century, and some of the laws designed for the commonweal became administrative codes of wide purpose and effect. This was true of the poor law system, codified (on the basis of earlier acts as well as experiments in various towns) in the two statutes of 1597 and 1601. These set up machinery for looking after those unable to work and for finding work, with punishment as an alternative, for those fit enough to labour – a system unique to England and satisfactory until the great changes in population and employment of the later eighteenth century. Another code worth mentioning was the so-called Statute of Artificers (1563) which fixed wages and organized training in industrial enterprises. By no means all of the flood of paternalistic legislation which inundated England after 1536 for something like a century sprang from the initiatives of the Council, which often adopted measures promoted by sectional or private interests, but it all added up to a general intervention and supervision under its eye.

The degree of control, of course, is another matter: how effective was all this legislation? Here everything depended on the ability of the Council to assert itself in the country at large, and this ability varied a good deal. The most hierarchic of the laws – those sumptuary regulations that tried to reserve expensive clothing to the richer sort – never worked at all well, whereas the poor law seems to have been really pretty effective, even in times of severe distress. The trouble was that while Elizabethan government could rely on a body of professional administrators at the centre, it had virtually nothing of the sort in the shires and hardly anything in the towns. True, there were still the sheriffs, still an essential cog in the machinery of law and justice; the county lord lieutenancies, regularized in the course of Elizabeth's reign as a means of organizing the shire militia, added a further element of central supervision. But the main agencies of administration in the localities were not bureaucratic, and even though supposedly organized by commissioning from the crown could not be readily coerced into obedience. Government in the shires depended on the justices of the peace, and in the towns on mayors and councils locally elected but usually also tied into the peace commissions. Here Council and secretaries could act only by constant vigilance, sending instructions and exhortations (another of Cromwell's innovations) and backing statute with royal proclamations that kept the justices' duties ever in their minds. From the 1570s,

printed Books of Orders were quite regularly sent out to all
local authorities, explaining their duties and possible courses of
action.[15] It may appear to have been a ramshackle system, but it
worked well, for two reasons. Local gentlemen and noblemen
wanted to run ordrly shires because they preferred order and also
wished to please a queen's government from which they could
hope to draw benefits of wealth and office. Secondly, the rulers of
the realm shared background and opinion with the rulers of the
localities, took trouble to keep in touch with opinion there, and
did not overplay their hands. The system worked because people
wanted it to work and because by and large care was taken not to
overstrain it at potential breaking points.

Parliament and Law

The essence, therefore, of Tudor England, despite the unques-
tioned difficulties, lay in national awareness and allegiance:
social and economic strains could be controlled, and even
differences over religion diminished the common loyalties only
for a small number of extreme Protestants and entrenched
Catholics. In the first place, of course, these loyalties centred
upon the monarch, indeed on the dynasty. Mary's easy triumph
over the duke of Northumberland's attempt in 1558 to pass the
crown to Lady Jane Grey conclusively demonstrated that
descent in the family overcame all other considerations.[16] The
house of Tudor posed a number of problems, more especially
because it proved exceptionally incompetent at providing an
heir in every generation. Henry VII left three adult offspring of
whom the only male succeeded with no difficulty at all; indeed,
the outburst of joyous welcome that greeted his accession
proved the triumph of one dynasty after all the battles for the
throne that had been going on since 1378. But though Henry
ran to six wives he had only one son, Edward VI, who died too

[15] P. Slack, 'Books of Orders: The Making of English Social Policy, 1577–1631',
TRHS (1980), 1–22.
[16] Mary's rights had been threatened when she was bastardized by act of Parliament
in 1536, but Henry VIII's will of 1543 (itself authorized by statute) restored her
legitimate claims.

young to marry, which brought the two daughters in succession
to the throne. Mary also failed to produce a child, which left the
crown to a sister who was certain to put an end to the attempt
to restore the English Church to Rome and the papacy, and
Elizabeth solved the succession problem by refusing to admit its
existence and living an unexpectedly long life. The fact is that
accident disguised the reality: the Tudors lived uncertain lives,
and the throne looked again and again to be open to a
competition which only good fortune averted. Astonishingly
enough, England was ruled by queens for a whole half-century,
but all levels of the nation accepted this uncommon experience
with devotion rather than unease. Elizabeth, of course, managed to create a kind of love affair with her people, partly by
playing the role of Gloriana and partly by emotionally
identifying with her formidable (indeed, appalling) father. From
1509 till 1603, the occupants of the throne overcame all sorts of
threats to their hold on their nation, mainly because that nation
wanted the peace and reassurance that continuity in power
brought, but in great part only because no monarchs had ever
acted the part better than Henry VIII and his daughter.

It is no wonder that for a long time historians spoke of a
Tudor despotism, an interpretation to which both the monarchs' massive personalities and the frequent savageries of the
regime seemed to give approval. Of course, the weakness of the
rule of both Edward VI, when noble faction dominated, and of
Mary I, increasingly dependent on her Spanish husband, might
be thought to have arrested despotic tendencies, in the manner
in which the reigns of weak kings following on strong ones had
saved England hitherto from true despotism. But in the
sixteenth century the possibility of a despotism was deliberately
and with care demolished, and this too was the work of Thomas
Cromwell. In his younger days, Henry VIII inclined to claims
which looked distinctly tyrannical, nor did Wolsey, determin-
edly committed to his king, moderate such tendencies. But the
king who in the beginning of his reign talked freely of his
personal imperial position – a line of argument that scared his
more reflective subjects[17] – in 1542 declared that he never stood
higher in his kingship than when associated with the Lords and

[17] T. F. Mayer, 'Tournai and Tyranny: Imperial Kingship and Critical Humanism',
HJ 34 (1991), 257–77.

Commons in his Parliament in 'one body politic'.[18] Whether Henry realized the essential change in his constitutional position which this politically inspired definition implied may well be doubted but does not matter. The imperial crown of the monarch had come to be absorbed in that 'empire' of England of which Cromwell spoke when, in the act prohibiting appeals to Rome (1533), he framed his definition of the unitary realm under one king but a king bound by law.

When Cromwell resolved to demonstrate that the problems of king and realm could be solved in only one way, namely by the law-making power of a Parliament which ceased to be the king's high court by incorporating the king within itself, he in effect established the fact of legislative sovereignty (omni-competent in all matters touching the realm of England, spiritual as well as secular) and placed it in the hands of a mixed sovereign. The Parliament that emerged from the 1530s was manifestly descended from its medieval ancestor but had undergone a major transformation, a fact confirmed by the frequency of meetings down to 1572 and the mass of statutes, public and private, enacted in those forty years. Thereafter, frequency of meetings slackened off slightly but there was never the remotest prospect that parliamentary occasions might revert to the limited activity that characterized the years 1470–1523.[19] The meetings of the assembly in its two Houses, at long last reckoned equal in the constitutional scheme, and with the king as a third member marked the coming together of the nation in a joint enterprise intended to result in agreed action. Of course, such meetings could and did provide opportunities for disagreement, even on occasion genuine opposition to the policy of the crown; we remember the speeches in support of Catherine of Aragon, the difficulties that Mary encountered, the puritan attempts, especially in 1571 and 1586, to procure drastic changes in the Church, or the agitation against mon-opolies in 1597 and 1601. But behind this occasional noise, which as a rule was easily silenced by management, stood a common purpose organized from the top but criticized and

---

[18] G. R. Elton, *The Tudor Constitution* (2nd edn, 1982), 277.

[19] The very frequent Parliaments of the thirteenth and fourteenth centuries were not bearers of legislative sovereignty but instruments of purely royal government being rendered pointless by factional and regional opposition.

amended by voices in both Houses, and many an apparent dispute really signified disagreements in the Privy Council transferred to the convenient stage of Parliament. The reality of Parliament after Cromwell's work on it lay in the fact of a tripartite sovereign body, levying taxes by consent and making laws by joint action. There was no rise of the House of Commons as a body nor any entrenchment of opposition in this institution, but there was also an end to the purely personal and potentially despotic monarchy.

Parliament was one of the medieval heirlooms that Cromwell pointed to a new role – the role of the nation in action. The other instrument, equally important in defining the nature of the English kingdom, was the common law. The establishment of legislative sovereignty terminated the independence of the Church's own courts – limited before this but still essentially subject to rule from Rome – and by stages extended the dominance of the common law also over the Church: a Church which in effect became a department of state. Canonistic principles and practices survived quite strongly into the seventeenth century, but whenever statute and common law addressed themselves to ecclesiastical affairs they obtained obedience.[20] The common law, as we have seen, had a long history behind it before the Tudor century, so much that at one time it was treated as though unchanged from time immemorial. In fact, in order effectively to serve the refashioned national community it had to undergo quite considerable changes.

The medieval common law had grown into a complex system depending on the services of a trained profession of advocates from whose ranks the judges were chosen. Practically, it bore the characteristics of a mystery and showed signs of obsolescence, so much so that at one time historians used to think it 'ossified' by the end of the fifteenth century and capable of renewal only through drastic action from outside. It was not

[20] R. H. Helmholz, *Roman Canon Law in Reformation England* (1990), demonstrates the continued importance of the old law of the Church; R. Houlbrooke, *Church Courts and the People during the English Reformation, 1520–1570* (1979), and M. Ingram, *Church Courts, Sex and Marriage in England, 1570–1640* (1987), document the continued role of the Church courts in the ordinary lives of the nation. Both Houlbrooke and Ingram also underline the increasing part played by parliamentary statute in the law administered in the Church courts.

well equipped in matters criminal; though felonies, carrying the
death penalty, were readily punished, the larger area of
malfeasances – misdemeanours including such things as riot or
slander – remained poorly ordered and usually escaped the law.
In civil matters the law was weak on contract; arrangements
between parties to any transaction left too much open to
unresolved and unresolvable disputes. The law was strongest on
tenure of land and on debt: disputes in these fields commanded
a wide range of remedies, most of them hampered by
technicalities. The law had in effect got sadly out of date thanks
to the switch of rights by seisin (tried in Common Pleas) to
landholding by enfeoffment to uses, unknown to the common
law and therefore picked up by the equitable jurisdiction of
Chancery, whose decisions always left room for further
litigation by reserving parties' rights at law if they could put any
forward.[21] By 1500, Common Pleas in fact dealt predominantly
with cases of debt.[22] There was enough dissatisfaction around
to provoke demands for real change; the revival of classical
learning led to repeated calls for the substitution of the
supposedly scientific Roman civil law for the allegedly barbaric
law of England, with its absurdities, delays and peculiar
language (corrupt French). Some of the needs of the community
were met by setting up new courts drawn out of the king's
Council with its power to receive and pronounce upon
petitions. Both Star Chamber and Requests received a degree of
organization under Wolsey's guidance, though they remained
ill-defined institutionally and had not settled to a proper and
specific area of practice. In this they copied the Court of
Chancery of Wolsey's day. All were tribunals offering equitable
answers to problems which the law either did not recognize or
took far too long, and proceeded too expensively, to deal
with,[23] and all therefore looked like threatening the dominance
of the common law.

However, that law reacted triumphantly, mainly from within itself. In the half-century down to about 1540 a silent,

[21] Above, p. 102.

[22] D. J. Guth, 'The Age of Debt, the Reformation and English Law', in *Tudor Rule
and Revolution*, ed. D. J. Guth and J. W. McKenna (1982), 69–86.

[23] J. A. Guy, *The Cardinal's Court* (1977); F. Metzger, 'The Last Phase of the
Medieval Chancery', in *Law-Making and Law-Makers in British History*, ed.
A. Harding (1980), 79–89.

behind-the-scenes, revolution renovated the old law, mainly by using the flexible action on the case to provide new remedies for new needs. The old writs continued in existence but fell into disuse. Thus disputes over rights in land sought the help of the action of ejectment, markedly more simple than the old possessory assizes; though in theory it only established whether an unlawful dispossession had taken place it came to be used to settle claims arising from inheritance or purchase. Fundamental changes took place in the conduct of trials, in the principles of pleading, in the provision of remedies sought by litigants, and in the refinement of the criminal law – all in the first place worked out in discussions, in and out of court, between the bar and the bench, though in due course many of these developments were settled, *ex post facto*, by act of Parliament.[24] This self-renewal enabled the theorists of the law to maintain their belief in an unchanging and immemorial law, whereas in truth the law of 1550 differed in everything that concerned the litigant quite drastically from the law of 1450. But though this veritable revolution was generated from within the profession it needed the administration of Thomas Cromwell to secure it. Cromwell was himself a common lawyer, as were his assistants in government: the system that he constructed rested firmly on the old law now refreshed, and his decade terminated the possibility that the civil law might be 'received' to replace the native law, as it did in France and Germany. Of course, Cromwell did not do this single-handedly. When Thomas More succeeded Thomas Wolsey as chancellor (1529) he began the rule of common lawyers in what had been a virtual preserve of ecclesiastics, and the incorporation of the equity of Chancery in the law – as an aid rather than an enemy to the common law – was set out in Christopher St German's treatise on *The Doctor and Student* (final version published in 1531).

By the latter part of the century, Chancery was a normal and settled court of the realm, applying precedent-settled principles of equity adjusted to the primacy of the law: old ideas of rivalry and enmity must be forgotten.[25] And it was in Cromwell's decade that the conciliar courts of Star Chamber and Requests

[24] See J. H. Baker's splendid introduction in vol. 2 of his edition of *The Reports of Sir John Spelman* (Selden Society, 1978).
[25] W. J. Jones, *The Elizabethan Court of Chancery* (1967).

settled as regular institutions largely staffed by common lawyers, and it was Cromwell's use of statute that promoted the codification of changes. The Statute of Uses (1536) and that of Wills (1540) restored the law's rule over rights of landowner-ship on principles which discarded out-of-date relics of feudal tenure. In the education of lawyers the 1530s also marked a new start: where hitherto lectures at the Inns had concentrated on the statutes of the thirteenth and fourteenth centuries, explaining the case law that had grown up around them, from about 1540 onwards teaching addressed itself increasingly to the acts of Henry VIII's time. The new style of *Reports* replaced the Year Books with a more systematic analysis and concen-trated on matters of law rather than pleading; the *Reports* received the assistance of a proliferation of legal texts also promoted by profit-seeking publishers. The decline in business that had befallen the old central courts began to reverse itself; in the course of the century there developed the remarkable fictions which enabled King's Bench and Exchequer to cut in on the cases between party and party that had been the preserve of Common Pleas, though the vast increase in the amount of litigation meant that all the courts were doing well.[26] It was Cromwell's administration that turned the occasional com-missions of oyer and terminer, appointed to try crimes in this or that locality, into the regular criminal jurisdiction of the assizes in the counties.[27] Thus the age of Thomas Cromwell stands out as the central phase of drastic changes that preserved the supremacy of the common law in a much changed and changing society, rendering it capable of facing further changes and remaining the law of England.

A Unitary State

Thus the 1530s, exploiting both past achievements and recent thinking on the needs of the commonwealth, initiated the

[26] King's Bench used the procedure of Bill of Middlesex, which by a fiction enabled litigants to raise all issues from all over the realm in this court; Exchequer used *quominus* (the pretence that a debt owed to him disabled a creditor to pay his dues to the Crown) to establish jurisdiction over private debts.

[27] Amanda Bevan, 'The Henrician Assizes and the Enforcement of the Reformation', in *The Political Context of Law*, ed. R. Eales and D. Sullivan (1987), 61–76.

reconstruction of society which continued actively down to the end of the century and spasmodically thereafter. A 'modern' England emerged from its medieval predecessor without visible breaks except – a major exception – for the incorporation of the separate English Church within the unitary English state. But this state did not exist in solitary splendour. It had contained within itself parts that had never been properly integrated; it faced the problem of communities within the islands that were not even parts of the kingdom of England; and it operated within an international complex of powers that in this era spread from Europe across the globe. In all these respects, the Tudor century witnessed developments which again started in the age of Thomas Cromwell, though what happened thereafter differed in various ways.

One thing that Cromwell positively achieved was the absorption of all England into his concept of a unitary state. An act of Parliament of 1536 terminated the relative independence of palatinates and franchisal territories, an end the more readily achieved because most of the lands in question (especially the duchy of Lancaster and many marcher lordships) had become vested in the crown before the accession of Henry VIII. Of the palatinates only Durham remained nominally separate, but episcopal rights were the rights of agents of the supreme head of the Church: no political problem there. Cromwell overhauled the regional councils of the North and the Welsh Marches, set up under Wolsey as means to control the borderlands; he made them into regional courts of justice firmly under the hand of the central government. Above all, utilizing the desires of the dominant elements in Wales, Cromwell put through the so-called Union of that country with England in statutes which terminated the separate existence of principality and lordships, reorganized the whole region in shires, and in effect put Wales under English law administered by English-style judges and justices of the peace. Though the transformation was not complete until 1543, the policy was proclaimed in 1536.[28] Of course, things did not happen in the schematic fashion this way of putting it might suggest: there were hiccups and difficulties. But it remains true that Cromwell planned the incorporation of

[28] P. R. Roberts, 'The "Act of Union" in Welsh History', *Trans. of the Hon. Soc. of Cymmrodorion* (1972–3).

Wales which had eluded the medieval kings and that after 1540 the region posed no further problems. At last, Offa's Dyke was filled in and the English found that the Welsh had joined the nation. In the latter part of the century, a new Welsh traditionalism put its head above the parapet here and there; Welsh translations appeared of the Bible and the Prayer Book; memories of bards and of King Arthur drew some nourishment from the somewhat unreal Welsh ancestry of the reigning house. However, the Union described the reality. Cromwell also undertook to incorporate Calais with England (like Wales and Cheshire, Calais was made to send members to the Parliament) but that endeavour, of course, came to an end in 1558 when England lost that last remnant of ancient conquests in France.

Ireland posed a very different problem.[29] It had never been integrated in any way with the English crown, which yet claimed suzerainty there; though Norman and English settlers had come to occupy considerable parts of the island organized in earldoms, larger parts remained in the hands of the Gaelic population adhering to its laws, customs and ruling families. The crown's administration at Dublin did exercise control over variable sectors, but efforts to impose a more direct government had been abandoned in favour of letting the Anglo-Irish nobility exercise rule, a device which saved the king of England from having to sink money in the maintenance of order in Ireland. By the reign of Henry VIII this meant that Ireland was managed for the king by the Fitzgeralds of Kildare, regularly at odds and sometimes at war with other families, more especially the Butlers of Ormond; the Gaelic regions, especially Connaught and Ulster, remained outside the system. And even though government was at times effective enough to keep the peace, the general condition of Ireland remained at best confused and confusing – just the sort of state of affairs that was likely to irritate Cromwell into action. There remain differences of opinion,[30] but everybody agrees that the Kildare rebellion of 1534, suppressed with difficulty and at considerable cost, called

---

[29] The best survey of Irish history in this period is S. E. Ellis, *Tudor Ireland* (1985).

[30] B. I. Bradshaw, 'Cromwellian Reform and the Origins of the Kildare Rebellion', *TRHS* (1977), 69–93, argues for intervention from 1532 leading to the conflict; S. E. Ellis, 'Thomas Cromwell and Ireland, 1532–1540', *HJ* 23 (1980), 497–519, argues for a less purposeful and more haphazard policy but agrees that after 1536 Cromwell tried to solve the Irish problem.

forth a serious attempt to settle Ireland. Here Cromwell faced an unusual degree of personal concern and interference from his king, much exercised over the new need to finance Irish government from England and much influenced by Cromwell's enemies on the Council, but he did succeed in establishing English rule controlled from London over the Pale and the great lordships. Like any English statesman over the centuries, Cromwell too could chalk up Ireland as the main failure in his policy.

After his fall, different methods were tried. The conversion of the lordship vested in Henry into a royal crown (1541) amounted to a consummation of Cromwell's policy, but the efforts of the new deputy, Sir Anthony St Leger, to turn the Gaelic lords into English noblemen were not given enough time. After Henry VIII's death the Irish problem altered completely: instead of assimilating that second kingdom to the style and principles of its senior partner, private interests intervened in a spirit of rapacious colonialism. By stages, new English arrivals (landed owners) replaced the old Anglo-Irish nobility, and several large-scale settlements (plantations) organized from England introduced powerful new forces especially into Munster, Leix, Offaly, and ultimately also Ulster. The results were predictable: revolt and endemic war which in the end (1601) led to a new and complete English conquest. Though there seems to be no truth in the notion that Irish resistance to England was inspired by a refusal to accept the Reformation of the Church – the Irish dissolved their monasteries more eagerly than did the English and appealed on occasion to the papacy for strictly political reasons – the fact of conquest worked against any progress for the new religion among the indigenous population. Behind the long war there stood not only Irish rebellion but also international complications: of this more in a moment. Even so, in the reign of James I an English-controlled administration settled Ireland along English and common-law lines, and on the face of it that kingdom appeared to have ceased to pose a threat to the king and people of England. The face of it misled.

Scotland also posed a problem, but again a very different one. Here the clumsy attempts of the Plantagenets to establish an overlordship had produced only an independent, coherent and relentlessly hostile kingdom – a permanent threat to the insular security of England aggravated by the 'ould alliance' with England's enemy France. The Scottish threat was responsible for the semi-military organization of the northern border counties, expensive in itself and a refuge for both overmighty subjects and escaping criminals. Henry VII had tried to solve the problem in the time-honoured way by marrying his elder daughter Margaret to the king of Scots, but this – though it produced an answer nearly a century later – had no beneficial effect in the short run. Indeed, James IV tried to assist his old allies when Henry went to war with France in 1513; his death at Flodden terminated the family connection and restored the traditional state of entrenched hostility. In the 1523 Parliament Cromwell advocated settling the north before any further adventures in France, but in his years of power he found the Scottish problem quiescent and contented himself with advancing the incorporation of northern England into the unitary state. The revival of glory-seeking war in 1542 at once renewed the pincer threat from France and Scotland; once again, the king of Scots died after defeat at Solway Moss, leaving an infant successor, Mary; and Henry tried to impose English suzerainty by forcing a treaty on the Scots which they at once repudiated. War in Scotland was part of Henry's bequest, and it helped to destroy Edward Seymour, the Protector Somerset, who advanced the major economic crisis of the 1550s by his efforts to take a victorious army into and out of Scotland. Instead, the French moved in very positively, placing a permanent garrison at Edinburgh and carrying off the Scottish queen to marry the dauphin of France. On Elizabeth's accession, the Scottish problem looked as insoluble as it had been for some 250 years.

What altered things totally were two events, one predictable but the other not. The predictable event was the Reformation guided by John Knox: by 1560, Scotland was in essence a Protestant, indeed a Calvinist, country, though the full working out of this new character took its time. The unpredictable event was the idiotic behaviour of Mary Queen of Scots which helped to destroy political peace in Scotland, promoted the ascendancy of a party inclined to an English alliance, and after 1568 left Mary a refugee and prisoner in England. None of this had happened without the active participation of the government of Queen Elizabeth, especially William Cecil who in 1560 settled

Plate 21 *Elizabeth I in procession, c.1582. (The Mansell Collection, London.)*

relations in the treaty of Leith – once again following up on ideas first put out by Cromwell. Although Scotland itself remained in a state of occasional turbulence, with noble faction strife and plots against King James VI, the era of wars with England looked to be over. It took the Stuart kings of both kingdoms briefly to revive it.

From the point of view of the English, the end of the northern threat and the existence of a neighbouring enemy who cultivated an alliance with more distant enemies came not a moment too soon. By the 1580s England faced a novel threat looming across the Channel. The war with Spain sprang from a double root – religion and colonial expansion. In the European confrontation of Valois and Habsburg – France on the one side, Spain and at times the Empire on the other – England had normally sided with the latter. Wolsey's brief flirtation with France in 1527 had been abandoned when it was seen to threaten English trade with Antwerp, and the preference for Habsburg had survived even the Emperor Charles V's efforts to protect the cause of his aunt, Catherine of Aragon. The Spanish connection reached its peak with Mary's marriage to the Archduke Philip, but this was also the end of it. Elizabeth managed to keep Philip from hostile action until Spain's military intervention in the 1560s destroyed the prosperity of Antwerp and so released England from urgent economic ties just as co-operation with the Habsburg power became ideologically problematical. With France convulsed by religious disputes, unable to hold the balance, and with Spain backing the papal bull against Elizabeth (1570) and offering support to English Catholic exiles, the new confrontation took shape in the 1570s. Philip II made himself the champion of the Counter-Reformation just as England emerged as the chief Protestant power in Europe: the conflict, which turned into war after 1587, rested in the first place on the religious split, and thereafter English patriotism (chauvinism?) fed on the conviction that Spain and its hated Inquisition stood behind constant plots to subvert the Reformation in England. One decisive result of this constellation was the support, intermittent and rarely effective, which England offered to the revolt of the Netherlands against Spanish rule.

Spanish enmity certainly derived in great part from this

Plate 22 *Engraving of the Armada, with English admirals depicted around border, from* The Tapestry Hangings of the House of Lords: representing the several Engagements between the English and Spanish Fleets, *by John Pine, Engraver, London.* *(The Bodleian Library, Oxford.)*

conflict over the faith, but it drew strength also from resentment at English raids into the American empire upon which Spanish wealth, and therefore military capacity, depended. The reign of Elizabeth witnessed the serious beginnings of English expansion overseas, though for the time being it was confined to maritime voyaging westward and trading by organized companies to the east (Russia 1555, the Levant 1581). It will not do to overrate these early stages of empire-building: much talk there was, some determined propaganda, the exploits of John Hawkins, Francis Drake and Martin Frobisher, but the eyes of queen and Council remained firmly fixed on Europe, the more so because attempts to settle colonies in the New World all came to rapid grief. The administration of the Royal Navy, revived tentatively by Henry VIII, underwent some reform, but England was still some way off being a true maritime power, and when involved in naval engagements always had to rely on the help of private vessels roped in for the occasion. The execution of Mary Queen of Scots, found guilty of participation in Catholic plots, started the declared war with Spain in 1587; in the following year, good fortune rather than exceptional skill removed the threat of the Spanish Armada; and for the rest of Elizabeth's reign England and Spain remained at war, a war fought in the Netherlands, later in France, and now and again by means of futile but annoying raids on the Spanish mainland. The reconquest of Ireland belongs to this war; though immediately provoked by rebellion in Munster and especially by the earl of Tyrone in Ulster, it became inescapable when Spain tried to use Ireland as a base for attacking England. The English by stages produced quite a competent army, and Mountjoy's victory in Ireland was over Spaniards as much as over Irishmen, but the chief effect of it all was the enormous cost. Because of the wars, the Tudor regime handed on massive debts to its successor, a good excuse for subsequent maladministration.

The Stuart Succession

When the old queen at last died in 1603, events moved with an unexpected smoothness that testified to the essential soundness of both the nation and its system of government. The accession of James VI of Scotland and I of England had been carefully prepared by English politicians maintaining regular contacts north of the border, and the new king entered his new kingdom in a kind of dun-coloured triumph. His easy takeover once again demonstrated the primacy of the principle of legitimacy: James was the true heir by birth, being descended from Henry VIII's elder sister, but he represented a renewal of the foreign presence on the throne and moreover had been excluded by the settlement of the succession which Henry had set out in 1543, as empowered by Parliament. In actual fact, there was no one else who would have done. In many ways, as the English discovered before later ages listened too exclusively to malicious gossip, James proved himself to be a good king: sensible, adaptable, peace-loving, and more especially eager to put an end to religious disputes that were undermining national unity and public order. He opened his reign with a conference of rival divines at Hampton Court where in effect he showed himself determined to continue the ecclesiastical policy of the middle way that he inherited from Elizabeth, though he was more positively Protestant than she had ever been. He also inherited her Privy Council, which he enlarged unduly with men of his own choice as well as the leading statesman of the queen's dying years, Robert Cecil, created earl of Salisbury in 1605. At the time, it appeared as though the nation had passed with ease through what might have been a traumatic shock with the end of the Tudors.

One aspect of public life grew if anything even more resplendent than before. The latter part of Elizabeth's reign and the thirty years that followed it became the greatest age of English poetry – the age of Shakespeare, with Marlowe before him and Ben Jonson after him. By some mysterious alchemy the language had reached its peak – flexible, melodious, equipped with an enormous vocabulary that was still adding to itself, and usable beyond the power of earlier or later ages in every conceivable way. Why, even the sermons of the day were often beautiful in language. One proper use was demonstrated with the appearance in 1611 of the Authorized Version of the Bible which rounded off the efforts begun by William Tyndale and Thomas Cromwell in a triumph of language and learning. The visual arts, as always in fog-bound England, trailed a little

Plate 23 William Shakespeare, from his Comedies, Histories and Tragedies, 1623. *(The Mansell Collection, London.)*

behind the achievement in poetry, prose and indeed music, but James's reign saw the rise of Inigo Jones, and the age of Charles I allowed England to catch up in this form of culture as well. After all, Charles was just about the leading collector of paintings then searching the ateliers of Europe, and in 1629 Peter Paul Rubens deserted his native Flanders for England, a knighthood and the ceiling of the Banqueting House built by Jones. The troubles of the mid-century seem to have cast a pall over these decades during which the English at last caught up with the civilization of the European Renaissance and indeed outranked all competitors in their poetry and prose. One strand in this notable outburst must be sought in the weighty growth of sheer learning. It was in the sixteenth century that Cambridge reached equal European status with Oxford, and that both became the breeding-ground of scholarship and public virtue. That characteristic English phenomenon, the politician trained in the classics at school and university, made his appearance in the reign of Elizabeth, incidentally (if somewhat improbably) fulfilling yet another part of Thomas Cromwell's programme. William Cecil, Lord Burghley, may be best remembered as a secretary of state and lord treasurer, but he also collected works of learning, promoted scholars and was a very active chancellor of Cambridge. Henry Howard, brother to the fourth duke of Norfolk, lectured at Cambridge in the 1570s before transferring to James's court and gaining the earldom of Northampton in 1604. The clerical profession no longer monopolized the world of learning.

Above all else, James's accession brought peace – peace with Spain (1604) after close on two decades of war at sea and danger on land, the settling of reconquered Ireland[31] and the end of any possible armed disputes around the Tweed. And it brought at least the possibility that new merit would now reap the reward which the old queen, unable to come to terms with a new generation, had withheld from it. The omens looked good. Yet the omens turned out to be wrong: the reign of James I quickly fell into a querulous discontent which allowed that of Elizabeth to gain a spurious glory that it never quite lost. From the first, the train of Scotsmen that followed James into England

[31] H. S.Pawlisch, *Sir John Davies and the Conquest of Ireland: A Study in Legal Imperialism* (1985).

called forth chauvinistic resentment and loud charges that they took too much of the king's favour and resources. James's very wise hope for a proper union of his two kingdoms foundered on these gut reactions in the parliamentary session of 1606. His hopes for religious peace were shattered by puritan refusal to accept the conformity put forward at Hampton Court (1604), and Archbishop Bancroft's anti-puritan policy led in the first six years of the reign to the most considerable deprivation of ministers of the Church yet seen. At the same time, hopes of peace with the Catholic resistance fell victim to the absurd Gunpowder Plot of 1605 which fully revived popular dread of popery.[32]

James made life more difficult for himself by an addiction to not very satisfactory favourites, almost as though he hoped to go one better than Edward II. His attachment to George Villiers, a handsome young man made duke of Buckingham, was the worst misjudgement of the reign, the more so because Buckingham also extended his sway over the next holder of the crown. James also displayed an eagerness to pontificate on all sorts of topics that in itself is rather engaging. What he said, repeatedly, about the nature of kingship, the true faith, the behaviour of some people in Parliament, and so forth was nearly always sensible, often witty and sometimes wise; nothing is further from the truth than the old view that he did not understand the kingdom he had inherited. But a voluble king naturally provoked contradiction and argument. The first Parliament of the reign deteriorated into a series of mismanaged clashes, while the next two (1614 and 1620–1) failed to pass any bills at all, to the disgust of the many interests seeking private acts. The government rallied in the last Parliament of the reign (1624), but by then an atmosphere of supposedly principled discontent had grown up which was beginning to undermine the essential unity of the nation. James was accessible, shrewd and often engaging, but Elizabeth's remote and formidable air had been wiser. Nor did his councillors come up to the standard of a Thomas Cromwell or Lord Burghley. Corruption unquestionably increased; trading in

[32] M. Nicholls, *Investigating Gunpowder Plot* (1991), should at last put an end to romantic speculation about an anti-Catholic conspiracy hatched by the English government.

offices grew alarmingly, and the creation of a supposed honour, the baronetcy, for the purpose of bringing in money by sales lowered the general tone further. Even the united front of the common law behind the king's government broke in the quarrel between Lord Chancellor Ellesmere and Chief Justice Coke; Coke managed to give his disappointment in his hunt for advancement the veneer of a principled defence of the rule of law. James did not even know how to utilize the ready service that Francis Bacon was willing to give. The renown of the law did decline in this age.

Behind the often petty ups and downs of affairs two more serious problems threatened the security of the nation under a working royal government. For one thing, James faced financial problems of devastating size. He inherited a fairly massive debt but also compensatory claims on Dutch and French debtors to the English crown, and he did not face serious inflation until the late teens of the century. The end of the war terminated the worst drain on his resources. Yet the difficulties mounted all the time. James turned out to be quite exceptionally spendthrift and never managed to raise an income to feed his joy at having come to a rich country after years of penury in a poor one. His family of wife and three children naturally vastly increased the costs of the Royal Household, but it mattered more that James showed no understanding of the need to save and loved distributing largesse. Yet once peace was made, it proved much harder to extract parliamentary subsidies whose yield slumped further as taxpayers kept cheating the collectors. Salisbury tried various measures, such as an increase in customs duties (impositions) and a more stringent exploitation of royal rights of wardship, all justified in themselves but productive of disaffection and loud protests; wardship was one of the grievances that led to the abortive Form of Apology (1604), a loud-mouthed statement of constitutional principle by a parliamentary faction, and the storm over impositions did much to frustrate Salisbury's imaginative attempt in 1610 to convert the burdensome and outdated feudal income of the crown into negotiated levies on the counties (Great Contract). After 1617, Lionel Cranfield, applying a merchant's experience, managed to reduce wasteful spending at court, to the active resentment of courtiers insufficiently restrained by an ageing king, but he too could not

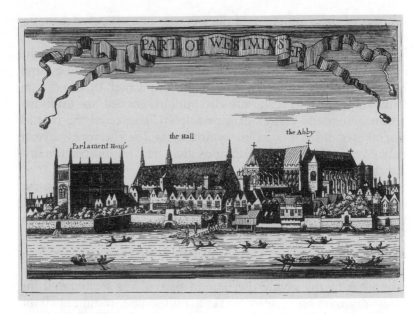

Plate 24 An engraving of Westminster, depicting Parliament House, the Hall and the Abbey. (The Bodleian Library, Oxford.)

increase the income of the crown and in 1622 fell victim to the people whose interests he had offended.

Right at the end of the reign, in the 1624 Parliament, a proper grant of taxation was obtained, but the reasons behind this unexpected co-operation involved the second inescapable burden upon James's rule. He was one king in Europe, seeking the company of others: he had a foreign policy to fashion at a time when Europe was slipping towards a war which in part stemmed from religious divisions and was to last for thirty years. England would in any case have been concerned, but her involvement turned out to be more immediate. In 1613, James's daughter Elizabeth, only seventeen years old, had married Frederick, count palatine, and when in 1620 Frederick lost the crown of Bohemia, taking refuge with his wife at the Hague, the problems of monarchic and religious policies began to menace James's relations with his people. He remained determined against war, but with Habsburgs ascendant again in Europe and Spanish troops occupying the Rhenish Palatinate, active men in England's ruling order increasingly called for intervention in support of the Protestant cause. James's court became a centre for diplomatic intrigue, as the king joined forces with the Spanish ambassador, the count of Gondomar, in an effort to preserve the peace and possibly marry the heir to the throne to a Spanish princess; Gondomar's influence helped to secure the failure of the 1621 Parliament which shouted for military action. However, that call suited Buckingham's ambitions, and when Charles I succeeded to the throne in 1625 a more forward policy became probable. But all that came of it was the duke's disastrous expedition to the Ile de Ré, supposedly in support of French Protestants. England stood exposed as forgettable in the European scene. The financial crisis moved Charles to demand a forced loan in 1627, and though most of the people affected paid up, the exaction left much bad blood in the localities and a small group of determined protesters gained unexpected sympathy when they were arrested. Buckingham wrecked the general support which the Tudor crown had received from magnates and gentry when he built himself an exclusive party of supporters and in the process alienated far more men of influence than he attracted. Out of this unholy mess came the Parliament of 1628–9, forcing the king to accept an essentially pointless protest called the Petition of Right and in the end, by organizing a piece of needless chicanery, enabling him to dismiss that tiresome body and embark on a positive and personal policy in reorganizing the kingdom.

The eleven years without a Parliament (1629–40) proved in many ways to be quite successful in England, where the king's position could still command a traditional loyalty, eroded but not dead. However, those years worked against the principles upon which the unitary state had been fashioned a century before. Cromwell had seen in Parliament both a means to make laws and an instrument for keeping king and people in informed contact, and in competent hands this had worked well enough. Charles, however, saw in Parliament only a platform for tiresome opponents and decided he did not need it; in consequence, when the crunch came, he proved to be quite inadequately informed on the state of opinion in his realm. Thomas Cromwell had believed in a *via media* in the ecclesiastical policy of the crown with outward conformity covering often passionate differences of belief, and this concept had served the age of Elizabeth well. Charles, on the other hand, threw his weight behind one of the factions in the Church which, under the guidance of bishops like Robert Neile and William Laud, tried to remove hard-core Calvinism and attract the people to 'the beauty of holiness'. Instead it created a powerful separatism hostile to the crown, which for the first time gave to puritanism the aspect of an organized movement. And Charles, still unable to raise the necessary money, failed to do anything about the danger to Protestantism in Europe, a danger resurgent after the death of the Swedish King Gustavus Adolphus (1632), who for a time took over the leadership of the cause that many Englishmen demanded should be exercised by them. Laud came to be seen, quite falsely, as a potential papist, and Charles was not without reason suspected of dealing with Rome. The active propaganda of a few — especially William Prynne, a furious pamphleteer who lost his ears and suffered internal exile in 1634–7 — created a set of convictions concerning the fatal policy of this king that remained dominant in English opinion for centuries. Yet much was done or attempted in those eleven years that deserves respect, not least Laud's efforts to produce a united and peaceful Church. What undid the good work was a remarkable degree of carelessness concerning the impression created. Good intentions and just measures wilted before the king's plain stupidity.

However, it was not the condition of England or the growth of a popular, perhaps puritan, opposition in that country, that in the end resulted in the civil wars, the execution of Laud (1645) and Charles I (1649), the abolition of monarchy, the setting up of a republic taken over by the military dictatorship of a second Cromwell. The turmoil of those twenty years has naturally attracted enormous attention from historians, lawyers, romancers and so forth, but the explanatory theories put forward all fall down in the face of facts. It has not even proved possible to agree on what turned men into supporters of either the king or the Parliament, and the general theories err in seeking profound causes for what in truth was a series of accidents tied together by a quite small number of personalities on either side. There have in effect been three theories, and while all of them contain little bits of truth, they are in the main somewhat tendentious fictions. The earliest, promoted by the

Plate 25 Engraving of the trial of Charles I, from A Journal of the Proceedings of the High Court of Justice, *1650. (The Bodleian Library, Oxford.)*

rebellious Long Parliament itself, maintained that the House of Commons rose to the defence of constitutional liberty against a tyrannical king: this became the Whig theory much cherished by lawyers. The second, convinced that higher principles still must have been at issue, spoke of the puritan revolution against a draconian regime of papist or quasi-papist conspirators. And the third, which has commanded most support ever since Marx

Plate 26 A naïve contemporary engraving of the execution of Charles I. (The Mansell Collection, London.)

and Engels first adumbrated it, held it to be a successful bourgeois revolution against the dominance of feudal land-owners supporting a feudal king. This last scheme has been further burdened with an attempted but unsuccessful demo-cratic revolution on behalf of the oppressed classes below the bourgeoisie.[33]

Now it is quite true that in the course of the twenty years' upheaval a lot was said about the fundamental law and a royal abuse of power, but in actual fact the Long Parliament and the Protectorate of Oliver Cromwell regularly ignored the details of law and liberty in the battle for victory. The new excise tax, which helped to finance the Parliament's war, proved to be a heavier and more enduring burden than anything Tudor or Stuart kings had tried. It is also true that the wars broke the hold of the episcopal Church on English Christians, enabling various sects – ranging from tyrannical Presbyterians to

[33] C. Hill, *The World Turned Upside Down* (1972).

chiliastic Quakers – to claim the right to worship their God in their own fashion, but the main part of the people (of all ranks) adhered essentially to the religion of the Church of England, though without bishops. The revolutionary regimes favoured the interfering and demanding claims of puritanism, but it all stayed on the surface and England did not turn puritan. The Marxist interpretation is the least convincing of the lot, if only because England had no body of people that could be called a bourgeois class, but also because the victors and the defeated of the civil wars believed in the same facts of economic life: the landowning classes were no more 'feudal' than the merchants of the towns. Much of the seemingly pervasive revolutionary air arose not from political action or military victory but from an enormous outpouring of the printed word. Levellers wrote volumes about rights and freedoms and put forward outline constitutions, but in the end were easily kept under control; Gerald Winstanley preached the cause of the common man and led his little band of Diggers, but no one paid much heed; Grub Street invented the extreme sect of the Ranters to titillate prurient opinion.[34] It is a mistake to judge that age by reviewing its pamphlet literature, especially when no attempt is made to count readers.

That there must be something wrong with all those great revolutionary theories is strongly suggested by even a brief look at the two ends of the story – at the effects the revolutionary era left behind and the circumstances that led to the convulsion in the first place.[35] When, in 1660, it was all over, it was not only the king that came back: in all its political and social aspects the old order returned virtually unchanged. Even the sensible modernization of the law which the Protectorate had undertaken disappeared again, and if the Star Chamber was not revived that was less a recognition that it had supported tyranny than an admission of the fact that even by the 1630s it had become somewhat superfluous. The England that emerged from the revolutionary era was still the England that Thomas Cromwell had launched on its career: a unitary realm under the

---

[34] J. C. Davis, *Fear, Myth and History: The Ranters and the Historians* (1986).
[35] For a useful review of changing opinions see B. Coward, 'Was there an English revolution?' in *Politics and People in Revolutionary England*, ed. C. Jones et al. (1986), 9–39.

legislative sovereignty of the king in Parliament, governed by the king in Council under the common law, and held together by the common interests of centre and localities – of the king, his ministers, and the gentry and nobility of the shires, with the communities of the towns fitted into the community of the counties. Even in the history of the two Houses of Parliament the interlude of war and revolution organized from within them produced no change in standing or function: after 1660, the Parliament was again that part of the royal government it had been down to 1640.[36] Did Oliver Cromwell vanish as though he had never been? He left behind the conquest of Jamaica, but this was simply in line with the colonial expansion that had begun in the years between 1580 and 1630 in which the true landmarks were the incorporation of the East India Company (1600), the settlement of Virginia (by 1619), and the other colonies of the American north-east. In nothing was continuity more obviously restored than in the Church which, by pushing dissent off into ineffectual sects, restored the middle-way principles of Cranmer, Parker, Andrewes and even Laud, shedding the temporary aberration of a ruthlessly predestinarian Calvinism and the effort to construct a Presbyterian government. Even the upward movement of the population, much the most powerful solvent of tradition, which for unknown reasons had slackened off in the earlier seventeenth century, resumed again after about 1670, leading the way to the immense economic expansion which had started in Elizabethan agriculture and the diversification of manufacture. The only two positively new features of the scene were the beginnings of a standing army and the searing memories of the wild times, both effective warnings in future to preserve the peace and avoid disruption.

Nor had the great storm begun as a manifestly revolutionary phase in the history of the English. If Charles I had been king of the English only, there would have been no rebellion or civil war. It all started because he was also king of Scotland and attempted to force upon that kingdom the kind of Church he governed in England. It was the Bishops' Wars and the Scottish invasion of England (1637–40) that provoked the crisis by demonstrating to Charles how tenuous was the loyal support he

[36] Sheila Lambert, 'Committees, Religion and Parliamentary Encroachment on Royal Authority in Early Stuart England', *EHR* 105 (1990), 60–95.

1653.
OLIVER CROMWELL
LORD PROTECTOR
of England Scotland
and Ireland.

QVERITVR BELLO

From a most excellent Limning, done by Samuel Cooper, in the possession of the Hon.ble Sr. Thomas Frankland Bart.

Plate 27 Engraving of Oliver Cromwell as Lord Protector of England, Scotland and Ireland, after Samuel Cooper. (The Bodleian Library, Oxford.)

still commanded and by forcing him to accept the demands of a powerful group of nobles to recall Parliament and behave like a constitutional king. The collapse of the army somehow got together against the Scots and the refusal of London to find the

Plate 28 Engraving of Cromwell's Scottish border campaigns. (The Bodleian Library, Oxford.)

money to buy them off showed up weaknesses which the king had not known to exist.[37] When the Long Parliament met in November 1640 it behaved in a strictly traditional manner – critical but with never a hint of revolutionary ambitions;[38] in the end (1642) it even enabled the king to pay the Scots to leave. That seemingly prophetic exercise, the impeachment in 1641 of Thomas Wentworth, earl of Strafford, conducted by the alleged leader of parliamentary revolution, John Pym, really forecast quite another truth. Strafford was attacked not because he symbolized Charles's tyranny but because he was hated by the third earl of Essex, enemy to the Stuart court, and Essex became in effect substitute king as figurehead of an aristocratic group determined to reduce the king to impotence. The civil war started as a somewhat belated baronial revolt disconcertingly reminiscent of what had happened in the reign of Edward II, though what ensued was very different. Hostile policies turned

[37] Cf. R. Ashton, *The City and the Court 1603–1643* (1979), for a revealing study of the king's failure in public relations.
[38] Sheila Lambert, 'The Opening of the Long Parliament', *HJ* 27 (1984), 265–87.

to war because Charles I, time and again demonstrating that his word could not be trusted, resolved to recover monarchic ascendancy. It was he who started the fighting when he raised his banner at Nottingham in 1642. Typically, he forgot that a party in a civil war which left London to the enemy could not hope to win, and London had by this time rid itself of the king's friends among its leadership.

Not that the war moved inexorably to a foregone conclusion: it was a bitter struggle and long before the end several regions tried to withdraw from it and keep the criss-crossing armies at more than arm's length. The kind of war it became had to do with the presence on both sides of veterans of the European conflicts who brought professional standards to what might have been armed rabbles; it also had to do with Charles's third kingdom, when the Irish rebellion of 1641 turned English uncertainties into relentless hostility to a king who recruited Catholics into his army. Once the wars had started and were pursued all over the kingdom they must not be written down: they killed many, destroyed much, released and confirmed all sorts of hatreds and ambitions, and in 1649, when both king and House of Lords vanished, looked like producing a true revolution. But, as I have said, in the end and despite Oliver Cromwell's energetic rule, there was no revolution. In a way, by restoring order the second Cromwell restored the world that the first Cromwell had set on its career in history. And by his conquest of Scotland and Ireland, maintained by the royal regime thereafter, he even completed the first Cromwell's work where it had been least successful.

5

The Long Eighteenth Century

Not so long ago it looked as though the history of the English and the territories they had incorporated into the kingdom could after the upheavals of the seventeenth century be summed up in agreed, indeed in soporific, terms. The implied verdict of the Civil War and the Interregnum against a dominant monarchy did have to be pronounced once more in the Glorious and Bloodless Revolution of 1688, but after that the path was clear. It led, by stages of violent party strife before 1714 to the Whig stability of the age of Walpole; it gradually removed kingship from the reality of government; it passed onwards into a growth of radical ambitions and reforms culminating in the Reform Act of 1832. That is to say, during those 150 years or so the dominant note was first the onset and finally the achievement of a liberal and democratic constitution, in its way the recognition of parliamentary victory in 1648 and supposedly the characteristic of Great Britain ever since. At the same time, society underwent a major transformation summed up in the concept of an Industrial Revolution mainly occurring in the years after 1760, a revolution which transformed a predominantly agrarian society into a factory-based economy exploiting technological change and innovation. This transformation witnessed (at last) the triumph of a middle class of industrialists and businessmen over the old ascendancy of a landed class of nobility and gentry. Indeed, the decline of that ascendancy was often seen foreshadowed in the commercial and colonial expansion that seemed to begin with the Restoration, though historians differed about the speed and totality of the bourgeois triumph. But in general it was agreed that in the eighteenth century the English emerged from their medieval condition into a state of affairs familiar to the later nineteenth century. The people by stages took hold of political power; the middle classes by stages took hold of economic power; a rural people moved into the towns and began to pose novel problems of order, employment and control. The Church and religion ceased to play the major role that had been theirs down to the failure of the puritan revolution. And it was clear that all this took its origin in the later seventeenth century and had by the early nineteenth occupied the foreground.

Of this well-established and coherent picture very little seems now to survive.[1] Instead we are presented with a nation returning almost thankfully to tradition and generally speaking sticking conservatively to its faith in the Anglican Church, a people still structured – despite changes in the economy – in the old hierarchical ways. The eighteenth century now looks again like what first impressions had always suggested it was – the great age of an aristocracy relatively small in numbers and relatively very rich in land and property. It has even been argued that so far from receiving new blood this aristocracy became as exclusive as were similar bodies on the Continent, and while this is a manifest exaggeration, the special place of the nobles rather than the rise of anything to be called bourgeois must not be denied.[2] Taken too far, these new views face the usual problem of revisionist history: in demonstrating the errors that had been adduced in teleologically explaining later events and conditions they come close to making it impossible to see how those later events and conditions could ever have come about. Here the new version will be treated as nearer the truth, but it cannot be swallowed uncritically and some balance will have to be struck.

One incontestable fact lies at the heart of the story: England

---

[1] The reconstruction of the period is mainly the work of J. C. D. Clark whose *English Society 1688–1832* (1985) lays out the plan, while his *Revolution and Rebellion: State and Society in England in the 17th and 18th Centuries* (1986) argues the case in a review of the historiographical record. I am persuaded that the traditional scheme will not do but cannot accept Dr Clark unreservedly.

[2] Lawrence and Jeanne C. F. Stone, *An Open Elite? England 1540–1880* (1984); for a friendly but fairly devastating critique see H. Perkin in *JBS* 24 (1985), 496–501. And see below, p. 204.

experienced a rapid and extraordinary increase in the size of its population. Whatever else may be true about the English in this era, the fact is that at the end of it there were far more of them. Population nearly doubled between 1681 and 1791 and nearly doubled again in the next forty years: by 1831 there were some thirteen million people living in England, at least twice as many as had faced the devastating onset of the Black Death in 1348. And this figure does not allow for the drain occasioned by the peopling of the North American colonies, an emigration not at this stage balanced by mass immigration into the country, though in the course of the century ever more people came from Scotland and Ireland to seek work and to settle. Some of the increase no doubt resulted from the decline of epidemic disease. The Great Plague of 1665 was also the last outbreak of bubonic plague, which vanished after three centuries during which it had been an ever imminent threat; smallpox was being controlled by Edward Jenner and inoculation; there appears to have been no serious attack of influenza (familiar in the sixteenth century). Nevertheless, the latest opinion points to a rising birth rate rather than a decline in the death rate as the main cause of this drastic upswing in numbers, and it ascribes that phenomenon to a noticeably lower age of marriage.[3] Since that datum depended in the main on the relative prosperity of the intending partners, it follows that the people as a whole must have been experiencing an improvement in living conditions; since the increase in numbers owed most to a rising birth rate, it follows that the people as a whole grew younger. Both consequences supported enterprise and initiative; indeed, they called for enterprise and initiative if the larger population was to make a go of living in a country whose size had not changed.

Expansion Overseas

In these 150 years the English became, not quite for the first time, an imperial nation, but this new empire extended beyond the bounds of Europe. At the heart of things, the long-standing ambition to unite the British Isles under one rule finally achieved

[3] E. A. Wrigley, 'The Growth of Population in Eighteenth-Century England: A Conundrum Resolved', *PP* 98 (1983), 121–50.

fulfilment: in 1707, the kingdoms of England and Scotland were united, and in 1801 Ireland went the same way. Instead of wearing three separate crowns and presiding over three separate realms with their own Parliaments, the monarchs were by the latter date kings of a realm now known as Great Britain and Ireland, and the Westminster Parliament included representatives from the previously separate territories. The union with Scotland had of course been presaged by the arrival of a Scottish dynasty on the English throne, but the decision finally to bring about what had been denied to James I in 1606 resulted less from imperial ambitions than from the endless difficulties emanating from a Scotland riven by the rivalry of magnates relying on their clans and aggravated by the survival of Stuart loyalties (Jacobitism) after the collapse of James II's monarchy. Ireland remained in effect on the margins of English concerns – and therefore left separate though increasingly governed indirectly from London – until rebellion promoted by France in her struggle with an England set to arrest the triumph of the French Revolution forced William Pitt to organize that second union. While peaceful coexistence became the order of the day between England and Scotland, with the old border finally disappearing, the Irish union never worked so well, in part at least because religious disputes stood in the way. The Scottish Kirk and the Church of England could co-operate; Catholic Ireland remained unreconciled behind the façade of a Protestant Englishry which ruled but did not represent that people. Moreover, Scotland benefited considerably in trade and in prospects for a thrusting nation from being able to treat England as a territory open to colonization; in Ireland the Union came too late to arrest the economic decline fostered during a century of apparent independence.[4]

The expansion of the English over the globe was highly peculiar: the age witnessed the acquisition of two empires and the loss of one of them. Settlement in North America began in the reign of James I. Originally promoted by private (but chartered) companies exploiting the search for land that moved

---

[4] Cf. D. Szechi and D. Hayton, 'John Bull's Other Kingdoms: The Government of Scotland and Ireland', in *Britain in the First Age of Party 1680–1750*, ed. C. Jones (1987), 241–80; J. C. Beckett, *The Making of Modern Ireland 1603–1923* (1966), chs 8–14.

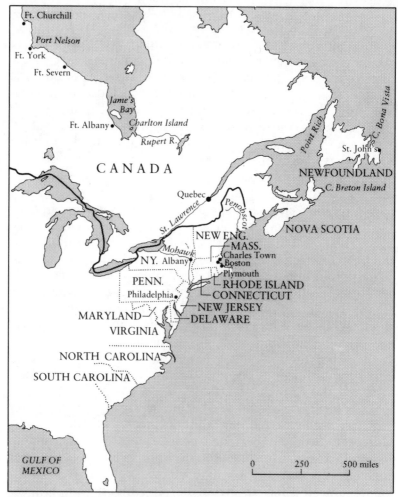

Figure 7 The North American colonies (from G. N. Clark, The Later Stuarts 1660–1714, Oxford University Press (1934), repr. 1940. Reprinted by permission of Oxford University Press.)

an increasing population, assisted by the attraction of the fishing grounds of Newfoundland, and further exploited by the emigration of religious dissidents seeking freedom to worship as they pleased and to deny such freedom to others, it had produced by the reign of Queen Anne a chain of colonies all down the eastern seaboard and was beginning to extend inland towards the Appalachian ranges. Virginia was conclusively settled by 1625 when it became a crown colony; in 1632–3, Catholic settlers occupied Maryland; in the reign of Charles II the Carolinas were opened up by more tobacco growers. Meanwhile, the enterprise of the so-called pilgrims had settled New England further north, and their intolerance hived off a new colony in Rhode Island. Victory in the Second Dutch War converted Dutch New Amsterdam into English New York (1664), and the visionary enterprise of that unusual Quaker, William Penn, founded Pennsylvania (1681–2). Victory in Europe sealed in the Treaty of Utrecht (1713) in effect registered the triumph of English expansion over that of their rival France, though further territories waited to be mopped up in the course of the Seven Years War when, in 1757, an English army under James Wolfe captured Quebec and opened the route inland up the St Lawrence River. Throughout the seventeenth century, similar contests between England and France, but really directed by both against the declining empire of Spain, established bases in the Caribbean islands. In short, the British empire in North America, organized in territorial units under governors and councils appointed by the crown, but also possessed of reasonably representative assemblies, appeared to be solidly established by the time that the Peace of Paris (1763) acknowledged English predominance. Emigration supported by the transportation of criminals and of indentured servants maintained the outflow of population, and until the reign of George III the colonies and colonists appeared to be safely English.

Of course, it did not last; by 1783, the American Revolution, or War of Independence, had removed the first colonial empire from the scene, though remnants survived in Canada and the West Indies to form a basis for renewed expansion. From the point of view of the English, however, the first American empire had produced two unexpected and lasting results. By extending the range of the language to regions potentially Spanish or French, it could be said to have acted as the first seed-bed for the universal rule that the debased Anglo-Saxon, reformed in the ages of Chaucer and Shakespeare and Samuel Johnson, was ultimately to exercise over a large part of the globe. (True, it was to undergo further debasement in the process of turning American.) And secondly, the empire had enormously extended the territory ruled by the common law of England, turning it into one of the only two major legal systems in a world increasingly dominated by Europe. The American colonies, and the United States of America after them, virtually all used the common law and in the process granted a degree of influence and standing to its practitioners which exceeded anything bestowed by the older society. The consequences of this worship of a law no longer simply common to the king's dominions have been various and by no means all satisfactory, but even after 200 years of separate developments the common ancestry is not forgotten.

One by-product of the gaining and losing of the American empire deserves special mention. Unlike the Spanish settlers in Mexico and Peru, the conquerors of the North American territories and the West Indian islands had found the indigenous population totally unwilling to settle down to labouring for their new masters. Out of this refusal grew the enormous expansion of the trade in African slaves, more especially to work the cotton and tobacco plantations of Virginia, the Carolinas, Maryland and in due course Georgia, but also the sugar plantations of the Caribbean. Now slavery was a very ancient fact of life – as old as history – and though Lord Mansfield in 1772 declared a fugitive slave free in England he did not 'abolish' slavery even in England. He rejected attempts at a theoretical justification of the institution but recognized the commercial importance of the trade in slaves – outside the British Isles.[5] But the days of this ancient, profitable and altogether horrible enterprise were in fact numbered. In 1787, a small group of humanitarian idealists, led in Parliament by William Wilberforce, began to campaign for its abolition, and twenty years later, after several failures, the necessary bill passed both Houses. It used to be said that it did so because the collapse of the sugar interests removed the obstacle of profitability, but this is not true. The West Indies interests were deliberately overruled in this remarkable victory of principle over profit.[6] But it does not seem likely that Wilberforce and his

---

[5] For the most recent comment on this famous case see James Oldham, 'New Light on Mansfield and Slavery', *JBS* 27 (1988), 45–68.

[6] R. Anstey, *The Atlantic Slave Trade and British Abolition, 1760–1810* (1985); S. Drescher, *Econocide: British Slavery in the Age of Abolition* (1977).

associates could also have overcome the opposition of slave-owners on the mainland and the traders supplying them, so that the end of the slave trade owed a good deal to the loss of the American colonies. As it was, from 1807 onwards frigates of the Royal Navy for several decades spent much time enforcing the act of abolition on the high seas, at a standing risk of international warfare.

The other tangential result of the American Revolution is less well known: it created among American scholars a seemingly permanent investment in the Whig historiography of the seventeenth-century civil wars. Across the Atlantic the legend that the whole business resulted from a struggle for the people's freedom against tyranny is still defended, for the events of 1776 and after can be called legitimate only if they can be read as effectively renewing the battles waged by Jefferson's and Washington's ancestors against the wickedness of kings.

While colonial enterprise, emerging from the staging-post of Ireland, occupied an empire in the west, another kind of empire was being constructed in the east. The East India Company, founded in 1600, was an association of merchants trading into the Indian Ocean, with a special ambition to cut in on the spice trade which, hitherto largely in the hands of the Portuguese, was in fact being taken over by the Dutch. After the Dutch secured their monopoly over the spice islands by killing off English and Japanese interlopers (Amboyna massacre, 1623), English interests switched to mainland India but for a long time remained confined to trading and trading posts. Of these, the most important was Madras, effectively constructed by the Company from 1641 onwards. Accident brought a foothold on the other side of the subcontinent when Charles II's Portuguese wife presented him with Bombay as part of her dowry (1661). Though trade continued it also ran into very considerable difficulties in bad times and when Indian princes decided to be hostile. In 1708 the Company underwent a very necessary reconstruction, and English interests in India once again began to grow, largely by agreements with such princes, until Robert Clive's victory at Plassey (1757) totally altered the scene. Now the English were in effect masters of Bengal and the mouth of the Ganges, though the governments of George III could not persuade themselves to draw the logical consequences. India,

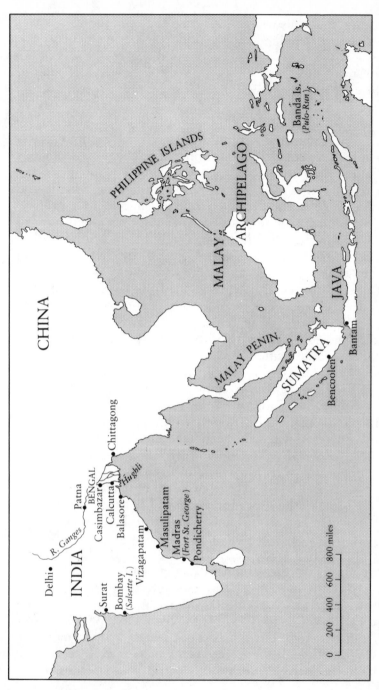

Figure 8 The East Indies (from G. N. Clark, The Later Stuarts 1660–1714, Oxford University Press (1934), repr. 1940. Reprinted by permission of Oxford University Press.)

after all, was not a colony; it possessed established political
organizations of its own, and the continued presence of French
interests prevented a total takeover by Britain. So the Regu-
lating Act of 1773 maintained the Company but equipped it
with some of the functions of colonial rule without exercising a
proper control. The English were lucky in that the first
governor-general under the act was Warren Hastings (1773–
85), a highly efficient and thoughtful promoter of imperial
policies that extended what was still in name the influence of the
Company over much of western as well as eastern India. By way
of reward he was met upon his return home by an endless
impeachment trial which concluded with a far too much
delayed acquittal. (The cause of India enabled Edmund Burke to
take up the second liberal cause of his life on which he was none
too well informed: after vainly supporting American resistance
to the king's government, he now tried in vain to convict the
late governor-general of corruption in office.) Pitt's India Act of
1784 at last recognized reality by imposing the intervention of
the royal government in the affairs of the new empire, though
the full building up of that empire belonged to the next century.
Anyway, it came conveniently to distract the attention of
expansionist ambitions from the failure of things in North
America – a failure in any case modified by the prospect of
opening up Canada.

European Wars and the Armed Forces

Expansion overseas in part sprang from conflict nearer home
and in any case usually brought such conflict in its wake. The
English had not known so much war in Europe since the distant
but no doubt glorious days of Henry V. The wars fell fairly
precisely into two very different stages. First there came the
three conflicts with the United Provinces (the Netherlands),
beginning in the days of the Rump Parliament and ending in the
collapse of Charles II's attempt to restore absolutism and
Catholicism with the assistance of Louis XIV of France.[7] These
quarrels arose out of commercial rivalry with the far more

[7] J. R. Jones, *Britain and the World 1649–1815* (1980), ch. 4, gives as full an
account of this interlude as is needed.

. t veroveren van 't Eylandt Shepey, en 't Fort Shirenaffe op den 20 Iunÿ A.° 166

Plate 29 Burning of English ships at Sheerness, 1667, in the mouth of the Medway. Contemporary Dutch print. (The Mansell Collection, London.)

successful Dutch and out of the astonished realization that these rivals had ceased to regard themselves as the clients England had thought them to be during their war of independence from Spain starting in Elizabeth's reign. Oliver Cromwell, still inclined to think in terms of a Protestant alliance, brought the first Dutch War to an inconclusive end (1652–4); various political intrigues promoted by a bunch of courtiers given to conspiracies in a manner inordinate even for their like brought about the second war (1665–7); Charles II's secret agreement with France led to the third (1672–4). The wars demonstrated rather strikingly that the Restoration had put an end to the military and political competence of England's government: while the first war witnessed English triumphs at sea and a peace concluded on English initiative, the second saw the Dutch fleet in the Medway and the third proved both militarily and financially disastrous. All that those wars achieved was to re-emphasize Dutch superiority in commerce and French dominance in the affairs of Europe; in addition they for the time being convinced the English that it was wisest to keep out of Europe's wars.

However, the choice ceased to be open to them when they rebelled against James II, ally of France, because they could rid themselves of that king only with the assistance of William of Orange, who took the throne of England (by dint of being his predecessor's son-in-law). From 1689 to 1815, England found herself repeatedly at war with France. King William's war (1689–97) led off, to be followed by the long struggle over the Spanish Succession (1701–13); a minor conflict once more over France's hold on Spain occurred in 1717–19; there followed the twenty years' peace commonly ascribed to the statesmanship of Sir Robert Walpole, a peace which ended with the war of Jenkins's Ear (against Spain once more, with France for once not involved: 1739–48), but this drifted into the war over the Austrian Succession in which Britain supported Austria against France and Prussia (1740–8); after a brief breathing-space the alliances reshaped themselves into the line-up of the Seven Years War (with Prussia against Austria and France: 1756–63); even the war started by the American rebellion drew in France (1778–83); and from 1793 to 1815 Great Britain battled almost continuously with the France of the Revolution and of the Napoleonic empire. War was really endemic in this age, but in the end Great Britain emerged as pretty much the leading world power – a world in which France, having temporarily recovered from insidious decline, retreated again into inferiority at the Congress of Vienna (1815). It is worth notice that all those wars took place while Britain was ruled by foreign kings (Orange and Hanoverian: Anne's reign forms an exception); yet the only conflict in which the primary concerns touched interests other than British was the war of King William, and even then the need to prevent the restoration of James II provided a specifically British interest. There was much talk at the time of England trailing on Hanoverian coat tails, but it was simply not true: the wars of George I and II, like the later ones, sprang from the specific concerns of the island kingdom, and in them the particular problems of the north German principality played almost no part. Even the British entry into the war against the French Revolution owed nothing to either anti-revolutionary sentiment (though that made much noise in parliamentary debate) or the threat to Habsburg and Hohenzollern; what ended Pitt's determination to stay out of the war was the French conquest of Belgium and the French threat to the Netherlands – the ancient principle of protecting the sea-flank of the kingdom.

The experience of war extended beyond statesmen and politicians – those always brought on stage in descriptions of these events – to the people at large. The eighteenth century settled one thing: England – Great Britain – needed and got a standing army and a regular navy. A people who had produced the general fyrd of Anglo-Saxon times, the organized feudal levy of the Norman kings, and the professional companies that waged the Hundred Years War against the French showed a somewhat surprising hostility to the work of a soldier. True, an act of Mary I's last Parliament (1558) organized the county militia under the control of the lords lieutenant, and throughout Elizabeth's reign attempts continued to produce troops (trained bands) capable of engaging the highly professional Spanish *tercios*, but the common attitude is better displayed in Falstaff's recruiting campaign and a general dislike of men supposedly specializing in rapine and destruction. The English may have considered themselves martial, but they were distinctly not military. The Militia Act was repealed in James I's first Parliament, and thereafter the king's right to call the nation to arms remained much disputed, especially as he could do so only if he got taxes out of Parliament. The problems of billeting soldiers awaiting transport overseas, of controlling them by the law martial, and of the money needed for war became urgent in the inefficient efforts of Charles I and Buckingham to intervene in the continental disputes of the 1620s; no wonder that all those issues loomed large in the attacks on arbitrary royal government summed up in the Petition of Right (1628). However, it was the civil wars that really crystallized the issues and transformed attitudes. While the king tried to give his county levies a backbone of Irish troops officered by Catholics, the Parliament first reverted to the one military element that had always been respected by the English – a fantasy of chivalry led by a supposedly martial aristocracy.[8] But the king enjoyed the services of professionals brought back from the Thirty Years War on the Continent (as, by the way, also did the Scottish army); the time had come for his opponents to emerge from the fourteenth century and the memories of Simon de Montfort and Thomas of Lancaster. The result was the New Model Army, a thoroughly professional body commanded by Sir Thomas Fairfax and Oliver Cromwell, the army which abolished the monarchy and supported the Protectorate. Its success in the Low Countries proved that Britain – the English – now had in their hands the real thing, long since worked out in Spain and France.

It was, of course, the very fact that the real army belonged to the enemies of the monarchy that after the Restoration made the very notion of a standing army in peacetime the subject of endless dispute.[9] Cromwell's army had destroyed monarchy and had been used, as was for ever remembered, to provide central control of local government and behaviour: the experiment of the major-generals became a standard part of the historical legend. Though Charles II retained the unchallenged command of the pretty useless county militia and managed to keep a regiment of Guards which in due course formed the nucleus of professionalization, the outcry, in Parliament and in pamphleteering, against a real army proved unending, and in the reign of James II received special strength from the fact that that king ignored all protests so as to keep a standing army largely officered by Catholics. James appeared to confirm the entrenched apprehensions that a standing army meant the promotion of tyranny and popery, but the ignominious collapse of the king's position in the face of Dutch William's invasion made no difference. Though William easily gained the support of such military forces as might have been mustered against him, he found those troops to be of little use in real war and at first relied on his Dutch to fight off Louis XIV. Still, by the end of that war (1697) he had a large standing army in England, and all the old songs of protest opened up afresh; even the man who had saved the English from Stuart despotism and a return to

[8] J. A. S. Adamson, 'The Baronial Control of the English Civil War', *TRHS* (1990), 93–120.

[9] Cf. Lois G. Schwoerer, *No Standing Armies* (1974).

Rome was compelled to cut down his army to a more or less ceremonial force.

That, however, was the end of it. With the outbreak of the War of the Spanish Succession the need for a real army and the willingness to maintain one became by stages understood, though each peace of course resulted in much temporary disbandment, and though blind conservatism found it possible throughout the century to protest against the hiring of Hessian troops, an alleged sign that Great Britain was made to dance to Hanoverian tunes (not true). In practice there now existed a standing British army: the king's army erected upon the agreement of parliamentary authority, an ultimate authority which appeared in the regular annual approval of appropriations for such purposes and in the annual Mutiny Acts which made it possible to maintain discipline.[10] This army provided careers for professional soldiers – commonly the younger and poorer offspring of the aristocracy and gentry – and thereby added a new profession to the existing ones of the Church and the law: a profession soon recognizable by the characteristics of an exclusive social club.[11] How very real this new state of affairs was appeared most manifestly in the beginnings of regimental traditions, especially the cherishing of battle honours: Blenheim and Rammillies, Dettingen and Quebec, assumed a charismatic air which affected also the civilian part of the nation. The defeat in America did not leave lasting scars because it was followed by the ultimate triumphs against Napoleon in Spain and Belgium. The army, which, assisted by sizeable detachments from other partners in the alliance, won the battle of Waterloo, had established its hold on the nation. Indeed, both nation and army soon fell victims to a common British disease in such matters: self-satisfaction and refusal to see that one cannot stay put for ever upon a little summit reached in the past. The special fears of the seventeenth century – those memories of Cromwell's troopers – soon evaporated as it became clear that neither government nor army wished to set

[10] But I should like to testify that in the Second World War it would not have been easy to find any serving soldiers who thought that their army was owned by the Parliament.
[11] A. N. Gilbert, 'Law and Honour among Eighteenth-Century British Army Officers', *HJ* 19 (1976), 75–87.

up a military dictatorship. Oddly enough, it was at the beginning and end of this century of war that military men moved into highly influential political roles: the dukes of Marlborough and Wellington remained for ever after the only men to take a reputation made on the battlefield into the civil concerns of the nation.

The century of wars also made the fortunes of the Royal Navy. Legend, of course, calls King Alfred its founder, but as a matter of fact the English relied for centuries on hand-to-mouth arrangements for the maritime defence of their island. It was only in the reign of Henry VIII, with the setting up of the Navy Board, that serious beginnings were made for the creation of a national navy, and the royal dockyards did then establish a most important foundation. But though Queen Elizabeth owned some ships and more good seamen, the Royal Navy remained somewhat rudimentary. Even in the Armada campaign and the various expeditions to the Iberian peninsula undertaken in the war that followed, her lord admiral had to rely on converting privately owned vessels temporarily to royal use. Still, when Charles I during the 1630s tried to build himself a larger navy by raising contributions (ship money) from inland counties, he gave his opponents a handy cry. In naval matters, too, the governments of the republican Interregnum opened a new phase with Robert Blake's victories over the Dutch, the leading seapower of the age. But it was not until the frequent wars of the eighteenth century that the British Navy took its modern appearance: regular ships staffed by professional captains and worked by professional seamen (admittedly at times of need reinforced by the untrained victims of the pressgang) gradually established an uncontested dominance on the seas. A remarkable series of successful admirals culminated in the legendary career of Horatio Nelson, and Trafalgar (1805) did for naval warfare what Waterloo achieved on land. When peace came, the Royal Navy did indeed rule the waves, often to the fury of other nations' ships, a state of affairs that made the attack on slave trading and slavery possible (while also infuriating other nations).

The Management of Finance

The acquisition of world power status cost money, and perhaps the most impressive achievement of the age lay in the solution of the age-old problem of financing the work of ruling the realm. Considering that the English monarchy had been in its early days exceptionally rich and able to impose regular taxation on the people, the unending difficulties encountered in the sixteenth and seventeenth centuries ought to be thought surprising, but the day of Danegeld and scutage were long gone. The French wars of the Middle Ages had enabled kings to call for taxes, but they had had to concede the right to consent to the Commons in their Parliaments, a right which fortified the conviction that taxation could be called for only on special occasions of need caused by war. Yet government required money also in peacetime. By the later fifteenth century a newish principle had acquired the spurious patina of tradition: the king, as Edward IV said he would, should live of his own, that is to say, rely on the resources normally vested in the monarchy. Thomas Cromwell had tried to wean the realm from this conviction when in 1534 he had secured a tax justified by the normal and peacetime needs of government, but two things prevented an immediate exploitation of this new start. The renewal of conflict made the regular demands of Elizabeth (who called for supply in twelve of her thirteen parliamentary sessions) appear as money for purposes of defence, and the drastic decline in the yield of taxation, as those liable to pay adjusted their tax returns, rendered parliamentary grants of secondary importance to the early Stuarts. Money remained a very touchy and difficult problem.

In this area too the needs created by the civil wars opened up a new phase. The Parliament and the Protectorate financed their business in the main from two new devices. The excise added a levy on internal trade in named products (especially beer and soon also spirits) to the established levy on trade passing in and out of the country (the customs). And the monthly assessment, allocated among the counties, replaced a tax whose yield depended on the willingness of the wealthy to pay by one whose yield was fixed beforehand. Efforts to continue the advantages embodied in these demands after the restoration of the monarchy produced three decades of furious debate, with new ideas tried and dropped, as well as old ones revived.[12] The excise survived and its principle was extended to placing a levy on the number of hearths in every house, a transparent attempt to avoid admitting the truth, namely that here was an annual standing tax upon the subject; small wonder that the hearth tax was one of the victims of the Glorious Revolution. All the old revenues of the crown came back in 1660, as did — rather meaninglessly — the talk of the king living of his own, and since a revival of the discredited Tudor subsidy proved pointless the monarchy tried to make the assessment acceptable. However, opposition to regular taxation was one thing that overcame even feelings of loyalty to a restored king, and Charles's restless extravagance did not help. The so-called stop of the Exchequer (1672), when the crown reneged on interest payments on loans, forms the only example of state bankruptcy in English history; other kingdoms had done this sort of thing quite frequently before this and did it again later. Even sizeable windfalls like the dowry that Charles's queen brought from Portugal or the subsidies transferred by Louis XIV from France in the hope that Charles would nerve himself to promote royal absolutism and toleration for Catholics only staved off near-disasters. The one thing that the reign produced was a much more competent organization for the administration of the money available in the hands of a new department, the Treasury Board, presided over by the lord treasurer or by a commission whose first lord was in effect the king's chief minister.[13] (These first lords controlled the various branches of the revenue very much in the way that Thomas Cromwell and Lord Burghley had done.) The Privy Council relinquished control, and the ancient Exchequer survived as a law court and an administrative absurdity till an act of Parliament abolished it in 1833. Knocked on the head so unceremoniously after some seven centuries of existence it had its revenge: the accumulation of wooden tallies, burned in 1834 in the fireplace of the House of Lords, set fire to the palace of Westminster of which only Henry III's Hall survived.

[12] C. D. Chandaman, *The English Public Revenue 1660–1688* (1973).
[13] Below, p. 189.

The reign of James II, a more careful manager than his brother, seemed to show that the financial resources of the government were adequate, but that appearance was created by the king's ability to raise supply to deal with major rebellions in England (Monmouth) and Scotland (Argyle). The last decade of the seventeenth century offered proof that things still called for remedy but it also at last provided some that worked. It had by then become manifest that any pretence that the finances of government were strictly personal to the king had long ceased to have any reality. The revolution of 1689 set the seal on that recognition, though the fact itself went back into the sixteenth century. James II had been deposed by an alliance of magnates, but magnates very positively relying on the Parliament, and in many ways those events certified the nationalization of the governmental system. The money to run it would therefore also have to come from the nation, and that manifestly so: there had to be an end to any pretence that it was the king's private endowment. This meant in the first place the provision of a regular levy, a tax approved annually by Parliament but in fact known to be permanent. Of course, the indirect taxation already in existence would continue: the customs and excise remained on the permanent agenda and in the course of the century were progressively organized in government departments under the supervision of the Treasury. And direct taxation would at last once again become a normal aspect of life in England. In the years 1693–7, the land tax – a rate on land values payable by owners and tenants which, poorly administered, never really reflected the actual distribution of national wealth[14] – was introduced. However, when the share of wealth not to be tapped in this way manifestly increased as time went on, the land tax began to look distinctly unfair, and in 1797 it was replaced by William Pitt's personal income tax. Needless to say, this was announced as an emergency measure demanded by the French wars, and for quite a long while ideas continued to float about that it might cease; it lapsed in 1816 but returned in 1842; if ever a thing proved to have eternal life it was this flexible and exploitable levy.

In many ways the income tax picked up the principles behind

[14] J. V. Beckett and D. K. Smith, 'The Land Tax Returns as a Source for Studying the English Economy in the Eighteenth Century', *BIHR* 54 (1981), 54–61.

the early Tudor subsidy, but from the first the administration resorted to official assessment, thus avoiding the erosion which had before the end of Elizabeth's reign rendered that earlier tax so useless. After much controversy dating from 1698 onwards, reality at last received full recognition early in George III's reign when the establishment of the Civil List funded on tax money separated the maintenance of king and court from the running of the realm.[15] Thomas Cromwell's concept had taken its time to win, but win it did in the end.

The other badly needed reform arose from the fundamental truth about English government finance: it had for a long time depended on deficit financing for the simple reason that calls upon money always rolled in before the money did. The last administration to have created a reserve was that of Lord Burghley, and the outbreak of war with Spain at once wiped that off the books. Financing government meant borrowing on the strength of the tax money expected to come in: it meant living with and servicing a standing debt. Throughout the Stuart period, English government had relied on native lenders, and the London money market had by stages organized itself for the purpose, but until 1694 arrangements remained diffuse and somewhat haphazard. In that year, the foundation of the Bank of England charged with organizing the advancing of loans and with managing the debt settled things on the kind of safe base which encouraged investment in government stocks and kept the interest rate low.[16] The days of borrowing at Antwerp at 14 per cent (Henry VIII) or fixing the lawful rate at 10 per cent (Elizabeth to Charles I) were over, and 'on the whole, eighteenth-century England was blessed with cheap money.'[17] The rate virtually never rose above 4 per cent, and in times of peace could be as low as 3 per cent. Certainly, there were crises like the speculative mania known as the South Sea Bubble, but the institution of a sinking fund into which part of the tax

[15] E. A. Reitan, 'The Civil List in Eighteenth-Century British Politics: Parliamentary Supremacy versus the Independence of the Crown', *HJ* 9 (1966), 318–37.

[16] Cf. on the whole subject of public credit: P. M. G. Dickson, *The Financial Revolution in England* (1967). As Heinrich Heine pointed out in the early nineteenth century, in England everything was royal (Army, Navy, even Society), but the debt was National.

[17] T. S. Ashton, *An Economic History of England: The Eighteenth Century* (1955), 29.

revenue was regularly paid as a guarantee for investors maintained an unaccustomed equilibrium in government financing. War remained a cause of heavy expenditure, the more so because in the wars of coalitions against revolutionary France and Napoleon, England's major contribution consisted of subsidies to allies only too likely to default on their debts. But though times could be difficult, the general air was one of hitherto unaccustomed financial security.

Agriculture, Industry and Trade

That imposing equilibrium and successful management naturally depended on the economic well-being of the realm. At one time, one would have ascribed this to a cataclysmic transformation called the Industrial Revolution, but both term and fact have lost respect.[18] It is plain that the older interpretation relied too exclusively on what happened in two sectors of the economy (textiles and metal trades); in actual fact, the industrial scene accommodated a great variety of enterprises, underwent a slow and haphazard development, and remained essentially fragmented. Above all, it is a mistake to look exclusively for new inventions and the growth of a factory system. Instead, we might heed the four conclusions arrived at in a recent study of the eighteenth century.[19] One: industrial growth took place throughout the period and there was no explosive revolution in the years 1760–1820, as used to be argued. Two: technical change also occurred throughout, and innovation did not necessarily mean mechanization. Three: by industrialization we should understand all forms of the reorganization of manufacture, much of which involved decentralization and the use of small workshops staffed by sweated labour rather than factories operated by skilled labour using power-driven machinery. Four: the impact of change varied greatly both regionally and in the supposed characteristics of the new

[18] M. Fores, 'The Myth of the British Industrial Revolution', *History* 66 (1981), 181– 98, demonstrates the error in terminology; J. Hoppit's review article, 'Understanding the Industrial Revolution', *HJ* 30 (1987), 211–24, tries to sort out what really happened.
[19] Maxime Berg, *The Age of Manufactures 1700–1820* (1985), 315–19.

order (division of labour, trained skills, source of employment). In other words, there is no single story to tell.

Nevertheless, it is possible to attempt a concise survey of that multicoloured scene. One thing is clear: the use of wealth changed markedly, and the eighteenth century saw the arrival of the professional consumer at the top of the social scale. Labour both profited and lost in the process. It profited because the manufacturers increased output by relying on more hands rather than on cutting down on people by introducing expensive labour-saving machinery, a preference which found employment for women and children (both domestically and in workshops) while it absorbed the growing number of men no longer employable on the land; but it lost because the abundance of labour badly depressed the payment offered, especially to women. The agrarian sector continued to dominate the scene in the numbers employed, but maintaining profitable farming increasingly called for an ever heavier investment in improving all practices, which led to a redistribution of landed wealth: estates grew much larger at the top and the smallholder began to disappear. Even the gentry at times faced great difficulties, and with population increasing, a bad harvest could mean hunger to a degree previously unknown. There certainly were riots (over the price of bread, but increasingly for other sorts of food reckoned to be too dear), especially in the 1760s, but the notion once put forward that they hid a class-conscious form of politicizing behind complaints about dearth has turned out misleading.[20]

The main impression must, in any case, be that English agriculture (this is true of neither Scotland nor Ireland) enormously increased its output: by mid-century, a country that had before this barely covered its own needs was regularly exporting large quantities of corn and supplying an eager domestic and foreign market with meat. In the second half of the century the bulk of farmland hitherto organized on the open-field plan was by stages enclosed; the movement contrasted with similar efforts some 200 years earlier by covering

---

[20] D. E. Williams, 'Were "Hunger" Rioters Really Hungry? Some Demographic Evidence', *PP* 71 (1976), 70–5; J. Stevenson, 'The "Moral Economy" of the English Crowd: Myth and Reality', in *Order and Disorder in Early Modern England*, ed. A. Fletcher and J. Stevenson (1985), 218–38.

most of the realm and being achieved by agreements registered
in private acts of Parliament rather than expropriation imposed
from above. The social structure of the agrarian sector settled
into the form towards which it had been moving ever since the
late fifteenth century. Men of noble and gentle status owned
virtually all the land and exploited it in the main by offering it
on longish leases to farmers who employed a paid and landless
labour force. The call was for rationalization and efficiency, and
the call was sufficiently heeded to enable England to maintain a
vastly greater population on what was on the whole a better
diet. Scotland benefited from the English demand for beef cattle,
and Ireland switched its food production to the potato.

A similar steady growth attended the manufacturing sector.
This was true of both the old-established and the new
industries. Thus the making of worsteds (in effect replacing the
older broadcloth) expanded more particularly in the West
Riding of Yorkshire, while the new textile enterprise in cotton
(concentrating on Lancashire) rose rapidly to pre-eminence in
consumption both at home and abroad. Iron and steel, utilizing
a lot of imported raw material, benefited enormously from the
growing addiction to new machinery, as did coal. The Staffordshire potteries took a lead in the world's production of china
and stoneware. England built more ships than all the rest of
Europe put together. The English abandoned the making of
linens, leaving that sector to the Irish, but they made all other
goods of consumption and imported virtually only raw materials and some luxuries. Though we must no longer speak of
an industrial revolution, and though the majority of the
population continued to live on the land, we must recognize
that by about 1820 England was an industrial power – the
leading industrial power in Europe. It owed that position in part
to technological innovations especially in spinning, smelting
and the supply of power (jennies, coke ovens and steam
engines), as a result of which the industrial worker's productive
capacity grew enormously. But it owed it also to the vast
improvement in internal communications. The new network of
canals began to be constructed in the 1750s, making the cheap
transport of goods throughout the country very much easier,
but more especially providing access to sea ports to landlocked
manufacturing towns. Between them, turnpike roads and the

invention of macadamized surfaces gave England the first satisfactory road network since the departure of the Romans had allowed paved highways to decline into far too common quagmires. The railway age was still to come, but even so communications had most strikingly improved. Through most of the century production relied on domestic labour and the putting out of work by organizing middlemen, a method which helped to preserve the regional character of both agriculture and industry. But by the third decade of the nineteenth century the factory or mill dominated the industrial scene; the balance of productive labour had shifted from the south and east to the north; more and more people crowded into often very insalubrious towns where employment was to be found; and the regions of England had at last amalgamated into a single national economy.

The line of progress did not, of course, run consistently upwards; there were quite a few bad spells of unemployment and of hunger, caused in the main by harvest failure and by war. The wars between 1793 and 1815 threatened the new economic structure several times, especially when Napoleon's Continental Blockade came near to stopping all British trade with Europe. There has been a long debate about the so-called standard of living: did industrialization and urbanization mark a crisis of subsistence for the labouring people or help to advance their condition? This debate will probably never cease because the disputants defend articles of faith quite as much as the results of research, but to the outsider coming late to this dubious feast it does look as though the optimists have the right of it – despite that sadly overrated poet, William Blake. At any rate, without the great changes in agriculture and manufacture the population explosion would have resulted in true disaster. National wealth unquestionably grew, and before very long the benefits of this growth filtered down below the entrepreneurial middle classes. Much depended on the willingness of the richer part to offer reform and assistance to the rest, in better housing, for instance, and more appropriate poor relief, though the rapid growth of population in the towns held back till the twentieth century the real achievements of the often proclaimed social improvements. At the same time, a good many workers began to form self-helping societies that forecast the development of

trade-unionism. Though poverty remained endemic the buoy-
ant economy managed to absorb the larger population without
really bad disasters; the English (increasingly pale town
dwellers rather than the rosy-cheeked farmworkers of the
nostalgic imagination) remained well off by the standards of the
rest of Europe and continued to attract immigrants, especially
the Irishmen who, before settling in Liverpool, built so many
roads and factories.

Everything, however, in the end depended on overseas trade.
It was this that both stimulated expanding enterprise and
promoted wealth at home, quite apart from forming the
foundation of the English command of the seas.[21] Though, of
course, England had for centuries exported wool and cloth to
Europe and in the sixteenth century took part in opening up the
fishing grounds of Europe, it was really after the Restoration
that the world-wide trade took off with the growth of the re-
export of colonial products (especially sugar from the West
Indies, tobacco from Virginia, and calicoes from India). The
decline of manufactures in the Mediterranean opened that
region to English trade, and by 1689 England had wrested the
primacy from the Dutch. Two particular developments assisted
thereafter. The settling of North America created not only an
important source of importable raw materials but also a major
market for English manufactures, and English activity in India
by stages monopolized that important area of exchange.
Secondly, from about 1689 onwards most of the various
trading monopolies that had been set up in the earlier centuries
were abolished step by step, so that trade across the seas became
open to any enterprising merchant. The tonnage of shipping
being built and used increased by leaps and bounds, and in its
wake there followed quite feverish activities in marine in-
surance, brokerage activities and a vast expansion of specialized
employment both in the ports and on board the ships. It appears
that the customs accounts are insufficiently reliable to provide
firm statistics, but roughly one can say that between 1700 and
1800 imports quadrupled and exports grew sixfold; most
important was the fact that the latter always ran well ahead of
the former. The value of the trade is the more difficult to

[21] R. Davis, *English Overseas Trade 1500–1700* (1973); Ashton, *Economic History*,
ch. 5.

establish because much of it was handled by highly professional smugglers who, for instance, took care of a large part of the import of such novel luxuries as brandy and tea.[22] The frequent armed clashes between the smugglers and the revenue men at sea and on land seem to have favoured the evaders of those ever-rising customs duties on imports. Small wonder that in that age the gentlemen who rode by took the place of Robin Hood as popular heroes flouting tedious authority.

At any rate, and despite intermittent difficulties caused for instance by the escape of the American colonies into independence and the wars with Napoleon, by the end of the era here under review England, with her Scottish and Irish appendages in tow, had become the world's leading trading and manufacturing nation. The resultant wealth benefited producers and middlemen as well as landowners, and it helped to maintain an ever-growing population usually above the level of mere subsistence. Food production, manufacture and world trade would not have grown the way they did if the domestic purchasing power – the demands of the consumer – had not provided driving-power. The position of leadership was in this age still maintained by that policy of protective rules, special bounties and navigation acts adverse to foreign competition which is usually summed up under the name of mercantilism, but the flag of a free and open trade was being hoisted over the land. In 1776 there appeared the treatise which laid the foundations of modern economic science, Adam Smith's *The Wealth of Nations*. Smith was a product of Glasgow University and lectured on philosophy, a background which surprisingly enough enabled him to see past the muddle of age-old and recent practice to the hard realities of the situation. Two of his prescriptions especially turned out to be essential to the economic health of the nation: the division of labour exploiting specialized skills in the setting of factories, and the freeing of trade so that the demand of the market should determine what was done. Full free trade, as indeed the fully developed factory system, did not arrive until the 1840s, but the practice of manufacturers and merchants, as well as the occasional policy

[22] G. D. Ramsay, *English Overseas Trade during the Centuries of Emergence* (1957), ch. 6.

of governments in undermining restrictive monopolies, set the scene long before that time.

Eighteenth-Century Government

It may be thought that all this paints too rosy a picture: back to the myth of the ever-improving condition of England. This is not my intention, even if a concise summary cannot avoid sounding rather optimistic. As has already been said, local unrest and rioting reflected discontent and fear of rising prices, especially of food. The English continued to be a people hard to govern and given to protesting.[23] Nor was anything done to improve the machinery of control, except for the Riot Act (1715) which enabled magistrates to call on military help in dispersing rebellious mobs.[24] The law continued to be the general refuge of the reformers, and the eighteenth century witnessed an enormous output of parliamentary statutes supposedly dealing with crime. In theory, the chances of ending on a scaffold increased throughout this period, but as in earlier periods execution was far less common than rumour has it, the number being further reduced by the newly available penalty of transportation to the colonies. The only laws consistently enforced were those protecting game against poachers, though even in this respect conventional notions concerning the wickedness of the ruling classes have turned out to be mistaken.[25] This is particularly true of the so-called Waltham Black Act (1723), passed not in order to suppress legitimate protest but because organized gangs were destroying deer and planning a Jacobite rising.[26] The popular press, especially the *Newgate Calendar*, spreading awed respect for professional criminals like Jonathan Wild (1682–1735), has left the im-

[23] There is a useful outline of the question in the Introduction to Fletcher and Stevenson, *Order and Disorder*.

[24] W. Nippel, ' "Reading the Riot Act": The Discourse of Law-Enforcement in Eighteenth Century England', *History and Anthropology* 1 (1985), 401–26.

[25] P. Munsche, *Gentlemen and Poachers: The English Game Laws 1671–1831* (1981).

[26] The argument to the contrary (E. P. Thompson, *Whigs and Hunters* [1975]) has been thoroughly disproved by E. Cruickshank and H. Erskine-Hill, 'The Waltham Black Act and Jacobitism', *JBS* 24 (1985), 358–65, and by J. Broad, 'Whigs and Deer-Stealers in Other Guises: A Return to the Origin of the Black Act', *PP* 119 (1988), 56–72.

pression that the people were exceptionally given to per-petrating unlawful acts, especially theft and murder, and they may have been; at present the very active industry studying these problems has thrown up more questions than answers.[27]

Those multiplying parliamentary statutes did not, in fact, really reform or renew the law because they kept re-enacting as supposedly new provisions already embodied in the existing law. Much of that legislation reflected the fact that regular annual Parliaments would have the time to pass just about anything that this or that interest – an individual or a group – decided should go on the book, a state of affairs which produced the new profession of parliamentary agent.[28] Until we have much more complete and exacting studies of the laws made than have so far been attempted it would be rash to base any interpretation on the partial reading of the statutes that has so far been done. One thing is clear: the common law elaborated by this repetitive and bitty statute-making badly needed reform. The sensible changes introduced by the mid-seventeenth-century republic were all rescinded at the Resto-ration, and the rather mindless devotion to a tradition last seriously tackled in the age of Thomas Cromwell returned, with the hero figure of Sir Edward Coke continuing to preside over the concept of law as immemorial and existing in its own right rather than as the product of human minds coping with changing circumstances. There were some reforms, of course, especially Lord Chancellor Hardwicke's act of 1753 which put an end to clandestine marriages. The gradual acceptance of representation by counsel for persons accused of crimes may have advanced the proper examination of allegations.[29] One reform made splendid sense: in 1731, the common law at last abandoned its immersion in the dreadful concoction known as Law French; thenceforth cases were conducted in English.

[27] Joanna Innes and J. Styles, 'The Crime Wave: Recent Writing on Crime and Criminal Justice in Eighteenth-Century England', *JBS* 25 (1986), 380–435. On the notorious problem of cheap gin see P. Clark, 'The "Mother Gin" Controversy in Early Eighteenth-Century England', *TRHS* (1988), 63–84. For an informative discussion of trial procedure see J. H. Langbein, 'Shaping the Eighteenth-Century Criminal Trial: A View from the Ryder Sources', *University of Chicago Law Review* 50 (1983), 1–136.

[28] Sheila Lambert, *Bills and Acts: Legislative Procedure in Eighteenth-Century England* (1971).

[29] J. H. Langbein, 'The Criminal Trial before the Lawyers', *University of Chicago Law Review* 45 (1978), 263–316.

However, a new age was coyly dropping hints of arrival, and the publication of William Blackstone's *Commentaries* (1765–9), though far more influential in the America of both colonial and independent days, signalled the fact in its endeavour to escape from the strictly historical treatment of the law into the more analytical methods of the law of Rome. In the end, Blackstone stayed in the camp of Coke,[30] but by the beginning of the nineteenth century the concept of law as an instrument employed for changing social needs was starting on its ultimately victorious career.

Some of the rioting and disorder, of course, went well beyond the local protests, often well justified, called forth by some social distress. Politics and passion were behind the more serious outbreaks. Very few even of these amounted to a threat to the existing order. Memories of the great rebellion governed much public behaviour both by for ever calling up spectres of collapse and by frequently warning discontent not to go too far. Monmouth's rebellion against James II might have threatened that king if the rebel could have won support throughout the realm; as things turned out, the violent reaction of a victorious regime killed some thousands of people and reinforced the hesitation of potential rebels. In 1688–9, the end of James II was astonishingly achieved without any sort of violence, and the only major troubles arose in Scotland and Ireland. In the former, the two Jacobite risings of 1715 and 1745 really demonstrated the non-existence of a serious threat to the Hanoverian regime, and the battle of Culloden (1745) ended the ability and willingness of the Highland clans to fight against the government of Great Britain. In the latter, resistance, first overcome by William III's victory of the Boyne (1690), revived under the inspiration of the French Revolution, but the efforts of Wolfe Tone's United Irishmen were easily repulsed in 1796 and 1798, the only positive result being the incorporation of Ireland in the United Kingdom (1801). Religion of a sort provoked the uproar accompanying the absurdities of the Popish Plot (1678) and the drink-sodden Gordon Riots (1780), the worst upheaval in the capital; religion of another sort saw the mobs come out in support of Dr Henry Sacheverell, Tory

---

[30] M. Lobban, 'Blackstone and the Science of Law', *HJ* 30 (1987), 211–35.

attacker of Whig politicians and Dissenting sects (1710). Radical political ambitions called forth the rioting in support of John Wilkes (1768), the clash at St Peter's Fields over Henry Hunt, called the Orator (Manchester, 1819), and the urban disturbances, worst at Bristol (1831), which finally secured the passage of parliamentary reform; but only in England could collisions which cost six, eleven and twelve lives respectively be called massacres. Of course, all such deaths are tragic, but by comparison with the hecatombs of victims in the French Revolution the troubles do rather fade away. The English could be volatile and excitable, and they valued their independence sufficiently to stand up at times for the rights of the less well off, but in the upshot the centuries of effective royal government still made themselves felt.

That government underwent some changes in those 160 years, all of them in effect continuing to develop the principles introduced by Thomas Cromwell: heeding the model even to the point of never following through in every particular. Under the guidance of three determined politician-administrators – the earls of Danby (1673–9) and Rochester (1679–86), and Sidney lord Godolphin (1684 and with interruptions 1690–1710) – the control of the nation's finances was reorganized in the small and tightly professionalized department of the Treasury. Sir Robert Walpole, the first man to attract the informal title of prime minister (1721–42), and William Pitt the Younger (1783–1801) handled the state's money efficiently without having to introduce major administrative reform, but they and other premiers (not least the Elder Pitt, earl of Chatham, who won the Seven Years War) helped along the emergence of the Cabinet from the Privy Council, though this governing board remained nominally unofficial until 1916. And in 1782–4 the offices of the two secretaries of state were reorganized, with the duties henceforth divided between home and abroad. The growth and promotion of world-wide trade produced another outgrowth of a Council committee, the intermittent Board of Trade and Plantations, first formally organized in 1696 but not permanently integrated into the structure of government until 1786. The frequent wars certainly led to improvements in both army and navy, more especially in the Ordnance Office responsible for supplying artillery and gunpowder, but nothing fundamentally new was attempted. Compared with the reigns of Henry II or Henry VIII, reform of government was piecemeal and *ad hoc*, but it could afford to be so because of what those earlier reigns had done. Most noticeably, like Thomas Cromwell himself, the statesmen of the eighteenth century did not tackle local government, which remained in the hands of ancient counties and established boroughs, with ever more independent justices of the peace and urban oligarchies exercising local control.

Politics and Ideas

In the aftermath of the great rebellion and the restoration of the monarchy, everything appeared to be set fair for peaceful politics, but this appearance did not last long. A few regicides were quickly sacrificed to lingering hatreds. The so-called Cavalier Parliament (1661–79), often prorogued but never dissolved so as to avoid the uncertainties of an election, witnessed the rule, under the king, of a succession of politicians who mostly came to grief because they could not keep a firm hold on the Commons or avoid the personal intrigues rife in the Lords. Clarendon, friend of Charles's youth, in 1667 fled abroad to avoid a very unjust impeachment, but at least this event left us the legacy of his *History of the Rebellion* (the profits from which built up the Oxford University Press). The politicians gathered in the so-called Cabal broke up in confusion when Charles hoisted his flag of toleration for Catholics (Declaration of Indulgence, 1672) and thus provoked the violently anti-papist Test Act (1673) which drove James duke of York, the king's brother and likely heir, out of office and public life. And while the administration of Thomas Osborne, earl of Danby, seemed to have organized the control of government over Parliament by means of patronage and force, that interlude of peace collapsed in the aftermath of the Popish Plot and the crisis (Exclusion Crisis) promoted by opposition peers under the leadership of Anthony Ashley Cooper, earl of Shaftesbury. The battle concerned the prevention of a Roman Catholic succeeding to the throne and was waged in Parliament, but the outcome clearly proved that ideas of parliamentary control over the monarchy looked better in theory than in practice, at least as long as the king retained complete charge of the assembling of that body. Charles II, hitherto so inactive and accommodating, came out of his corner fighting furiously, and instead of the duke of York losing the chance of the crown Shaftesbury had to take refuge in Holland, where he died in 1683.

However, the battles of the Exclusion Parliaments did produce one lasting result. Shaftesbury organized his support not only in the Commons but also in the country at large, that is to say in parliamentary boroughs likely to prove useful. He thus brought into existence the first genuine political party with a nation-wide base, superseding the manipulating of court and magnate factions on which management of the Commons had relied ever since the reign of Henry VIII. Shaftesbury's party provoked a matching organization among his opponents, and those years of crisis thus left behind the Whig and Tory parties as genuine and lasting bodies. Naturally, their fortunes fluctuated thereafter, but they never disappeared altogether or were totally submerged into divisions between Court and Country – ins and outs. It was the Tories who backed James II even though his policy promoted popery and absolutism; it was the Whigs who secured William's throne in England; Whigs and Tories battled in the reign of Anne with the latter ascendant at her death; and though some Tories agreed to support the Hanoverian succession in 1714 those new kings trusted the Whigs better. By the mid-century the 'rage of parties' had ebbed into a degree of mutual toleration, but neither party ever disappeared: during the so-called Whig ascendancy of 1714–60 the Tories continued to cohere and operate, gradually abandoning an atavistic addiction to the Stuart claimants. Having lasted as identifiable parties into the 1750s, both underwent considerable changes in the reign of George III, when there emerged hard-core Whig factions opposing a general gathering of 'King's Friends' who included both old Whigs and Tories, but by the 1780s party structure once again solidified in the two traditionally named entities.[31]

The existence of these political parties, with a leadership in

[31] J. C. D. Clark, 'The Decline of Party, 1740–1760', *EHR* 93 (1978), 499–527; 'A General Theory of Party, Opposition and Government, 1688–1832', *HJ* 23 (1980), 295–325.

both Houses of Parliament, a set of avowed beliefs, and an organization extending into the country thus must not be doubted after 1680, but their real role and significance have too often been misunderstood. The chief reason for mistaken views was the revolution of 1688–9 which on the face of it altogether terminated the system that had prevailed under Tudor and Stuart monarchs: the system which made the king-in-Parliament the sovereign law-maker but committed government to the king at best in Council. The Bill of Rights and its aftermath not only strictly limited some aspects of monarchic power but seemed to prescribe a constitutional structure in which the executive crown was responsible (answerable) to the House of Commons, and the Parliament in turn was responsible to a national electorate organized in two parties putting forward candidates for election. Certainly Parliaments now met regularly every year, and the crown lost its absolute control over its assembling; in 1694 it became the law that Parliaments had to be dissolved and re-elected at least every three years, and though in 1716 the period was extended to seven years the maintenance of a convenient assembly by means of unending prorogations was over. The predominance of the Commons seemed secured by the need to get supply discussed and voted there every year. The Act of Settlement (1701) belatedly won the Exclusion battle by forbidding any person to sit on the throne who was not a communicant member of the Church of England.

Thus the apparent centre of political debate and action had unquestionably moved from the court to the Parliament, and many commentators in the eighteenth century, both native and foreign, professed to believe in the outward appearance of a government responsible to and ultimately controlled by the people. The revolution of 1689 did in fact finally settle the question of sovereignty in the law: it belonged where Thomas Cromwell had put it (to the king-in-Parliament), and the nibblings at royal absolutism that the Stuart kings had promoted and their clergy had tried to support were ruled out of court.[32] A good many 'commonwealth-men' went further

---

[32] H. T. Dickinson, 'The Eighteenth-Century Debate on the Sovereignty of Parliament', *TRHS* (1976), 189–210. The widespread confusion caused by an unwanted revolution is discussed in J. P. Kenyon, *Revolution Principles: The Politics of Party 1689–1720* (1977).

and kept proclaiming the supposedly populist principles of the Glorious Revolution, and even foreign observers regarded the English constitution as liberal and lawful to a degree, built as it seemed to be on the mixed sovereign power supposedly advocated by Aristotle. Such commentators as Charles Montesquieu in *L'Esprit des lois* (1748) fudged the scene further by discerning a strict division of functions between the executive, representative and judicial agencies of English government, a naïve misreading which was to affect and bedevil permanently the government of the United States of America. The reality was nearly always quite different. On the face of it, the executive (the king and his ministers) were dependent upon gaining majority votes in the House of Commons that represented the people. In actual fact, the executive continued so to organize the House of Commons as to be assured, as a rule, of that body's obedience, and in that exercise of management the crown continued to be able to use its patronage relationships with the members of the Upper House. This is not to overlook the fact that opposition existed in both Houses; debate could be fierce and management occasionally slipped, but it is to assert that it was not majority parties in either House of Parliament, produced by election, that created or terminated the power of any of the king's ministers. On the contrary, reconstructed ministries entrusted with power by the king created majorities for themselves in the Commons by regular management and sometimes by subsequent elections. The only new aspect of management lay in the fact that in creating such supporting blocks it was possible to utilize party groupings committed to members of the administration. In all other respects, Thomas Cromwell would still have recognized the familiar parliamentary scene 200 years after his death.

The easy removal of James II together with the conventional phrasing of the Bill of Rights misled interpreters into thinking that the end of Stuart absolutism equalled the end of kingly rule. So far from Parliament taking control of the kingdom, kings continued in control of the Parliaments. We have always respected William III (whose chief interests turned upon the protection of the Netherlands against French aggression) and Queen Anne has usually been regarded with a tolerant smile, but she took counsel advisedly at least as often as she took tay and herself chose her chief ministers. A real transformation has lately taken place in the reputation of the first three Georges, who have ceased to be the stupid provincials and limited pretenders of the liberal tradition. However much George I and II continued to act as electors of Hanover, with frequent visits to their German principality, they did not neglect their English commitments; until George III's final lapse into mental instability (1811) the monarchs continued to superintend English politics from within their courts.[33] True, the fourth George both as prince regent and as king forfeited both respect and power, but until then the ancient truth that England harboured a dominant monarchy – was a kingdom in the fullest sense – remained very definitely in being.

Furthermore, another ancient fact held good too: under the king, it was the aristocracy that counted, and even on the parliamentary scene it would still be a serious error to forget the House of Lords. This is where wealth foregathered, and wealth still signified those means of patronage that continued to construct political support for whatever ministry happened to govern.[34] Virtually all the leading politicians of the century sat in the Lords, though the exceptions – Robert Harley under Anne, Robert Walpole under George I and II, and the younger Pitt under George III – recall the leading roles played by Thomas Cromwell and William Cecil before elevation to the peerage. Those three statesmen have, rightly, attracted much attention, but they deserve that not so much because they stayed in the Commons but on account of their remarkable personal qualities as politicians and managers. Above all else, it must be understood that the existence of real parties did not control the making of ministerial appointments. The Whig alliance of Godolphin and Marlborough did not give way to the so-called Tory administration of Harley (1710) because that party won an election (the election followed the change of ministry) but

[33] Ragnhild Hatton, *George I, Elector and King* (1978); J. B. Owen, 'George II Reconsidered', in *Statesmen, Scholars and Merchants*, ed. A. Whiteman et al. (1973), 112–34; I. R. Christie, 'George III and the Historians – 30 Years On', *History* 71 (1986), 205–21; Linda Colley, 'The Apotheosis of George III: Loyalty, Royalty and the British Nation, 1760–1820', *PP* 102 (1984), 94–129.

[34] Cf. e.g. M. W. McCahill, 'The House of Lords in the 1760s', in *A Pillar of the Constitution: The House of Lords and British Politics, 1640–1784*, ed. C. Jones (1989), 165–98.

because the duchess of Marlborough lost Queen Anne's favour. Walpole's twenty years at the top of the tree depended not on the existence of an organized Whig party in the Commons: he organized support called Whig by means of the trust reposed in him by his monarchs, and when he lost that trust he lost office, less than a year into a recently elected seven-year Parliament. George III had to learn his trade and especially rid himself of his childhood mentor, Lord Bute, and in consequence had briefly to accept a narrowly Whig administration, but it was he and no one else who in 1783 launched Pitt on his two decades of ascendancy. The parties crystallized opinion and could be useful as an element in politicians' power bases, but they did not make or unmake ministries: kings did that. There were certainly enough protests against the corruption of a power structure exploited by individuals for their own benefits, and a number of offices under the crown came by stages to disqualify holders from sitting in the Commons, but the real fruits of patronage were found not in places in the customs service or stewardships of royal parks (as in earlier days) so much as in the social and financial advantages distributed with care by the king's managers. Details may have changed, but the essence of the old political structure survived the apparent death-blow dealt in 1689 with notable ease. There was never again to be a court of High Commission; judges would henceforth be appointed during good behaviour and not during pleasure; the crown's power to dispense from the operations of the law was limited to the area to which sound doctrine had confined it before James II abused it; a standing army would henceforth need the consent of Parliament. And after 1701 Roman Catholics would be excluded from the throne, as they still remain. In other words, the constitutional monarchy planned in the 1530s survived into the eighteenth century. The appearance of parliamentary control over that monarchy misled the observer because in fact that monarchy, through its agents, controlled the Parliament.

Not everybody, of course, at the time agreed with this: some read the signs differently and some wished to change them. Starry-eyed theorists talked as though 1689 had really subjected government to the people: they preserved the radical imaginings of James Harrington and Henry Neville in a celestial garb.[35]

[35] Caroline Robbins, *The Eighteenth-Century Commonwealth Men* (1961).

Others, though convinced of the claims of a popular involvement called civic humanism, came to realize that politics were
not like that and began to confine their dreams to a civilized life
away from politicians.[36] Even in the day-to-day battles of
Parliament and the press, the language of a backward-looking
radicalism left its mark: it proved attractive to attack the
manipulators of power with the kind of high-minded verbiage
that they usually employed to cover up the politics of
corruption. None of this, however, affected the realities of the
day, until towards the end of the century radical discontent
began to seek real change. The American Revolution opened the
eyes, or at least the mouths, of some English politicians and
restored a genuine Whiggery to such remnants of the old party
as the Rockingham faction and its spokesman Edmund Burke;
'no taxation without representation' was a slogan that crossed
the Atlantic eastward. John Wilkes found that the people – or at
least the London apprentices – could be roused to a spot of
rioting by demagogic propaganda, and from about 1780
onwards a movement for the reform of the electoral structure
(ostensibly to make government responsible to the electors)
began to gain strength. It was significantly enough accompanied
by the first efforts to claim a true political freedom for women:
in 1792, there appeared the prototype of feminist programmes,
Mary Wollstonecraft's *Vindication of the Rights of Women*.
Indeed, by the 1790s the sort of apprehensions of popular
unrest and threatening revolution that had been so strong a
century before revived within the governing order.

This novel air of purposeful action owed a good deal to the
growth of the public press without which loud voices would
have reverberated in an empty space. Regular news-sheets had
begun to appear before the civil wars but gained enormously
from the nation's desire to learn what was going on in those
wars. The proliferation of various 'Mercurii' induced Charles
II's government at last to make a reality of a censorship which
had hitherto been noticeably feeble. Unlike the repeated efforts
going back to a proclamation of 1538, the Licensing Act of
1662 did control the press, mainly because of the devoted
labours of Sir Roger L'Estrange, prototype of successful and

[36] M. M. Goldsmith, 'Liberty, Luxury and the Pursuit of Happiness', in *The Languages of Political Theory in Early Modern Europe*, ed. A. Pagden (1987), 225–91.

philistine censors. But this was another means of control that fell victim to the Glorious Revolution. The Licensing Act was repealed in 1695, and throughout the eighteenth century the public press – Grub Street as well as possibly more responsible journalism – grew apace in size, regularity and influence. Though London remained the centre of this kind of publicity, it was provincial newspapers that multiplied in number. Papers still today in regular production – *The Times* and the *Observer* – can claim a continuous existence from the last decade of the eighteenth century. The regular press benefited enormously from commercial needs seeking advertising space, but above all it offered a highly influential means to manipulate opinion. The radicals gained most from the end of censorship and the proliferation of newspapers.

The political impetus behind radical demands stemmed from the French Revolution and the ensuing wars, events which called forth two diametrically opposed reactions. One side took up the strictly patriotic position: revolutionary France was still France, only more so and worse. Patriotism also drew strength from religious fears of revolutionary atheism.[37] Even before the war broke out, that point of view had been memorably enshrined in Edmund Burke's *Reflections on the Revolution in France* (1790) with its accurate forecast of the disastrously destructive route which that much acclaimed event would take, though in the process Burke sentimentalized the dying days of the Bourbon monarchy beyond all reason. He received a reply from Thomas Paine – *The Rights of Man* – which shone with all the mindless admiration of abstract principles that tend to animate revolutionaries in countries not likely to adopt revolution. Paine, noble fellow, transferred himself to France, where he soon fell out with the regime of the Terror; he then escaped to America where he continued to find imperfections to denounce before he died in 1809. Meanwhile his example had helped to inspire two kinds of protester. The poor and unemployed began to turn associations of self-help into strike-prone trade unions that provoked the needlessly savage Combination Acts (1799). Among the educated upper classes a new phenomenon made its appearance – the Englishman who, so far

[37] W. Stafford, 'Religion and the Doctrine of Nationalism in England at the Time of the French Revolution and Napoleonic Wars', *SCH* 18 (1982), 381–95.

from despising all who are not English, will offer praise only to 'any country but his own'. In the Stalin era we have become so familiar with this type of high-minded protest that we do not seem to realize how new it was in the age of Charles James Fox, well-endowed scion of the ruling order who chose to worship Robespierre from afar. As George Canning soon pointed out in one of his contributions to the propaganda published in the *Anti-Jacobin*, such 'friends of humanity' would refuse even sixpence to a 'needy knife-grinder' who admitted that his torn breeches testified to an ale-house brawl and not to the oppression of the poor; only kicks were suitable for wretches whom 'no sense of wrong can rouse to vengeance'. For the first time the passions of high-minded anti-patriotism sounded their tin trumpets. The wars made certain that the existing order would face serious military and economic problems but could ignore the claims of moral outrage; generally speaking, the English, explaining that they would never be slaves, remained patriotic. But there was that small band of harbingers who saw virtue only abroad.

Religion

In all this turmoil of politics, which had started as a rage of parties but had lost the rage without abandoning of parties, the real issues that separated Whig from Tory revolved, oddly enough, around the fortunes of religion and the Church. Contrary to what has long been believed, a right constitution continued very generally to be thought of as inseparable from a right faith.[38] In 1660, with monarchy and Church restored, the immediate need called for the sorting out of attitudes to the recent victors, now separated off as Dissenters, and the immediate reaction involved a determined attempt to keep them out of any influence on affairs. Efforts to comprehend at least the Presbyterians within the national Church soon gave way to more vengeful feelings, and uniformity of the Anglican kind was in theory restored (1662) and then backed by the various measures of the so-called Clarendon Code (not of Clarendon's

[38] Cf. M. Goldie, 'The Civil Religion of James Harrington', in Pagden, *Languages of Political Theory*, 197–222, esp. at 199.

invention) that made life difficult for those refusing to join the club. However, Charles II's desire to offer some toleration to non-Anglicans (Declaration of Indulgence, 1672) backfired; read as mainly an attempt to promote the cause of Rome, it led to the Test Act but made Dissent look less terrible. Until the overthrow of James II, the part that religion played in politics increasingly meant a united front in Parliament against popery, and Shaftesbury's Whigs from the first formed links with the underprivileged Dissenters. And from that point the one undoubted plank in the Whig platform was toleration for all Protestants, a policy which produced the Toleration Act of 1689. This removed virtually all the disabilities that the statutes of the later Stuart reigns had imposed on Protestants who stood aside from the Church of England; what remained could be dealt with by the practice called Occasional Conformity – that is, attending communion in a parish church once a year. Almost of necessity, the Tories, having had to yield up their loyalty to a king who promoted popery, embraced a High Church policy which achieved success under Robert Harley's management. However, after some dithering the Hanoverians' Whigs settled for tolerant and latitudinarian principles,[39] and thereafter agitation from both sides kept the issues of religion and Church alive beyond either necessity or good sense. The commonest as well as least justified political cry was 'The Church in Danger': what was really at issue was not the survival of the Church but the degree to which it would accept Protestant variety in the realm.

On the face of it, admittedly, there appeared to be more serious dangers to the inherited faith and system. Truly conservative clergy and laity (especially among the gentry) abominated the supposedly latitudinarian (indifferent) attitudes of Whig politicians and the bishops they chose to appoint; it was always possible to denounce advocacy of a relaxed coexistence as treason to the only true faith. In fact, the soft line never relaxed all that far. It never exorcized ceremony and ritual and even bigoted fanaticism: the Church, swaying one way or another, survived within the framework of the Protestant

---

[39] G. M. Townsend, 'Religious Radicalism and Conservatism in the Whig Party under George I: The Repeal of Occasional Conformity and Schism Acts', *Parliamentary History* 7 (1988), 24–44.

Church first adumbrated in the early Reformation.[40] However, there were movements outside the Church, outside Dissent, and outside the gradually returning Roman Catholicism – movements of a positively secularist tinge. Antitrinitarian notions, whether Deist or strictly Unitarian, were heard and were received as the real threat to Christian orthodoxy that they had been held to be ever since the Arian heresies of the early centuries. And there were, or there were said to be, real atheists. What seemed to promote such aberrations was the great advance and the spread of natural science which had been on the move since the earlier seventeenth century – ever since Francis Bacon had proclaimed the need for an unprejudiced study of nature. To the age of Isaac Newton (1642–1727) there succeeded the age of Joseph Priestley (1733–1804) and Humphry Davy (1778–1829): the discovery of the laws of physics was followed by the unravelling of the truths of chemistry. All over the place, nature (as the phrase tended to go) began to reveal her secrets, and the Royal Society, properly founded in 1660, stood by to provide an organized home for the new learning. The point, in the present context, is not that the scientists were necessarily atheists or even antitrinitarians: Newton, for instance, abandoned the scientific work of his youth to immerse himself in some very old-fashioned magic and numerology.[41] But what the new science for the first time seemed to offer was an explanation of the universe which might dispense with a Creator; for the first time, atheism acquired some means to develop positive alternatives to religion.

In so far as the eighteenth century was the supposed age of Enlightenment, a strong dash of scepticism and doubt entered a good many minds. A philosopher like David Hume could deny all supernatural explanations and yet survive unpersecuted, and he and his like found guides and allies in France and Germany. But they never constituted more than a small band: Tory believers like Samuel Johnson were far more numerous and influential, and the Church never stood in danger

---

[40] F. C. Mather, 'Georgian Churchmanship Reconsidered: Some Variations in Anglican Public Worship 1714–1830', *JEH* 36 (1985), 255–83.

[41] I am not persuaded by the argument that in this Newton was typical of his age (cf. T. G. Ashplant and Adrian Wilson in *HJ* 31 [1988], 260). Other scientists in England and elsewhere stuck to their new-found guns.

of losing its hold upon the English people, especially once it had accepted that Protestant Dissenting sects could be regarded as friendly aliens sheltering under the same umbrella. In the 1770s, some steps were taken to relieve both Dissenters and Roman Catholics from some of the legal disabilities still round their necks,[42] though full-scale acceptance of toleration (especially the repeal of the Test Act) had to wait for the 1820s. Considering how persistent the view of that age as the age of reason has been, the really surprising things are the survival of High Church orthodoxy in the parishes of England, and the popular movements for an evangelical revival which marked the second half of the century. By the 1740s, John Wesley and his associates were preaching what came to be known as Methodism – a puritan revival proclaiming an Arminian theology of freeish will and goodish works.[43] At first resented by the men in power, who sometimes instigated mob attacks on the preachers, it proved ineradicable, especially after it directed its energies in the next century towards the conversion of the heathens of the new industrial towns of the north and Wales. Methodism split from the Church of England and thus greatly enlarged the catchment area of Nonconformity, but similar intellectually doubtful ambitions informed an evangelical revival within the established Church and the old sects. The movement for the abolition of slavery and the slave trade profited from the renewal of exaltation, and at first there was some connection between evangelical Christians and the advocates of radical reform; but the evangelicals tended to be pacifists, and in the era of war after 1793 tried to steer clear of public affairs.[44] At any rate, the possibility that religion might become a matter of individual choice and drop out of politics, a possibility that after the uproar of the seventeenth century some people had hoped for and some historians thought they saw growing in the century of the Enlightenment, had by the 1760s surrendered to an

---

[42] J. Gascoigne, 'Anglican Latitudinarianism and Political Radicalism in the Late Eighteenth Century', *History* 71 (1986), 22–38.

[43] J. D. Walsh, 'Origins of the Evangelical Revival', in *Essays in Modern Church History*, ed. G. V. Bennett and J. D. Walsh (1966), 132–62; 'Methodism and the Mob in the Eighteenth Century', *SCH* 8 (1972), 213–27.

[44] D. Lovegrove, 'English Evangelical Dissent and the European Conflict, 1789–1815', *SCH* 20 (1983), 263–76.

Plate 30 *John Wesley preaching on his father's tomb, Epworth Church, Humberside. (The Mansell Collection, London.)*

0000282920/CAM073/00003
CUSTOMER: 0000000000

1   83.98   UN   3.98

S799-(Used books at low prices)

SHIP/HAND   0.00
TAX (7.525% on $3.98)   0.30
TOTAL   4.28

PAYMENT TYPE
CASH   5.00
PAYMENT TOTAL $ 5.00
CHANGE DUE - CASH $ 0.72

THANK YOU!

Gift cards for everyone on your list!

END OF TRANSACTION

account. Merchandise paid for by check may be returned for cash after 12 business days and are then subject to the time limitations stated above.
Exchange or store credit will be issued for merchandise returned within 30 days with receipt. We reserve the right to limit or decline refunds or exchanges. Proper I.D. required.

*SOFTWARE POLICY: Returns accepted within 30 days with receipt for in-store credit only. Registerability is not guaranteed. All copyright laws observed.

HALF FRICE BOOKS RECORDS MAGAZINES REFUND POLICY

Cash refunds and charge card credits on all merchandise (except software*) are available within 7 days of purchase, with receipt. Merchandise charged to a credit card will be credited to your account. Merchandise paid for by check may be returned for cash after 12 business days and are then subject to the time limitations stated above.
Exchange or store credit will be issued for merchandise returned within 30 days with receipt. We reserve the right to limit or decline refunds or exchanges. Proper I.D. required.

*SOFTWARE POLICY: Returns accepted within 30 days with receipt for in-store credit only. Registerability is not guaranteed. All copyright laws observed.

entrenched conservatism assisted by a noisy revivalism. Odd perhaps, and rather sad.

English Society

The Church maintained its hold as much as anything by underwriting the alliance of squire and parson. Yet the predominant styles of life to be encountered in the laity were distinctly not spiritual – and the clergy pretty regularly copied the materialist behaviour of their leading parishioners. General opinion throughout remained attached to a hierarchically structured society; rank rather than class continued to be the prevalent concept, and even those who wished to remedy social injustices did not think it right to level the orders.[45] That general tone continued to be set by the aristocracy, both at court and in the revived local courts of the great houses which were being built all over the place.[46] Blenheim, Marlborough's reward for his services to king and queen and nation, was only the most extravagant of them. Now and again the building mania spelt ruin, and of the vast Tudor mansion at Audley End in Essex half was pulled down in the 1690s because the family could not afford the lot. Nor was the use and abuse of stone and brick confined to stately homes; the towns also renewed themselves, especially the great centres of trade like Bristol and Liverpool, and above all London which continued to grow quite out of proportion with the rest of the realm. The fashionable zeal of the Regency era created modern Bath and Brighton; the new industrial developments gave metropolitan status to country towns like Manchester, Leeds and Birmingham. And so forth. It was in the century after about 1750 that England both rural and urban, but more especially urban, assumed its later face.

The aristocracy may have set the standards of material ambition and of taste, but wealth accumulated also below its ranks. Profitable investment in trade, in manufacture and in

---

[45] P. J. Corfield, 'Class by Name and Number in Eighteenth-Century Britain', *History* 72 (1987), 38–61.

[46] J. Cannon, *Aristocratic Century: The Peerage of Eighteenth-Century England* (1984).

banking genuinely altered the age-old distribution of wealth and accumulated surpluses of cash which made possible victorious war and at a later date also increasing provision for the labouring classes. But while there was unquestionably a great increase in the number and influence of the inevitable middle classes, especially of the towns, the landed gentry really retreated somewhat from the position of ascendancy which it had erected on the exploitation of monastic lands and the profits to be made from feeding an ever-expanding population. The distance grew between the greater and the lesser land-owners, and it is no wonder that the ethos and habits of the age bear so strongly aristocratic a mark. Of course, that top layer of society also altered in composition. New wealth liked to gain new status, and the movement into noble ranks never ceased; indeed, buoyed up by political influence, the calls of patronage and the claims of potentially influential clients, it grew much more active after the middle of the century. In the half-century after 1775 the House of Lords rose in membership from 199 to 358, with some families dying out to hide the fact of over 200 new creations.[47] The newcomers for the first time included Scotsmen and Irishmen as members of the English peerage; also, where earlier creations (at least after 1689) commonly sweet-ened the retirement of servants of the crown, this later lot included many highly active politicians and entrepreneurs. That is to say, the aristocratic top layer not only continued to play a very active part in the life of the nation but in effect increased its hold on place and influence. Democracy got very tired waiting vainly in the wings.

It is high time a word was said about Englishwomen, though I must emphasize that most of what has been said about 'the English' does apply to them as well, more especially in those early days when queens and abbesses exercised quite as lasting an influence as did kings and abbots. True, the law of England granted real independence only to property-owning widows; daughters and wives in theory depended on fathers and husbands for their maintenance, though even the ribaldry of the ages reminds us of the fact that daughters and wives do not

[47] M. W. Cahill, 'Peerage Creations and the Changing Character of the British Nobility', *EHR* 91 (1981), 259–84. Facts like these support the view that the Stones' *An Open Elite?* is wrong.

always submit in convenient humility. At least from the reign of Elizabeth onwards the Chancery mitigated the rigour of the law,[48] and it would be a mistake to think that the technical subjection to their males described the real condition of women. In the Later Middle Ages and into the sixteenth century we find women independently in charge of some businesses, personally attending to the public sale of the products of dairies and bakeries they were running, and actively involved in administering lands they owned in their own rights or their husbands'. It would appear that by the beginning of the seventeenth century far fewer women were involved in such work; increasingly they concentrated on the management of their own households and families, where they unquestionably held command.[49] Even so, widows, especially in London, commonly carried on their late husbands' businesses, sometimes remarrying to unload the burden off their shoulders; this happened quite regularly in the printing trade. The civil wars shifted the running of many an estate on to the shoulders of the landowner's wife while he served in the army or languished in prison.[50] It was mothers who stood responsible for the raising of their children, especially their daughters, though those daughters' marriages were far more often in their own hands than tradition supposes. In the higher ranks of society, women, once married, enjoyed a good deal of true independence, especially in the reigns of queens looking for trustworthy companies of female attendants: women courtiers benefited as much as their male counterparts from places at the centre of affairs.

In the course of the sixteenth century, two developments assisted the active role of wives and mothers. The education of women in the intellectual arts, much demanded by humanist

---

[48] Marie I. Cioni, 'The Elizabethan Chancery and Women's Rights', in *Tudor Rule and Revolution*, ed. D. J. Guth and J. W. McKenna (1982), 159–82.

[49] For a case study see Marjorie K. McIntosh, *Autonomy and Community: The Royal Manor of Havering, 1200–1500* (1986), 171–5; *A Community Transformed: The Manor and Liberty of Havering, 1500–1620* (1991). In general, see Bridget Hill, *Women, Work and Social Politics in Eighteenth-Century England* (1989), and Jane Rendall, *Women in an Industrializing Society: England 1750–1880* (1990).

[50] Cf. the revealing correspondence between Sir Thomas Knyvett and his wife Katherine in the 1640s: *The Knyvett Letters 1620–44*, ed. B. Schofield (1949) – in themselves sufficient to dispose of the strange theory that the upper classes did not know conjugal love before the eighteenth century.

writers, became increasingly common once Thomas More's daughters had shown the way, and the upheavals in religion brought women to the front because official policy always treated female deviants and protesters with less severity than male ones. True, female rebels or heretics might suffer as sadly as their men, but a good many women got away with treasonable words that would have done for their husbands, and their public behaviour was less scrutinized. Thus the advance of puritan beliefs and the preservation of Catholic (recusant) tenets both owed much to the women of the households. Women lower down the social scale appear to have given up the running of businesses, but with the expansion of manufactures their work, especially in combing and spinning wool and cotton, though far too often sweated labour, assumed a vital role in the economy and produced a measure of personal freedom. And some outstanding individuals – women like Dorothy Osborne (1627–95) who married Sir William Temple and shared his political and entrepreneurial programme, or Aphra Behn (1640–89) who rivalled William Congreve as a playwright of contemporary renown – underline the fact that women were not irredeemably repressed by 'patriarchal' society.

Throughout the eighteenth century, in fact, women played major roles in politics and in the arts. It was Queen Caroline rather than her husband George II who supported Walpole's ministerial ascendancy, and (at a sort of opposite pole) actresses like Sarah Siddons (1755–1831) took their lawful place upon the stage where previously boys had been employed to play female roles. The 'Bluestockings' of the mid-century testified impressively to the increase in leisure and education that had come to the women of the middle classes.[51] The modern English novel may have been started by Samuel Richardson and Henry Fielding, but before the end of the century the most admired work was done by Fanny Burney and Jane Austen – and Jane Austen remains the only eighteenth-century novelist whom today one can read simply for pleasure. At this point, however, a rather strange thing happened. Until the 1780s or thereabouts women might earn respect or contempt by their individual

---

[51] P. Langford, *A Polite and Commercial People: England 1727–1783* (1989), 109–16.

behaviour, but it was the sort of respect or contempt that was bestowed on men as well. The ancient apprehension that women were sexually voracious and so threats to male virtue still persisted in some quarters and kept preachers at uttering their old conventional warnings. But as social mores in general grew more finicky, or if you like more decent, this fear and liking of the female insensibly changed into a conviction that 'good women' must be sheltered from the dangers of life (and especially of men); lack of such shelter came to stink of public depravity.[52] It was in the closing decades of the century that women began to be relegated to a pedestal, permanently isolated from 'real' life. At least that was the intention. The state of affairs that the feminist agitators of the next century battled against had really come about quite recently, a product of both increasing prudery and sentimental romanticism.

In fact, the tone of public and private discourse from the Restoration to the early nineteenth century in the main pursued a line of increasing propriety. The release from the high-minded and high-falutin moralizing of the puritan age immediately produced an exceptional measure of crude wit and sexual innuendo, much encouraged by Charles II's public behaviour and not much hampered by his brother's dislike of such airs. The age of Nell Gwyn could never have been prissy, but Restoration comedy enthusiastically picked up the threads of bawdry familiar enough on the Elizabethan and Jacobean stage. John Wilmot, earl of Rochester (1647–80), a fluent poet in several modes, made his name at court with the most explicit obscenity yet seen in print, and although he died young he left a legacy to be exploited. Daniel Defoe's Moll Flanders made no bones about the advantages of whoring, and John Cleland's Fanny Hill a generation later turned earthy fun into rather miserable pornography. However, the end of the Stuart regime gradually introduced a degree of restraint. The general desire for an outward improvement in morals and morale was summed up in one favourite adjective – polite. Politeness was to pervade everything – individual behaviour, relationships between men and women, even the play of politics where the notion of a free people came to be linked to the notion of a

[52] Ibid., 604–7 on the 'fear of licence'.

Plate 31 Frontispiece from The Chances: A Comedy, acted by Her Majesty's Servants at the Theatre-Royal, *written by the late Duke of Buckingham. A Restoration comedy which depicts Nell Gwyn in the centre stage. (The Bodleian Library, Oxford.)*

well-mannered ruling caste.[53] The (to me at least) mild tedium of the famous essayists – Joseph Addison, for instance, or Richard Steele – certainly polished away the cruder outpourings of earlier pamphleteers, though it also tended to emasculate the language. Politeness did not, of course, win everywhere and every time; more particularly it never affected the great age of political caricature in the reign of George III when James Gillray and Thomas Rowlandson set standards of furious but funny obscenity which it took the mid-Victorian era quite some time to get away from. But the dominant desire was for the smooth,

[53] L. E. Klein, 'Liberty, Manners, and Politeness in Early Eighteenth-Century England', *HJ* 32 (1989), 588–605.

Plate 32 The Gordon Riots in Broad Street, 7 June 1780. (The Mansell Collection, London.)

uninvolved, courteous selfishness of the polite world which the fourth earl of Chesterfield preached in his advice to his grandson while at the same time practising disabling contempt on Dr Johnson. To tell the truth, the eighteenth century remained at heart reasonably crude and distant from refinement, but it spent a lot of money and time to build the polite façade behind which reality might hide. At least the top layers of society did so; the bulk of the English seems to have remained unaffected by the antics of their betters.

The nobility also led the laity into the schools and universities originally created for the making of clergy but turned by stages (with some difficulty) into institutions for the formation of gentlemen. Oxford and Cambridge did not exactly flourish in this period; the Scottish universities, for instance, served the intellectual needs of the nation very much better, as Adam

Smith proved. But neither were they in so pitiful a decline as tradition used to allege. They continued to provide good instruction in such unprofitable skills as the composing of Greek and Latin verse; they provided havens for some highly original scholars like Richard Bentley (1662–1742) on the Cam or Thomas Hearne (1673–1735) on the Isis; and they did assist in the making of an upper-class culture which provided an important social glue for people of varying opinions. This was the age of clubs and coffee-houses – places where men of like background and upbringing but different attitudes could meet to sort things out without drawing swords. For the offspring of parents not in the Anglican communion the Dissenting Academies are supposed to have provided a much better education which made their exclusion from the universities a profitable blessing. However, this would seem to be less than true: if Presbyterians, Congregationalists and Baptists avoided the universities it was because they thought their teaching irrelevant to the lives of merchants and civic worthies: philistine good sense rather than deprivation dictated their choice. They certainly did not stay away from the Inns of Court, where the same religious barriers were supposed to exist; indeed, many lawyers stemmed from origins that benefited from the very lax enforcement of the penal legislation.[54] In these respects as in most others, the century endeavoured to be polite – relaxed, unfanatical, intent on social peace. In due course, the evangelical revival put an end to a peace partly maintained by blessed indifference and in due course also assisted a radical revival following the ideas of Jeremy Bentham, still sitting today embalmed in the corridors of London's University College.

Georgian England attracted much attention from abroad; a part of the world which the top layer of English society increasingly knew at first hand as the grand tour through France and Italy, first tried in the age of Elizabeth, became a necessary stage in a gentleman's education. Experience in France and Italy reinforced the outburst of taste – in pictures, in china and silver, in buildings and gardens – which absorbed so much aristocratic wealth but also cast a truly attractive glow over the age. Much of Europe turned Anglophil in this period, a reaction in part to

[54] Cf. for all this D. L. Wykes, 'Religious Dissent and the Penal Laws: An Explanation of Business Success?' *History* 75 (1990), 39–62.

Plate 33 Vauxhall Gardens, *after Rowlandson.* (*The Mansell Collection, London.*)

the benefits that English tourists brought to innkeepers and sellers of artefacts, but in greater part to the entrenched conviction that the English constitution – that Aristotelian mixture of monarchy, aristocracy and democracy – represented the ultimate ideal to be striven for.[55] The fact that the admiration, shared for instance by a mind as sharp as Voltaire's, pretty thoroughly misjudged the truth of the somewhat haphazard system by which Britain was governed matters not at all, even if that foreign respect helped to anchor the Whiggish self-satisfaction which outlasted the movement for reform and in retrospect endowed the eighteenth century with political virtues it never possessed.[56] But at least after the foreign involvements of Normans and Plantagenets, after the dangers and rebellions of the Tudor age, and after the furies and upheavals of the seventeenth century, the English now set an example of a settled and sensible peace. In any case, Anglomania did not endure. Instead there grew up in the 1790s throughout much of Europe a hatred for Englishmen, who allegedly stood in the way of liberty and fought for their interests with the lives of other peoples.[57] Perfidious Albion soon discovered the cost in repute which triumph on land and sea brought with it.

In view of this later reaction, it is worth notice that all visitors to England agreed on one thing: English inns and English public transport surpassed anything known at home, and the food was beyond all cavil. *Sic*, alas, *transit gloria*.

---

[55] Cannon, *Aristocratic Century*, 155–7.

[56] Linda Colley, 'The Politics of Eighteenth-Century British History', *JBS* 25 (1986), 359–79, emphasizes the artistic and social successes of the age but argues that power rather than accommodation preserved the peace.

[57] A. D. Harvey, 'European Attitudes to Britain during the French Revolutionary and Napoleonic Era', *History* 63 (1978), 356–65; T. C. W. Blanning, *The Origins of the French Revolutionary Wars* (1986), 131–2.

6

The Great Climacteric[1]

We have now brought the English through a thousand and more years of history, and despite all the often drastic changes in circumstances and behaviour the main features of the scene have proved surprisingly continuous. Formed into one people out of diverse war-bands and farmers, they quite early acquired what can fairly be called a sense of nationhood. This sense grew steadily more positive in the face of Celtic remnants on the fringes, of foreign invaders and alien rulers, of frequent wars at first on home grounds but increasingly on other people's territories. They preserved the Germanic origins of their language and absorbed into it any other elements that came their way, creating in the process a singularly flexible and adaptable means of discourse, and they managed the curious double achievement of unity at home in the face of persisting regional diversity. They acquired and retained an unquestioning conviction of superiority over outsiders from whom they nevertheless learned a great deal while developing their nation. They remained a predominantly rural people who yet from an early date promoted forms of trade and manufacture which gave them an edge in the European markets, and they several times built and lost external empires without ever abandoning their inchoate sense of imperial destiny.

These enduring features owed most to two mechanisms which imposed themselves upon the people rather than emerging from them. The English possessed a monarchy which

[1] This chapter of necessity confines itself to an outline and survey; anything more searching would require another book.

created power and control at a very early date by the standards
of European experience, and that monarchy provided both an
administration and a law which quite rapidly supplied both
bone structure and outer skin to the fact of nationhood. Of
course, all these details underwent frequent change but the
changes operated within the larger continuum. There were
moments of deliberate and positive reconstruction, and there
were detailed alterations in the wake of events, but between
them these mechanisms settled the facts of a self-aware people
ruled by kings and the law and the organized spirituality of the
Church. Not even the intermittent weakness of kings or the
failure of the law to eliminate violence could permanently
damage those basic conditions, a fact fully brought home to
everybody's understanding when even the abolition of the
monarchy, the capture of the law by a faction, and the
disappearance of the Church proved to be only a temporary
break in the continuity. The things done away with were
restored with astonishing ease. Thus the ultimate truth of the
English people's existence lay in that mixture of order enforced
by authority with freedom exercised under authority which was
not to be found anywhere else.

That structural duality made for enduring facts of life. It
backed the social ascendancy of an aristocracy which hardly
ever became politically oppressive because it served under the
crown; periods of exception, of course, occurred but again were
strangely short-lived. That duality eased the transition from
serfdom to freedom which benefited from the English sense of
individual rights guaranteed by the law; breaches of that
principle were again rarer than elsewhere and more readily
remedied. The duality encouraged a society and a people
structured by degrees, a structure that was very rarely brought
into question and never seriously damaged. Of course there
were occasions when aristocrats thought they might win the
powers of an oligarchy, or when lower orders tried to break the
bonds of obedience, but none of those occasions produced
enduring consequences; before very long, the English were
every time back with their well-understood variety of status
under king, law and Church. Ten centuries of human existence
are bound to witness much turmoil and strife. It is therefore
important to see that so far as the English were concerned all

that turmoil and strife played itself out against a surprisingly unchanging backcloth of accepted and shared authority.

The time of true change finally arrived in the early nineteenth century. At the start of this new phase a number of ancient ambitions had at last been realized, more especially in the union of the two islands and three kingdoms under a single crown. The loss of the North American colonies had been made up by the virtual occupation of an empire in India and by the established ascendancy in the Caribbean; moreover, the United States remained an important trading partner (the American railroads later in the century were largely built with British money and in part by British engineers). Even the injury to *amour propre* had been somewhat repaired by the burning of Washington in the half-witted war of 1812. In England itself, agriculture benefited from the pressures of the French wars and manufacture was in the process of being industrialized. World trade and shipping were largely concentrated in English hands.

Plate 34 The Death of Nelson at Trafalgar *by Benjamin West. (The Mansell Collection, London.)*

Plate 35 Wellington at Waterloo, engraving by John W. Cook after Alexander Sauerweid. (The Mansell Collection, London.)

On the face of it, the year 1815, with peace at last restored, looked like a springboard for unrestrained development in wealth and possibly contentment. As usual in history, things did not quite turn out that way. Even though in the long run the nineteenth century was to be the age of English, or rather British, world dominance, immediately troubles easily out-weighed contentment, especially as experience made it increa-singly plain that the long age of the English tradition was at an end. In a way, the aftermath of the victory over Napoleonic France formed a warning signal. Instead of sitting back to enjoy the fruits of a triumph after more than twenty years of war, blockade, high taxation and much distress, the country fell at once into a major slump as governments were forced to reduce taxes and therefore spending, faced the return to civilian life and for preference to employment of hundreds of thousands that had served in the army and navy, saw themselves forced to satisfy the powerful agricultural interest by protecting laws that kept food prices high, and faced a prolonged depression which produced a rash of rioting especially of machine-breakers (Luddites). The new age began in a mess of troubles, and although the English in due course recovered and entered upon a successful career as the workshop of the world and the rulers of a global empire, the nineteenth century witnessed a sequence of economic troubles, renewed in the twentieth, that spurred on a succession of radical protests. The reign of Queen Victoria looks peaceful and universally prosperous only in retrospect, though in actual fact the general standard of life and living did improve throughout the nation.

The main problem facing the realm lay in the astounding expansion of the population. A country that in a thousand years had never more than seven million souls suddenly exploded. By mid-century England and Wales alone held twenty million with another nine million in Scotland and Ireland, though that last country was losing people after the miseries of the great famine of 1845–9. By the end of the century, the figures had again doubled and by 1950 (wars notwithstanding) they had reached their present level of over fifty million. It was the beginning of this explosion that produced the doom-laden analysis put forward by Thomas Malthus (1766–1834), who held that, if unchecked, the number of people would expand at a rate that was bound to outstrip the growth of the available means of subsistence. His figures were well calculated but failed to take into account the astonishing consequences of a more intensive food production. The English did not starve because that production kept pace with needs until the 1870s, when the flood of imports from such producers as North America and New Zealand ruined English agriculture while greatly improving the feeding of the English. The population explosion easily overcame cholera epidemics and other diseases, not to mention a very high rate of infant mortality: the English were breeding like rabbits, with large families forming the standard ambition at all social levels. Most of the increase came from within the nation, though there was also a fair amount of immigration, mostly Irish. In the 1890s, England became a refuge for Jews driven from Russia by persecution, an event which changed the face of London's East End. The empire channelled West Indian blacks and East Indian browns into parts of England: I vividly remember my naïve amazement at seeing the many non-European faces I encountered in London after seventeen years of life in central Europe. Astonishingly enough, until the break-up of the empire deposited sizeable communities especially of Muslims in England, those external additions were quite well assimilated within the English community; the second generation looked like turning English. Of course there were some bad reactions, but it should be stressed that, compared with the normal behaviour of societies faced by alien invasions, the English treatment of the new arrivals was generous and creditable.

The population explosion had several consequences that changed the face of the country and the living habits of the people. The most obvious and most immediate effect was urbanization: the English moved into rapidly expanding towns. By the middle of the nineteenth century a people who had always thought of themselves as country dwellers, indeed as rustics, and had looked with suspicion upon the impersonal collectivities of the cities had mostly turned into town dwellers – though sentimental romanticism preserved illusions about the superiority of rural idylls. With London continuing in the lead, all the towns grew steadily, with considerable profit to the building trades. The novel ease of communications brought by

Plate 36 *Stoke Place, Buckinghamshire, a typical Regency country house, which depicts the importance of perspective between buildings and lake, from* Views of Country Seats. *(The Bodleian Library, Oxford.)*

the rapidly developed railway network assisted in these moves into the towns. It also assisted tidal waves of transfers in the regions. In the nineteenth century, large numbers of people drifted into the industrial areas of the north, while in the twentieth industrial decline reversed the flow and the south-east grew fastest; although regional differences and self-consciousness continued to make themselves felt, generally speaking the unification of the realm beyond anything known in the past became manifest. The swollen towns posed all sorts of administrative problems: accommodation, security, health and sanitation demanded attention at a rate that the administrators were rarely able to meet. The nineteenth-century towns offered advantages in numbers, weatherproofing, food supply, shopping facilities, but they also carried an air of gloom and dirt. Urbanization was going forward much too fast for it to be truly civilized, and just when the towns had at last managed to organize themselves properly the age of the motor-car arrived to put new — and so far unsolved — problems in the way of urban living. However, it should be remembered that on balance town life clearly won over village and farmstead. The main effect of it

Plate 37   *The effects of the Industrial Revolution as shown in this engraving of Leeds, 1858. (The Mansell Collection, London.)*

all was totally to alter the setting and experience within which the English now lived.

England became an industrial economy: manufacture and the factory moved to the top of the tree. The agricultural interest remained powerful but underwent some vicissitudes. Though after the repeal of the corn laws in 1846 it never again dictated policy as until then it had done, it survived the great depression of the later nineteenth century and revived in the wars of the twentieth. But the proportion of the people who lived on the land dropped rapidly, while those who worked in the new factories and lived in the new towns (at first often in slums) increased all the time. The new industries absorbed also women and children in their labour force, but this led to a series of enactments which in effect eliminated most of this source of cheap labour. Actually, the biggest demand for the work of women came from the employers of domestic servants, a very large body of people down to the First World War and eliminated from middle-class households only after the second.

Factories and the domestic demand reorganized the social structure of the people, and the ancient divisions by orders and degree began in the 1830s to be replaced by the new divisions of class. Yet it should be noted that the correct terms are not middle class or working class but middle classes and working classes: these bodies of English people never acquired a single group identity but contained within their ranks widely differing standards of wealth, employment and sectional interests. Nevertheless the familiar structure of society that had effectively endured into the later eighteenth century had a century later been replaced by one still familiar today. The reality of this transformation was to some extent hidden by the relatively slow growth of the new system and by the preservation of some of the old order's outward appearances. England retained both monarchy and aristocracy into the age of democracy, but neither is today what it used to be. The monarchy lost its political function and became a national symbol – extremely useful in that role because the top of the social tree could thus be removed from the demands and accidents of politics. Though some monarchs tried to react against this reduction, the long reigns of two queens have greatly assisted this retreat into the role of a visible figurehead. The aristocracy survives in two

forms – hereditary peers and life peers – but after about 1900 it
ceased to command the political lead that it had still enjoyed (at
times intermittently) in the age of Palmerston, Russell and
Salisbury. It was notoriously the rule in nineteenth-century
England that every cabinet should include one duke, even if he
did no work. Three shocks in the end destroyed aristocratic
government. The death duties imposed by the Liberal government of the 1890s reduced noble wealth; the Parliament Act of
1911 removed the Lords' veto in politics; and the killings of the
Great War removed shoals of natural claimants to political
power. But even as the ceremonial role of monarchy was very
well worth preserving, so that of the aristocracy continued to
serve a useful purpose. Other countries, afflicted by revolutions,
abolished noble titles and had to find other means of rewarding
merit or satisfying blackmail, means that did far more harm to
their nations than making lords out of middle-class manufacturers, capitalists, newspaper proprietors or even university
dons ever did to the English. A man or a woman can hold a title
without affecting the wealth of the nation or reducing its moral
standards. The alternative example of the USA shows how
sensible the English were to hold on to the accidentals of
nobility into an age that had at last abandoned the reality.

The social transformation both followed upon and led to a
major change in political language. The new industrial society
produced enormous new social problems, greatly aggravated by
the explosion in numbers. Economic depressions occurred with
tiresome frequency in an economy which depended on ever-
growing wealth, at home and abroad, to absorb the manufacturing output, but even in good times increasing numbers of the
English, driven into towns, faced poverty, sickness and periodic
unemployment. The English divided not into the classes of
Marxist imagining but into regular haves and far too regular
have-nots, both kinds being found in the middle layers as well
as the working classes. Out of this situation grew two
phenomena which, though able to look back to earlier roots,
changed so drastically as to contribute massively to the
transformation of the English: a radical demand for change and
even revolution, and a paternalistic reorganization of the state's
function in the lives of the people.

We have become so accustomed to the existence of radical

pressure groups and the flood of radical criticism of the existing order in books, pamphlets and newspapers that we find it difficult to realize how greatly these protests changed public life in England. Expressions of this critical spirit range over an extraordinarily wide spectrum, embracing genuine revolutionary movements like Chartism, working-class organizations for the improvement of living conditions (trade unions), political parties dedicated to programmes of detailed reform, and thinkers and writers who may be profound or merely bigoted. The subjects of these protestations varied with time and circumstances. Thus the demands of the 1830s and 1840s sought to solve all problems by reforming Parliament so as to make it the true agent of 'the people'. The agitation of the Anti-Corn-Law League exploited the prevalent doctrine of non-interference (*laissez-faire*) supposedly derived from Adam Smith and Jeremy Bentham; a little later, acquaintance with the noise made by Karl Marx and Friedrich Engels converted some of the dissatisfied to socialism. In England, socialism turned out to be comfortably adaptable, finding a home for a romantic dreamer like William Morris as well as for an embittered Tory like Henry Hyndman. The growth of unsolved social problems provoked agitation for interference which culminated in the programme of the Labour Party but left no sector of the political nation unaffected. Perhaps the most unexpected aspect of the radical wave emerged in the later nineteenth century, when it became fashionable to find virtue only in some foreign country or its system (most commonly France); the curious theory that only the English have a class system is still found put forward by some victims of that bug. In fact, though the English in the main remained fairly chauvinistic patriots, an increasing number began to feel a shamefaced regret for the excesses of their imperial past, unaware as they tended to be how much better they had done than other imperial powers. True, this complex of reactions was always better visible among the so-called intellectuals than among the mass of the people, who allowed national consciousness to override class antagonisms. In fact, radical protests never turned into class war. The bulk of the working classes, even when organized in socialist trade unions, remained conservative even in politics, and the leadership of the agitators for reform was always dominated by a large contingent of well-off members of the middle class (remember the Webbs or G. D. H. Cole!). It should not be forgotten that the loyal strength of the Labour Party had always lain in Wales and Scotland; in England, not many even of the workers embraced that party as a matter of faith. The fact that the communist movement always remained pretty exiguous, even when communism was briefly seen as an ally in the battle with Nazi Germany, underlines the entrenched conservatism of the modern English — so different from other European countries where the parties of extreme right and left flourished. Unlike the radicalism of the seventeenth-century sects or the friends of revolutionary France, native radicalism in England turned out to be widespread, angry, noisy — and non-revolutionary. When, in 1848, Europe exploded in revolutions Chartism stood at one of its high points: yet it never tried to link up with the true revolutionaries of France or Germany; when post-war depressions promoted the growth of fascist violence, the British Union of Fascists remained singularly unimportant.

The reason for this failure to take protest all the way must in great part be sought in the growth of the paternal state. Action in the transformation of the nation came in the main from above, even if the above often responded to pressure from below. Though the intellectual climate of protest and reform changed drastically from the *laissez-faire* stance of Benthamism in the early nineteenth century to the fundamentally socialist body of ideas that has dominated the later twentieth, ·the practical effects were surprisingly similar. They were so because all the dissatisfied in and out of government regarded their function as defined by the discovery and remedy of defects in society. The governing sort did not distance themselves from the governed. In this respect they continued a relationship that had been endemic in English society throughout the centuries, but the enormous changes in that society produced a distinctly novel reaction to the duties that being in charge imposed on a man. A rapidly changing nation called for rapid and frequent responses, so that reform became a continuous phenomenon — reform by political action in Parliament. However much some agitators might call for revolution (as the early makers of socialist parties habitually did), they always found themselves overtaken by action from above which appeared to satisfy the victims of society sufficiently to render revolution impossible. Time and again, confronted with aggressive trade unions, strikes and public disorder, politicians saw the spectre of revolution hover about their heads and those of industrialists and landowners; time and again it vanished with an expiring howl at the touch of what in retrospect must look like fairly inadequate reforms. Thus by cumulation rather than total upheaval, the English changed and changed their society.

Though the beginnings of state intervention in the interests of the poor and oppressed can be traced to the Factory Acts passed between 1804 and the 1840s, or the Poor Law Reform of 1834, those tentative and often unpopular measures did not greatly affect the social scene until the administration of Sir Robert Peel (1841–6). Even then, however, they stemmed from the initiatives of the privileged classes. It is not without meaning that the best remembered philanthropist is not an organizer of protest like Feargus O'Connor (who never achieved anything positive) but the seventh earl of Shaftesbury. Reform suffered less from an insufficient will to act than from the prevalent conditions of government inherited from the past – a general opposition to heavy spending and the exiguous size of the body of administrators.[2] These limitations began to disappear in the second half of the century, with the decline of *laissez-faire* economics (much advanced by John Stuart Mill's discovery of a moral duty vested in government), the irresistible expansion of the civil service that followed upon reform of recruitment in 1857, and the growing awareness of the often appalling living conditions of the working classes. The spread of socialist ideas provoked a hostile reaction which took the trouble to seek improvement without socialism.[3] Some administrators might continue to deplore policies which cost a lot of money and therefore demanded heavy taxation, but despite occasional pauses social amelioration by the action of the state became the norm after about 1870, culminating in the creation of the welfare state in the 1940s and 1950s. (The supposed effort to change all that

[2] N. McCord, 'Some Limitations of the Age of Reform', in *British Government and Administration*, ed. H. Hearder and H. R. Loyn (1974), 187–201.

[3] J. W. Mason, 'Political Recovery and the Response to Socialism in Britain, 1870–1914', *HJ* 23 (1980), 565–87. The failure of socialism among the leaders of the Labour Party is nicely described in J. Grainger, *Character and Style in English Politics* (1969), ch. 8.

that came with the 1980s recognized that the English could not afford a universal Santa Claus policy, but failed of its purpose because it did not succeed in reducing the size and power of the civil service.)

In the earlier stages of this irresistible development, one of the most powerful driving forces sprang from religion. The nineteenth century witnessed a striking revival of evangelical Christianity in all branches of that faith. Even the remarkable return of Rome[4] and the departure to Rome of such leading Anglican clergy as the later cardinals Henry Edward Manning and John Henry Newman profited from the anti-rational passions of evangelicalism. So did the appeal of Frederick Denison Maurice, another reforming cleric whom pious historiography has placed on a pedestal even though he remained loyal to the Church of England. In fact, Anglicanism, battling against both the growth of Methodism and the Romish leaning of the Oxford Movement, tried to persuade the English that it best represented their national (and imperial) character.[5] The Church found this the more difficult as well as necessary because Nonconformist movements included some determined imperialists.[6] In the process, the clergy accepted a degree of professionalism never reached before (professionalism in the ministry), and all forms of the Christian religion turned for a time against modernity, seeking the alleged truth in the Middle Ages. The Reformation got a bad name, and churches and chapels acquired a rather deplorable Gothic aspect. This sentimental renewal of the faith did, however, benefit reform because it encouraged the leadership – especially William Ewart Gladstone, a life-long High Churchman even when he turned political Liberal – to heed protesting voices from the ranks of the clergy. In due course, religion once again departed from public life, but this has left behind influences for social reform that were born out of the faith: both William Temple,

[4] Gerald Connolly, 'The Transubstantiation of a Myth: Towards a New Popular History of Nineteenth-Century Catholicism in England', *JEH* 35 (1984), 78–104, shows that the increasing strength of Rome in England did not derive from Irish immigration but constituted a genuine native revival.

[5] Keith Robbins, 'Religion and Identity in Modern British History', *SCH* 18 (1982), 465–87.

[6] Stephen Koss, 'Wesleyanism and Empire', *HJ* 18 (1975), 105–18. And cf. Clyde Binfield, 'English Free Churchmen and a National Style', *SCH* 18 (1982), 519–33.

assiduously socialist archbishop of Canterbury, and the bourgeois militancy of the Salvation Army take the mind back to those elderly convictions.

Between them, commonwealth principles of interference and evangelical Christianity do seem to suggest that the swelling movement for reform might have sprung naturally from the experience of the past: in a way, the later nineteenth century, despite its denunciation of the Reformation, reminds one of the age of Thomas Cromwell and William Cecil. But that appearance is entirely superficial and the bearers of modern reform were totally unaware of an earlier age when the state had decided to intervene.[7] Despite the notable growth of serious and learned history, the nation at large proved as ignorant of its true past as it has commonly been, the more so because many of the new guides continued to preach error until F. W. Maitland and T. F. Tout thrust scholars into the Public Record Office. For one thing, even the nineteenth-century historians sought salvation in sentimentalized Middle Ages and tended to read the sixteenth century as a time of despotic aberration; for another, the political pressures of the day altered altogether in the stages which produced a democratic electorate. The 'age of reform' opened with the First Reform Act (1832), and although this did not much alter the balance of political power in the realm it opened the door to the more comprehensive reforms of 1867, 1884, 1918 and 1928 which finally secured universal suffrage for men and women. In terms of politics, the arrival of democracy produced the inescapable ascendancy of organized national parties, effectively in control from about 1868, and with it a dominance of demagogues over their cabinet colleagues. It is arguable that as a mass electorate was created and parties became fully organized instruments for acquiring and exercising power, so have individual Englishmen and women progressively lost the power of influencing political action as independent individuals. But it should not be denied that the existence of parties seeking, at regular intervals, the approval of a mass electorate has maintained the reforming activity of the state: parties need programmes, and parties based on a democracy need programmes of active intervention.

[7] So unaware that when I rediscovered the Tudor use of the state I found myself accused of reading the twentieth century back into the sixteenth.

All this expansion of activity eventually called for a total overhaul of the machinery of government, in some ways the most striking break with the past. English government – the king's government – had been (as we have seen) one of the outstanding hallmarks of English society, a fact which again might suggest that the modern development grew naturally out of what went before. But it did not. At the centre, the growth of new departments and the vast expansion of the civil service put an end to the traditional reliance on a small and coherent body of officials, virtually a family affair; instead it inordinately increased both the powers and the anonymity of the operators – powers that in due course came to be used to hinder rather than promote efficient action. Routine often triumphed over sense. But it was local government that really broke with the past, starting with the reforms of the 1880s that terminated the rule of the justices of the peace.[8] Local government, in shires and towns, has predictably become a reflection of central government: a professional bureaucracy serving a politicized body of councillors.[9] Thus the practices which had restrained the centre's hold over the localities gave way to principles which linked the centre's rule to subordinate replicas of itself in the localities. When in the 1970s a somewhat idiotic revision of shire boundaries was undertaken which quite consciously abandoned a structure that had lasted for a thousand years, the decision to round off a revolution was given symbolic proof. In addition, all the machinery of government, local as well as central, found itself deprived of traditional interrelationships and in consequence saddled with that characteristic hallmark of the new machinery, the organized trade union. NALGO and NUPE say quite as much about the break with the past as do overstaffed council offices and party-political councillors.

However, the most enormous break with the past occurred in another aspect of local government, in the creation of a regular police force. From 1829, the whole country by stages acquired

[8] Maitland lamented a reform which sacrificed a man who 'is cheap, he is pure, he is capable' not for any sound reason but 'upon the altar of the spirit of the age' (H. A. L. Fisher, *Frederick William Maitland* [1910], 63–4).

[9] For a useful summary see J. P. D. Dunbabin, 'British Local Government Reform: The Nineteenth Century and After', *EHR* 92 (1977), 777–805.

the machinery for the discovery and prevention of crime, independently of the political structure and supposedly truly impartial. Despite recent departures from the sound principles developed in that century, it should be said that the British police – still the only force unaffected by electoral ties and also the only one to avoid the regular carrying of arms – constitutes one of the truly meritorious achievements of modern times. At least down to the 1960s, it succeeded in turning the English (not the Irish and perhaps not the Welsh and Scots) into a law-abiding and peaceful people, for the first time in their history. One curious part-consequence of this change also made its appearance in the later nineteenth century: crime became a major source of entertainment. Though police and detective forces had long been part of the scene on the continent of Europe, the detective story originated in England before it became one of the conquering exports of that country, striking root all over the place but especially, of course, in that outpost which had best preserved the pre-modern English attitude to crime, the United States of America.

As a matter of fact, the last two centuries have witnessed something truly new: that vast expansion of popular amusements and leisure activities which characteristically started in England and then spread over much of the globe, sometimes in the wake of imperial expansion but quite often simply by imitation. I have in mind both regular holidaying (the English invented both the seaside holiday at home and mountain climbing elsewhere) and organized sport, whether active or passive. Both greatly benefited from the new ease of movement about the country and ultimately the world which began with the railways and the steamship, both pioneered by England. In assessing the consequences of industrialization and urbanization, the miseries of unemployment and slum-dwelling must not be forgotten. But neither must the spread to the people at large of the pleasures of mind and body that in previous ages had been the preserve of the rich.[10] Linked to this expansion of experience was the equally striking expansion of the sources of

[10] It has been argued that what really structured the working class of the nineteenth century was ability to consume and display: Paul Johnson, 'Conspicuous Consumption and Working-Class Culture in Late-Victorian and Edwardian Britain', *TRHS* (1988), 27–42.

information. Newspapers and journals had been known since the seventeenth century, but what happened in the nineteenth constituted an explosion that permanently altered the relation of the people to their environment, their rulers, their view of themselves, and indeed their understanding of the greater world beyond. No need to elaborate the obvious, but it might just be noted that in the end the passive enjoyment of sport and display joined hands with the expansion of the information industry in the televised occasion which enabled the holiday-maker to stay at home.

Behind these manifestations of a popular will to take part stood another novel development which had not originally been designed for this purpose. The story of educational reform has been often enough outlined, though opinions will always differ as to its achievements. In this field, too, the state took over from private enterprise – enterprise which in the nineteenth century produced a proliferation of church-supported primary schools for the poor and a wide range of public schools for the rich. Acts of Parliament laid out comprehensive schemes for basic (1870) and secondary (1902 and 1944) education. Unquestionably the nation grew literate and up to a point numerate; the number of people willing to use their minds increased by leaps and bounds. The crudities of the old boarding schools did in part persist into the new era of self-consciously reformed schooling: Eton and Winchester took a while to learn from Rugby and Manchester Grammar School. Perhaps more striking still was the proliferation of new universities. After some 700 years the monopoly of Oxford and Cambridge (themselves drastically reformed several times) was broken by new foundations, with Durham and London leading the way in the 1830s, until by the 1980s it became possible to expect that a majority of the people would experience what is known as higher education. It might be remarked that probably the most enduring effect of all this was the creation of a teaching profession ranging through all these institutions; the fact that both schoolteachers and dons have continued to grumble incessantly should not hide the considerable increase in social respect that has come their way.

Proliferation in numbers and institutions was accompanied by a proliferation in study subjects. The English did learn a good deal from other nations, more especially the Germans who in the nineteenth century pioneered intellectual enterprise, but they retained idiosyncratic peculiarities which have often bewildered their neighbours. Among these was a touching belief in the moral virtues of a classical education; only in England did schoolboys still compose Latin verses on the eve of the Second World War. The 'public school spirit', bottled in various attractive containers, managed to survive the decline of the Christian religion which had in the first place produced it. But the universities and similar places moved relentlessly ahead, and by the 1950s it became for the first time more usual to ask a person where he or she had graduated rather than which school they had attended. The present situation took nearly 200 years of reform – reform imposed from outside and reform promoted from inside – to develop: by the looks of it, further reform from outside and inside, which has already reduced the educational success of the schools, may fairly soon put an end to this extraordinary age of true learning. The literary critics, speaking a language composed of French and American, are busy leading the way into incomprehensible mysticism: others may follow. It is therefore desirable at this point to record the triumphs in the natural sciences, in archaeology and history, in law and economics, which in the last two centuries have created a multicoloured fortress of learning in England. Perhaps it will survive the attentions of ignorant administrators and self-centred theorists.

In all this democratic spread – some fortunate, some less so – the most satisfactory transformation and the one that should receive nothing but a respectful welcome has been the recognition that women are people too. Although there will always be some men who think that female emancipation in politics and education has gone much too far, as well as some women who think it has gone nothing like far enough, in the present context the point to be recognized is that the ancient division into two sexes has in large part ceased to have any meaning outside the strictly sexual realm. We saw that early moves in this direction can be traced in the eighteenth century, even as in earlier times the peculiarly aseptic treatment of women proclaimed in the nineteenth century hardly existed. But even though there have long been women in business, in estate management, in the counsels of princes and potentates, and even in the world of learning, the democratization of emancipation has successfully removed barriers and differences which had become formidable only in the prurient age of Queen Victoria. If the men cannot cope with the strident feminists who see offence round every corner, that is just too bad.

Another area which has undergone drastic transformation is the law of England, especially relevant here because the common law (as we have seen) formed one of the enduring mainstays of the English people's identity from before the Norman Conquest till the age of Jeremy Bentham: at which point everything changed. The visible alterations responded to necessity. By this time, the law of England was burdened with a good deal of dead wood, especially with statutes that should have been repealed long since; the legislative prolixity of the eighteenth century had created much confusion, and the earlier attempt during the Protectorate to cleanse the slate had been reversed at the Restoration. So the nineteenth century set to, throwing out masses of outdated and unwanted lumber. In this respect, as well as in the rational reorganization of the central courts (the creation of the High Court in 1874, with its several divisions that at last integrated the Chancery in the normal system), the reign of Victoria did much highly necessary work without damaging the role of the law in the life of the nation. Copyhold lasted rather absurdly until 1925. In sum, the reforms at last eliminated the Middle Ages but maintained links to past principles and lines of development. Where they really altered fundamentals was in the whole concept of the law. Until the nineteenth century, the law had been thought of as an independent force within the organizing of life and of rights, independent of other aspects of society and absolute in its claims over its own area of operation. In the wake of Benthamite reform it came to be changed conceptually into an instrument of social control in the hands of government, at the service of whatever larger social purposes might be thought desirable at any given time. The sceptre turned into a screwdriver. Thus the law joined the monarchy in abdicating its self-contained claim to obedience and accepting a subordinate role. But while the crown became a symbol under which the new democracy could shelter, the law became a weapon for winning whatever new theory and new people's power asked to see put through. By the middle of the twentieth century the law had vacated the dominant place in the general consciousness that it had occupied for so long, and a knowledge of the law no longer assumed an understanding of that law's history: a barrier, intellectual as well as practical, had been set up between now and then. And the English had ceased to be a people of inveterate litigants – and that at least is a gain.

Change upon change: yet the English experienced the largest and most traumatic change when they turned into the British. The vast empire built in every part of the globe was rightly called British: its opening, settlement and management employed Scotsmen, Welshmen and Irishmen quite as much as Englishmen. The benefits of empire in trade and power also accrued to the British rather than the English. The futile attempt to keep the empire in being as a commonwealth similarly could not be called English. The armies that fought the wars in India and South Africa, and the armies and navies that fought the two World Wars, were British. And so forth. Of course, in that British amalgam the English formed the largest part; they continued to exist as a people, diverse in their classes and regions but manifestly distinguishable from the other components in the one political structure. But in all aspects of public life and activity the English were totally subsumed into the larger entity of the British – a nationality but not a nation, a gathering but not a people. They noticed this the less because in that agglomerate they retained numerical ascendancy, supplied the largest part of public servants and political activists, and retained the leadership in financial (though hardly in industrial) organization. The centre of power remained at Westminster, with Edinburgh and Dublin working under the dominance of the 'imperial' government and Parliament. However, as the world got used to the new term applicable to the people who had come forth from their island to exercise rule just about anywhere it did look as though the history of the English had come to an end. The age of triumph belonged to the British – in India, in Africa, in the white colonies turned into dominions, politically also in Europe. The English as English could but contribute to the amalgam; they could not and did not claim the scene for themselves.

Or so it was until the other day. Two World Wars have disposed of the British empire, and though most parts of it have bought the glories of independence at the cost of political decline and economic disaster, the red areas have permanently faded from the map. One day it will be possible to cast a usable balance sheet, but at present it is still too early for that. Oddly enough, of all the peoples involved, the English (not the British) may turn out to have been most indifferent to the ending of an era. Of course, it was quite agreeable to dominate so large a part of the globe, and the ruling order, which supplied the managers of those distant regions – governors, councillors and district commissioners – does miss the glory and the profit. But even among them the first generation of the post-imperial age has already forgotten India and Africa and the Caribbean (except as teams that play superior cricket), and for the generality of the people the empire never signified anything truly vital in their lives. They lived on in their towns and shires, before and during and after the imperial phase.

However, another imminent break-up affects them much more directly. The United Kingdom ceased to be properly united in 1922, when the larger part of Ireland acquired for the first time in its history a political identity and national image. Now we have separatist movements in Scotland and (less convincingly) in Wales. Perhaps the English are about to re-emerge from their British phase. There are some signs of a retreat into the past: crime is rampant again, as it was in the eighteenth century, and memories of an ungovernable people given to violence rise up in a new style of riot. The police have lost much of the trust of the middle classes, and the Churches are making all sorts of improbably backward-looking noises. Are the English on their way back to the old order (and disorder)? The answer to that question must, no doubt, be no: no people can rid itself altogether of two hundred years filled with drastic transformations. The democratic, property-owning rentiers of the twenty-first century will look very different from their hierarchically structured and highly enterprising ancestors. But perhaps they will manage to preserve the one characteristic which they gained in the centuries of a strong monarchy and a powerful system of legal rights, the one characteristic which marked them out among the nations. Perhaps they will retain the ability to tolerate variety and will once again come to respect the rights of the individual: the rights not of Man but of English men and women.

Further Reading

This is, of necessity, a very compressed list of books only (no articles) further reduced by the fact that hardly any of the works referred to in the footnotes are listed. The list and the footnotes should be used together.

General

S. H. Steinberg and I. N. E. Evans, *A New Dictionary of British History* (London, 1970).

G. R. Elton, *The Sources of History: England 1200–1640* (London, 1969).

J. H. Baker, *An Introduction to English Legal History* (2nd edn, London, 1979).

A. Macfarlane, *The Origins of English Individualism: The Family, Property and Social Transition* (Oxford, 1978).

Keith Thomas, *Religion and the Decline of Magic* (London, 1971).

L. Pollock, *Forgotten Children: Parent–Child Relations from 1500 to 1900* (Cambridge, 1983).

J. P. Kenyon, *The History Men: The Historical Profession in England since the Renaissance* (London, 1983).

Chapter 1

J. Campbell (ed.), *The Anglo-Saxons* (Oxford, 1982).

H. R. Loyn, *Anglo-Saxon England and the Norman Conquest* (London, 1962).

S. Bassett (ed.), *The Origins of Anglo-Saxon Kingdoms* (Leicester, 1989).

F. M. Stenton, *Anglo-Saxon England* (Oxford, 1947).

D. Whitelock, *The Beginnings of English Society* (Harmondsworth, 1952).

C. N. L. Brooke, *From Alfred to Henry III, 871–1272* (Edinburgh, 1961).

M. Deanesley, *The Pre-Conquest Church* (London, 1961).

H. R. Loyn, *The Government of Anglo-Saxon England 500–1087* (London, 1984).

H. Mayr-Harting, *The Coming of Christianity to Anglo-Saxon England* (London, 1972).

D. Knowles, *The Monastic Order in England* (2nd edn, Cambridge, 1963).

Chapter 2

F. Pollock and F. W. Maitland, *A History of English Law before the Time of Edward I* (reprinted Cambridge, 1968, with introduction by S. C. F. Milsom).

F. W. Maitland, *Selected Historical Essays*, ed. H. M. Cam (Cambridge, 1957).

E. Miller and J. Hatcher, *Medieval England: Rural Society and Economic Change 1086–1348* (London, 1978).

D. Knowles, *The Religious Orders in England*, I (Cambridge, 1948).

F. Barlow, *The Feudal Kingdom of England 1042–1216* (4th edn, London, 1988).

D. C. Douglas, *William the Conqueror* (London, 1964).

V. H. Galbraith, *The Making of Domesday Book* (Oxford, 1962).

E. Power, *Medieval Women* (Cambridge, 1975).

J. C. Holt, *Magna Carta* (Cambridge, 1965).

D. Crouch, *William Marshall: Court, Career and Chivalry in the Angevin Empire* (London, 1990).

Chapter 3

M. McKisack, *The Fourteenth Century 1307–1399* (Oxford, 1959).

B. Wilkinson, *Constitutional History of Medieval England*, II 1272–1399 (London, 1952).

C. Dyer, *Standards of Living in the Later Middle Ages: Social Change in England c.1200–1520* (Cambridge, 1989).

J. R. Lander, *Court and Community: England 1450–1509* (London, 1980).

F. R. H. Du Boulay, *An Age of Ambition* (London, 1970).

D. Knowles, *The Religious Orders in England*, II (Cambridge, 1955).

K. B. McFarlane, *The Nobility of Later Medieval England* (Oxford, 1973).

R. G. Davies and J. H. Denton (eds), *The English Parliament in the Middle Ages* (Manchester, 1981).

C. Ross, *Edward IV* (London, 1974).

C. Phythian-Adams, *Desolation of a City: Coventry and the Urban Crisis of the Late Middle Ages* (Cambridge, 1979).

Chapter 4

C. G. A. Clay, *Economic Expansion and Social Change: England 1500–1700* (2 vols, Cambridge, 1984).

G. R. Elton, *Reform and Reformation: England 1509–1558* (London, 1977).

W. T. MacCaffrey, *The Shaping of the Elizabethan Regime* (Princeton, 1968).

D. M. Palliser, *The Age of Elizabeth: England under the Later Tudors 1547–1603* (London, 1983).

R. Lockyer, *The Early Stuarts: A Political History* (London, 1989).

G. R. Elton, *Reform and Renewal: Thomas Cromwell and the Common Weal* (Cambridge, 1973).

C. Russell, *The Causes of the English Civil War* (Oxford, 1990).

J. S. Morrill (ed.), *Oliver Cromwell and the English Revolution* (London, 1990).

R. Hutton, *The Restoration: A Political and Religious History of England and Wales, 1658–1667* (Oxford, 1985).

J. Youings, *The Dissolution of the Monasteries* (London, 1977).

R. M. Warnicke, *Women of the English Renaissance and Reformation* (Wesport/London, 1983).

Chapter 5

J. C. D. Clark, *English Society 1688–1832: Ideology, Social Structure and Political Practice during the Ancien Régime* (Cambridge, 1985).

C. H. Wilson, *England's Apprenticeship 1603–1763* (London, 1965).

J. H. Plumb, *The Growth of Political Stability in England 1675–1725* (London, 1967).

G. S. Holmes (ed.), *Britain after the Glorious Revolution 1689–1714* (London, 1969).

W. A. Speck, *Stability and Strife: England 1714–1760* (London, 1977).

I. R. Christie, *Wars and Revolution: Britain 1760–1815* (London, 1982).

E. Cruikshanks and J. Black (eds), *The Jacobite Challenge* (Edinburgh, 1988).

N. McKendrick, J. Brewer and J. H. Plumb, *The Birth of a Consumer Society in Eighteenth-Century England* (London, 1982).

J. Brewer, *The Common People and Politics, 1750–1790* (Cambridge, 1986).

Chapter 6

F. M. L. Thompson, *The Rise of Respectable Society: A Social History of Victorian Britain, 1830–1899* (London, 1958).

H. Perkin, *The Rise of Professional Society: England since 1880* (London, 1989).

N. Gash, *Aristocracy and People: Britain 1815–1865* (London, 1979).

C. L. Mowat, *Britain Between the Wars 1918–1940* (London, 1955).

K. Morgan, *Labour in Power 1945–1951* (London, 1984).

J. Ehrman, *Cabinet Government and War 1890–1940* (London, 1958).

S. Rothblatt, *The Revolution of the Dons* (London, 1968).

Index